D0820614

Malcolm and the Cross

Malcolm and the Cross

The Nation of Islam, Malcolm X, and Christianity

Louis A. DeCaro, Jr.

L.C.C.C. LIBRARY

NEW YORK UNIVERSITY PRESS
New York and London

NEW YORK UNIVERSITY PRESS
New York and London

Copyright © 1998 by New York University
All rights reserved

Library of Congress Cataloging-in-Publication Data
DeCaro, Louis A., 1957–
Malcolm and the cross / Louis A. DeCaro, Jr.
p. cm.
Includes index.
ISBN 0-8147-1860-4 (acid-free paper)
1. X, Malcolm, 1925–1965—Religion. 2. Black Muslims.
3. Afro-Americans—Religion. 4. Islam—Relations—Christianity.
5. Christianity and other religions—Islam. I. Title.
BP223.Z8 L5733339   1998
297.8'7—ddc21   98–19687
                              CIP

New York University Press books are printed on acid-free paper,
and their binding materials are chosen for strength and durability.

Manufactured in the United States of America

10 9 8 7 6 5 4 3 2 1

For my godchildren

Britney Meteney
Shanae Smith
Zuri Cudjoe

New wine for new wineskins

BÉT 12230-Q 12-8-98 29.95

Contents

Preface

In this secular, not to say cynical, age few tasks present greater difficulty than that of compelling the well educated to take religious matters seriously.
—Eugene Genovese, *Roll, Jordan, Roll* (1974)

While I was preparing my first book, a religious biography of Malcolm X, I made the decision to put off discussing the Nation of Islam and Malcolm X in the context of Christianity and give primary focus to Islam. While this was an editorial expedient, I also recognized the importance of paying singular attention to Malcolm and Islam since this relationship is central to his life as a religious revolutionist. On the other hand, a religious analysis of Malcolm X is hardly complete without discussing his story in relation to Christianity. Although his eclectic religious upbringing blunts his own stylized claim to having been a Christian,[1] the issue of Malcolm and Christianity remains relevant. Malcolm never received an orthodox Christian upbringing and was consequently incredulous toward doctrinal Christianity from the time of his youth. Nevertheless, Malcolm was exposed to the Christian church—at least to the many denominations of Protestantism—and dealt with Christians throughout his life. As a leader, both in the Nation of Islam and as an independent activist, Malcolm apparently recognized that as long as the Christian church was relevant in the black community, it was worthy of critical attention. To be sure, Malcolm's analysis of the Christian church while in the Nation of Islam was bound up with the theological peculiarities of that movement. However, even after he was ejected from the Nation of Islam, Malcolm continued to make critical observations about Christianity, especially regarding its impact upon and relevance to the black community. In a different sense, Christianity was always of great interest to Elijah Muhammad's Nation of Islam—as is the case with its predecessor and successor movements of the same name. Despite his early rejection of Christianity, Elijah Muhammad, the founder of the second Nation of Islam, spent much of his time as a religious leader discussing Christianity and the Bible. Indeed, it was Elijah Muhammad's ostensible theology that provided Malcolm with the raw material he would need to fashion his own superlative polemic against white and black Christianity as the Nation of Islam's spokesman.

In discussing Martin Luther King, Jr., Nathan Huggins once noted that historians "are ill at ease with true religious phenomena." King believed in the Christian God, Huggins continued, "and his life was shaped by that fact, from the inside out. For most of us, that belief remains a mystery. We are products of a secular age in which religion is trivialized or popularized to make it palatable to all." Unfortunately, he concluded, "we have few scholarly examples to show us the way" to look deeper into the spiritual dimensions of Martin Luther King, Jr. Certainly the same could be said for Malcolm X and the Nation of Islam. Political science and psychology are not adequate in themselves to provide a complete understanding of the religious and spiritual issues undergirding this story and, as Huggins also pointed out, social scientists, historians, and other humanists are often "poorly equipped to discuss the inner terrain of spirit and mind" typified by pivotal religious experiences in the lives of great leaders.[2] Certainly, many of Malcolm's scholarly admirers and avowed political disciples seem inclined to deemphasize his religious life—a prejudice they unfortunately share with his critics. In a pluralistic society where religion is increasingly privatized, perhaps people are simply uncomfortable recognizing religious experience as worthy of critical study.

Some may object to my calling the Nation of Islam a cult and prefer the movement's self-justifying claim of being an Islamic movement tailored to the needs of African Americans.[3] Nevertheless, most

African American traditional Muslims have not required the cultic doctrines of the Nation of Islam as a prerequisite to accepting Islam, and some might even resent such a notion. Indeed, the claim that African Americans need a skewed version of Islam before accepting is also demeaning: as if black people are incapable of understanding the religion of Muhammad without some distorted version being fed to them first. Furthermore, the Nation of Islam's relationship to traditional Islam in some ways parallels the relationship of the Mormons to orthodox Christianity in the United States. All their claims to the contrary, the Black Muslims[4] and the Mormons have always existed outside the pale of the religions they tend to imitate.

Malcolm and the Cross is divided into two parts. The first is devoted to background material on the Nation of Islam movement. Those who have recognized the importance of observing the Nation of Islam in the context of Islam worldwide should also appreciate the value of understanding the birth and development of the movement in its Christian context. The second part is devoted to Malcolm's religious development, again with a focus on Christianity and his interaction with it.

Amiri Baraka has written that Malcolm "was a path, a way, into ourselves."[5] While he was undoubtedly writing from the perspective of black people in the United States, it is possible to expand his words to include all those who share an appreciation of Malcolm X and his life, development, and contributions. The sincere study of Malcolm X inevitably leads toward introspection, a gift that Malcolm seems to bestow even beyond the grave. Always a few steps ahead, Malcolm X is hard to catch up to, though one is surely a better human being for the pursuit, no matter what religious worldview one happens to embrace. What follows, then, are the reflections of one believer's sojourn with Malcolm X—if you will, an attempt at an *X-ology* of the cross.

Marana Tha

Acknowledgments

I would like to thank Niko Pfund, director of New York University Press, for encouraging me to follow up my first book on Malcolm X with a second book and then helping me to conceptualize it as a manuscript. Certainly, Despina Papazoglou Gimbel, managing editor of New York University Press, once again proved gracious and extremely helpful in bringing the manuscript to publication, and I would like to thank her as well. Indeed, I would like to express my thanks to all the staff at New York University Press for their kind assistance whenever I have called or stopped by during the preparation of this manuscript. Likewise, I am very grateful to Henry R. Lewis ("H.R.") for offering his advice, encouragement, and insightful perspective, not only on the subject, but on the author and his approach to the subject. Similarly, I greatly appreciate Paul Lee's unrelenting commitment to the betterment of my work—his generous assistance, his sometimes brusque criticisms, and his compelling devotion to the spiritual and scholarly disciplines of his work have proven that commitment. In my association with Messrs. Lewis and Lee over the past six years I have undoubtedly learned a great deal about a world quite foreign to the one in which I was born and came to manhood. As African American men with a reverent commitment to what Malcolm called "the black secret soul," they have treated me with a generosity of spirit apropos of the noblest of the ancestors.

I continue to be blessed in having access to and friendship with Wilfred Little Shabazz, who has patiently taken many phone calls from me, thoughtfully explaining and reflecting upon matters pertaining to his brother Malcolm and his family history. Wilfred personally models the principles of humanity and spirituality to which he subscribes, and I am blessed to know him. In Harlem, I have spent many hours discussing Malcolm and the Nation of Islam with the Rev. Charles Kenyatta (formerly Charles 37X Morris). I am grateful for his unselfish sharing of his recollections. In particular, I will never forget the day in June 1997 (only days before Dr. Betty Shabazz succumbed to the horrendous burns resulting from a tragic fire in her home) when Kenyatta and I drove north of New York City to visit Malcolm's grave. It had been two decades since Kenyatta had been to Ferncliff Cemetery and I proved to be of no help in locating the plot, even with a map. In my quest to find Malcolm's resting place, however, I remember looking up to see Kenyatta standing in the midst of the cemetery, his head turned in such a way as if he were listening once again to the voice of his friend. Slowly the elder moved to the exact site of the grave and called me to join him there. I am grateful for his friendship.

Harold Dean Trulear, a superb scholar, clergyman, and esteemed friend has allowed me to bounce many ideas off of him, and has challenged my thinking in many respects during the preparation of this book. Similarly, Andrea Clark and the members of the Racial Unity Ministry (R.U.M.) of the Redeemer Presbyterian Church in Manhattan have provided me great fellowship and encouragement. Finally, as I assumed the pulpit of my own pastorate, I have been greatly encouraged by my ordaining pastor, Archbishop Wilbert S. McKinley, of the Elim International Fellowship in Brooklyn, New York, who first welcomed me to his church in my days as a graduate student. In my quest to understand the black experience and the black church especially, Bishop McKinley spent many hours over many cups of coffee at Junior's Restaurant answering questions, and in a very real sense pointing me toward the study of Malcolm X. Without the four years I spent at Elim, learning to worship and also understand something of the black Christian experience and the breadth of the black diaspora, perhaps I could not have properly approached my work. Likewise, I have also been a part of Bethel Gospel Assembly in Harlem, where Bishop Ezra N. Williams is pastor, and Carlton Brown is associate pastor. My involvement in Bethel involved writing, teaching, and prison ministry, though I was enriched in ways far greater than anything I could have offered the church. The pastoral and ministry staff embraced me as a brother and nurtured my interests, exemplifying the kind of inclusiveness that the white Christian church has consistently failed to demonstrate in this society. Finally, I salute my congregation at the Vroom Street Evangelical Free Church for giving me room to write and extend my work while adjusting to new pastoral duties. I am blessed to have loving, supportive parishioners, and while some of them might not understand why their pastor would write about an infamous "Black Muslim," they have demonstrated a willingness to let me do my work as an aspect of my calling. Ultimately, I hope they will not be disappointed.

Introduction

The Nation of Islam and Christianity

Who in their native beauty most delight
And in contempt doe paint the Divell white.
> —"Jetty Coloured," 1621, in Winthrop Jordan,
> *The White Man's Burden* (1974)

Farrakhan knows that as soon as he says Jesus, he's lost. So he
goes about it differently.
> —Rabbi Jonathan Rosenblatt, in Guy Trebay,
> "Sins of Omission," *Village Voice*, October 2, 1996

One of the least noticed aspects of the legacy of the Nation of Islam is that in calling white people "the devil," belief in the metaphysical Satan is nullified. Of course, in a society where this and other doctrines so essential to traditional forms of Abramic religion (Judaism, Christianity, and Islam) have been discarded, perhaps the loss of the "personal devil" of the Bible seems irrelevant. However, given the fundamental religiosity of African American culture—so distinct from the prevalent "post-Christian" orientation among many European Americans—the denial of the biblical devil was quite a coup for the Black Muslims. From Sunday morning sermons to Friday night tales, the devil has always been perceived as a real person in the preponderantly Christian-oriented culture of black America. One day in 1930, however, a mysterious "white" man appeared in Detroit, Michigan, with a new cosmology—and a new devil. His legacy, passed down to and embellished by his black successors, was zealously crafted on behalf of African Americans. However, this legacy was as determinedly anti-Christian as it was anti-white, though for most journalists and historians the latter agenda has been its defining factor.

Given the lead of the media, we are often so focused on the Nation of Islam's "race hatred"[1] that few appreciate how decisively and thoroughly the teachings of the Nation of Islam have challenged the Christian church, manifesting itself as a dramatic *religious* alternative within the African American community. It is not merely that the Nation of Islam dismisses Christianity as "the white man's religion," though this characterization is central to its assault. Rather, the Black Muslim movement has also taught that Christianity is *doctrinally* incorrect—that it is in conflict with science and logic as well as with the supposed original revelation of Allah. In the religious sense, the Nation of Islam is not merely a movement, but a bona fide cultural phenomenon. The Black Muslims are not merely an occurrence—nor even a remarkable occurrence on the landscape of religious life in black America—but perhaps the most successful religious departure from classical black Christianity originating within the community itself.

African Americans have long been found in varying numbers along the full spectrum of religious life in the United States, and many have rejected doctrinal Christian belief in following one or another religious alternative, whether cult or mainstream. However, the Nation of Islam phenomenon perfected the previous experiments in black "Moslem" rebellion against Christianity and gave to African Americans a religious idea that has continued to work for the better part of a century—manifesting itself in three definitive Nation of Islam organizations and a number of lesser or related ones.[2] As distinct as Louis Farrakhan's present-day Nation of Islam is from Elijah Muhammad's organization, what links them is not only a fervent commitment to black nationalism but also the kind of apostasy (and I use this term in its pure definition) it represents with regard to the black Christian church and the Bible itself.

It seems that the founder of the Nation of Islam phenomenon was not soundly rooted in the religion of Muhammad ibn Abdullah. Though he claimed to be a descendant of and a spiritual successor to Islam's great prophet, the *paterfamilias* of the "Lost Tribe of Shabazz in the wilderness of North America" advocated an "Islam" that would prove to be as disturbing to believers in the Qur'an as to believers in the Bible. However, the difference between the founder's conflict with traditional Islam and his conflict with Christianity was that from the beginning the Nation of Islam was aggressively and openly anti-Christian and it was the influence of Christianity that he tried to up-root. Some would argue that the original intent behind the founding of the Nation of Islam was to prepare the way for an authentic Islamic endeavor among African Americans, but this seems more romance than historical fact. In its various manifestations since the beginning, the cultic nature of the Nation of Islam as a religious phenomenon is constant because the religious and spiritual DNA of the movement lacks the gene of orthodoxy in either the Muslim or Christian sense. To be sure, many Black Muslims eventually found their way into traditional Islam, and no one can deny the inclination the Nation of Islam provided toward traditional Islam for many of its adherents. Still, this says more about the orientation of the adherents than about the theological continuity of the Nation of Islam with traditional Islam. The Nation of Islam has never correctly taught its followers about the religion of the Qur'an, and neither has it ever encouraged them to become traditional Muslims. Those African Americans who moved from the Nation of Islam into traditional Islam might credit the Black Muslims for pointing them eastward, but they cannot retrospectively apply religious legitimacy to their Black Muslim experience in light of the teachings of the Qur'an. Furthermore, in many cases the move toward traditional Islam by former Black Muslims is equally a testimony to the religious bridges burning behind them. In other words, the Nation of Islam is far more proficient at demeaning Christianity than it is in introducing people to the religion of the Qur'an.[3] Indeed, the fact that former adherents like Malcolm X, Warith Mohammed (Elijah Muhammad's son), and Muhammad Ali all became zealous proponents of Sunni Islam does not prove the Nation of Islam is proto-Islamic but suggests rather that it is pseudo-Islamic. Malcolm and Warith both faced opposition from the Nation of Islam for raising the banner of Islam, and Ali later acknowledged that Malcolm had chosen the right path while he had chosen to remain with the Black Muslims. Less than a week before his assassination Malcolm told an audience that "what Elijah Muhammad is teaching is an insult to the entire Muslim world."[4] As Malcolm's story particularly demonstrates, then, the one who would understand and embrace the Qur'an will by necessity flee the shores of "the Nation." Those who continue to hope for a reconciliation between traditional Islam and the Nation of Islam have a long wait ahead.

There are those who would likewise blur the lines between the teachings of the Nation of Islam and those of the Christian church. In some instances Christian ministers have worked cooperatively with the Black Muslims. With the triumph (and it *was* a triumph) of the Million Man March in October 1995, Louis Farrakhan successfully gathered a million black men under his wing in Washington, D.C.— many of whom probably had Christian backgrounds and some of whom were Christian clergymen or laymen. And early in 1997, Benjamin F. Chavis, formerly of the NAACP and a Christian clergyman, announced he was joining Farrakhan's Nation of Islam. Standing before the assembled Black Muslims with a Bible in one hand and a Qur'an in the other, Chavis displayed an amazing amount of wishful thinking when he declared, "I find no theological contradiction between being a black Christian and a black Muslim." Even if Chavis (who wants to retain his credentials with the United Church of Christ) is successful keeping one foot in the church and one in the mosque, the "new paradigm for black leadership" he desires to demonstrate, religiously speaking, would be abortive.[5]

The undeniable favor enjoyed by the Black Muslims among African Americans today was foreshadowed a generation ago in the quiet and qualified sympathy of many blacks toward Elijah Muhammad and Malcolm X. The present popularity ranges from self-identified Christian clergy and laity who openly cooperate with and support the Black Muslims to those, like many of the brothers at the Million Man March, who would differentiate between the man who led the march and the unity and well-being of black people in the United

States. Fundamental to that distinction, however, is the moral high ground that has been claimed by Louis Farrakhan—not only as a social critic but as a minister who "works" the Bible so effectively that his rhetorical force is mistaken for theological and spiritual integrity. It is this confusion of force with integrity that is the defining theme of the rarely told story of the Nation of Islam and Christianity. When Louis Farrakhan credits Malcolm X as his teacher and Elijah Muhammad as "the Messenger," it is this religious sleight of hand that represents both the lesson and the message of the Nation of Islam.

As a leader in the black community, Louis Farrakhan longs for the very thing he shall never possess: the mantle of the black church. Like the leaders of the precursor Nation of Islam organizations, Farrakhan is hopelessly at odds with the black Christian church. He may win the hearts of individual Christian pastors and may even enjoy the arm's-length favor of many Christian people, but, like Simon Magus of old, he is caught in the galling trick bag of his own religious legacy. One discerning rabbi noted shortly after Farrakhan's World's Day of Atonement in October 1996:

> Let's face it, the Million Man March and the World's Day of Atonement are really about getting people to attach to Farrakhan religiously. The religious power buttons he's jealous of aren't really held by Jews. They're held by the black Christian leaders. That's the constellation he wants. Farrakhan knows that as soon as he says Jesus, he's lost. So he goes about it differently. He's not really after the Pharisees, he's after Jesus. Jews are just the effigy.[6]

No doubt, the black clergy recognize this also, but like Wyatt Tee Walker, pastor of Harlem's Canaan Baptist Church, they have perhaps refrained from fighting Farrakhan in the name of black solidarity or because they feel he is saying things that need to be said to whites. In "An Open Letter to Louis Farrakhan & Others," published not long before the Million Man March, Walker demanded that Farrakhan make public redress for "past intemperate remarks" about the black church "with a pledge to cease and desist in the future." Walker wrote:

> There is no way for me and others similarly situated, in the name of unity, to set aside the twenty-five years of caustic criticism that you

have leveled at Black Churches and Black preachers. If unity is the goal, then reconciliation must proceed first. I have always been offended by your criticism of Black [c]hurches and Black preachers but I held my peace in the name of unity. It was a mistake of judgment.[7]

According to one witness[8] to a meeting between Farrakhan, Walker, and other black clergy in New York City prior to the Million Man March, the former made some satisfactory gestures of reconciliation to Walker and the black church. They were apparently accepted, especially in light of the great opportunities afforded ministers who wished to appear with the Black Muslim leader at that momentous gathering in the nation's capital. However, Walker probably realized that as tempered and pacific as Farrakhan may present himself to the black church, his doctrines actually assume the Nation of Islam's perennial invective against Christianity. Detente may be possible for the black church and the Nation of Islam, but genuine reconciliation remains out of reach.

Well-attended marches and somber days of atonement notwithstanding, a Black Muslim cannot acquire the religious devotion that is entitled to the black Christian minister because African American Christians have always known the fundamental difference between *their* faith and that of the white Christian, just as they know the irreconcilable difference between Christianity and the Nation of Islam. In sheer chronology, the Nation of Islam was born too late, its founders and proponents appearing in history long after the black community recognized the duplicity of white Christianity in the spiritual wilderness of North America and decided to cling to Jesus nonetheless. This is something that Malcolm X came to learn and respect, especially after he was free of the "strait-jacket religion" of the Nation of Islam. The greatest defense against the simplistic charge that *Christianity* is the "white man's religion" and a "slave-making lie" is found in the integrity of black Christian faith. On the day of judgment it will be neither Moses nor Jesus who will rise up to rebuke Elijah Muhammad, but it will be David Walker, Harriet Tubman, and Sojourner Truth who will stand to make accusation.

The story of Malcolm X and Christianity, then, is instructive, first, because it represents an important if not essential aspect of his life as a religious revolutionist as well as the religious context in which Elijah Muhammad's Nation of Islam existed. Second, the Nation of Islam's religious themes continue to resound in the doctrines and preachments of Louis Farrakhan's contemporary Nation of Islam (along with his lesser known "Muslim" rivals). The story of Malcolm and Christianity, however, is unique, not identically resembling the experiences of those who abandoned the Christian church for "Islam." Malcolm's story rises above the cultic narrative of the Black Muslims, his quest for religious integrity—like his quest for human rights—having been compelled by sincerity, self-criticism, and a selfless agenda that have rarely been characteristic of the Nation of Islam or the people who have benefited most from it.

Malcolm X saw the Nation of Islam committing the most heinous sins at the point of its greatest institutional strength, and many of the same charges he once leveled at the black Christian church he ultimately was forced to aim at his former Black Muslim brethren. Even more tragically, in the end it was Elijah Muhammad's movement that brought about his death. Even factoring in government culpability by way of surveillance, infiltration, and propagandastic exacerbation, Malcolm's assassination was brought about by the same "Nation" he had helped to build. Louis Farrakhan may decry the shameful work of the FBI in provoking hatred for Malcolm within the Black Muslim movement, but almost three decades later he issued a stylistic rejoinder to those outside of the Nation of Islam that suggested the public tears he has shed for Malcolm contain more salt than sorrow: "Was Malcolm your traitor or was he ours? And if we dealt with him like a nation deals with a traitor what the hell business is it of yours?"[9]

The tragic fact remains that Malcolm was crushed, not by the cross but by the star and crescent of the Nation of Islam. The final irony is that Malcolm's death, almost messianic to many,[10] may also serve as a living, indeed dying reminder of the cultic dependence of the Black Muslims upon the Christian message and also the spiritual vitality that former black Christians have brought with them from the church into traditional Islam. Malcolm's altruism kept him from hiding comfortably and safely abroad while the Nation of Islam advanced its disingenuous "Islamic" message among African Americans. His integrity led him back to the United States and onto the stage of death where his final witness poured forth, not in words but in martyr's blood. In finding his own tragic death on behalf of others, then, Malcolm X perhaps drew closer to the cross than he had ever done in life.

Malcolm and the Cross will inevitably fall short of fully explaining this compelling "anti-quest" since, as St. Paul has written, "who among men knows the thoughts of a man except the spirit of a man, which is in him?"[11] With Malcolm gone we will never know many things about his inner pursuit of religious truth, especially in regard to Christianity. Nevertheless, this book may at least highlight a valuable facet of an extraordinary sojourn that ultimately transcended the often parochial worlds of race and religion—a journey that men and women will retrace in the pages of Malcolm's story for generations to come.

PART I

Fires Which Burnt Brightly
The Nation of Islam in a Christian World

Malice and habit have now won the day.
The honours we fought for are lost in the fray.

Once proud and truthful, now humbled and bent,
Fires which burnt brightly, now energies spent.

Our flowers and feathers as scarring as weapons.
Our poems and letters have turned to deceptions.
                    —Excerpted from Keith Reid's
                    "Fires (Which Burnt Brightly),"
                    from Procol Harum's *Grand Hotel*
                    (Chrysalis Records, 1973)

1

A Rumor from the East

The Fard Muhammad Movement and the Problem of the Bible

> But rumors from the East and from the North will disturb
> him, and he will go forth with great wrath to destroy and
> annihilate many.   —Daniel 11:44

Within a few years of his appearance in Detroit, Michigan, in 1930, the founder of the original Nation of Islam had become a divine icon.[1] Having first appeared in the urban black community in the guise of a peddler, he quickly implemented an agenda of proselytization and organization that likely reflected previous involvement in other movements.[2] Obviously a man with strong racial convictions, W. D. Fard, also known as Fard Muhammad, quickly sought to exert his influence among his customers. Guiding them from informal conversation to house groups, and finally to rented facilities, Fard molded his trusting followers into an organization within a short time. He trained assistants, devised a catechism, and recycled the frustration of racist victimization and the desperation of economic plight into the fuel needed to propel them out of the Christian world and into the world of "Islam."

Fard played the mysterioso to the hilt. Despite the fact that he qualified as a "white" man, he was not of European background and certainly held racial sentiments that were as foreign to most white Americans as the religion of Islam. His first success in the eyes of his followers was perhaps his own profile as a man who had peeled away the appearance of whiteness from the mentality of whiteness—a distinction Malcolm X would elevate many years later in his descriptions of "white" Muslims abroad. What could be more mysterious than a "white" man with religiously charged sentiments that easily rivaled the most militant "race men" of the era? Indeed, so successful was Fard at this profile that his followers accepted him as a virtual non-white. "Professor Fard had straight hair . . . and [he had] very light features," recalled the son of Fard's greatest follower. "He was not presented to us as a Caucasian, mind you, we were told that one of his relatives was Caucasian." As to his "white" relatives, Fard painted the most exotic family tree, telling some of his black followers that he was from the lineage of the Hashimide sheriffs of Mecca; he told others that he was from the tribe of Koreish, the tribe of the Prophet Muhammad. Interestingly, police records suggest that Fard was of a mixed racial background, being either of Hawaiian or Polynesian/British heritage, though other theories suggest Fard was of Syrian and Caribbean background, or of some other eastern extraction.[3]

The mystery of Fard's race was exceeded by the mystery of his past. Within the movement, Fard seems to have fed the fascination of his followers not only with tricks and illusions that gave him a mystical aura, but also by making himself out to be older than he actually was and by glamorizing his mission with claims about his accomplishments. He reportedly told some of his followers that he had studied for twenty years at the University of Southern California, Los Angeles, in preparation for his saving work among blacks. He elsewhere claimed that he had worked among dark people for twenty years before he "made himself known to them." Fard's past was not what he portrayed, though it may have been equally as interesting. Active on the West Coast, it appears he had mixed race politics with criminality and served three years at San Quentin before embarking eastward to Detroit.[4]

Still, Fard was a thoroughgoing "race man," and there is every reason to believe that his interest in black liberation was sincere and that his agenda, however peculiar, was informed by conviction. Understandably, Fard attacked the hypocrisy of white Christendom, but it was apparent that he was no religious reformer. Prior to Fard, Marcus Garvey had worked within a Christian context to counter white Christianity with a zealous form of black Christianity that was entirely at home in the Bible. In contrast to Garvey, a black American named Noble Drew Ali had founded the first "Moslem"-oriented movement, the Moorish Science Temple, in that same era. Drew Ali completely set aside the Bible, substituting it with his own *Holy Koran* (a cultic admixture of sectarian, apocryphal, and exotic religious writings). The genius of Fard's movement, therefore, was found in his refusal to go either the way of Garvey or Drew Ali with reference to the Bible. Apparently indifferent to Garvey's black Christianity, Fard nevertheless recognized the value of using the Bible in his campaign in the black community; perhaps he also observed that Drew Ali had enjoyed little success in wooing African Americans away from the Bible with his *Holy Koran*.[5]

Ironically, the Bible was as much Fard's greatest problem as it was his passport to success. While he later put an English interpretation of the real Qur'an in the hands of his followers, Fard apparently recognized that no successful liberation movement among African Americans could afford to divorce itself from the Bible as an authoritative canon. Fard's dilemma, then, was how to use the Bible to undermine the biblical doctrines upon which rested the integrity of the Christian faith and the black Christian church in particular. To Fard's advantage, many in his audience were not well-schooled. More specifically, most were not acquainted with the issues surrounding the theological and literary aspects of the Bible, except perhaps for the rich oral exegesis of the "Exodus" theme in black preaching—a characteristic typical of Elijah Muhammad's Nation of Islam audiences two decades later. Despite their personal devotion to the Bible as a divine oracle (which endures today among most African Americans, even among congregations with pastors who may hold more liberal beliefs regarding the sacred text), Fard was able to disrupt their devotion by employing what appeared to be a logical exposé of biblical fallibility.[6]

The result of Fard's turn-and-attack on the Bible put many of his followers into a virtual state of shock; it puzzled them because Fard had often used the Bible to vindicate his initial presentation. The testimony of one follower clearly illustrates how Fard's approach had radically disturbed his listeners, putting them in a frame of mind where they became dependent upon him: "The very first time I went to a meeting I heard him say: 'The Bible tells you that the sun rises and sets. That is not so. The sun stands still. All your lives you have been thinking that the earth never moved. Stand and look toward the sun and know that it is the earth that you are standing on which is moving.'" This man was quickly convinced by his teacher's argument, not discerning that Fard had set up a straw man of literalism that could be easily knocked down, and with lasting impact: "Up to that day I always went to the Baptist church. After I heard that sermon from the prophet, I was turned around completely. Just to think that the sun above me never moved at all and that the earth we are on was doing all the moving has changed everything for me."

Fard's unschooled follower was impressed by this seeming contradiction, but like many other disciples, this man was led into a cultic crisis that could only be resolved by a radical reordering of his religious life. "When I went home and heard that dinner was ready, I said: 'I don't want to eat dinner. I just want to go back to the meetings.' I wouldn't eat my meals but I goes back that night and I goes to every meeting after that. . . . That changed everything for me."[7] Unable to trust the Bible, the followers of Fard quickly became religious dependents who looked to his diatribes for revelation and increasingly found themselves alienated from the central social and spiritual institution of the black community, the Christian church.

Indeed, as Fard's authority increased, so did his acerbic treatment of the Bible. Along with the "white devil" epithet that would become a trademark of the Black Muslim phenomenon, Fard began to inject a bitter suspicion of the Christian canon into his teachings, labeling the Bible "the poisoned book." Along with his own catechism, which featured bizarre questions that appeared to be highly mathematic but were actually somewhat parabolic,[8] Fard initiated what might be considered an oral apocrypha of the Bible. His apocrypha, which was to be accepted as authoritative revelation, was actually a theological thrust at the heart of doctrinal Christianity:

He used to tell the story of Jesus when he preaches. He told the followers[:] "Mary's father was a rich man and therefore he refused to give Mary in marriage to her greatest lover, Joseph Al-Nejjar, because he was a poor man with nothing but a saw and a hammer, because he was a very poor carpenter. Being in love with Mary, hopeless of marrying her, Joseph had impregnated her with Jesus." And this is very reasonable and scientific.[9]

Clearly, Fard brought with him an anti-incarnational theology as it pertained to Christianity, though his claim that Jesus was actually the biological son of Joseph does not suggest Fard was advocating an Islamic perspective. Quite the contrary: in claiming that Jesus was the son of Joseph "Al-Nejjar" and Mary, Fard simultaneously violated the Bible and the Qur'an. His apocryphal assertion about the birth of Christ suggests that Fard had no intention of introducing black people to traditional Islam. Had he wished to do so, Fard could have easily drawn the Qur'anic distinction between the virgin birth of Christ as a creational miracle and the Christian conception of the virgin birth as an incarnational miracle.[10] By flouting the canons of Christianity and Islam in this manner, Fard not only sketched an enduring self-portrait of religious distortion, he also set a precedent for fictionalizing on biblical texts for the next Nation of Islam movement.

An early observer of the first Nation of Islam noted that Fard's "message was characterized by his ability to utilize to the fullest measure the environment of his followers." Fard consequently supplemented his teaching with other cultural and historical sources, including Freemasonry and its symbolism. However, since the reading skills of most of Fard's followers were limited, they relied on his explanations of these supplemental sources. As was the case with his use of the Bible, Fard explained to his followers that all of the sources he recommended were "symbolic" and couldn't be understood without his revelations provided during temple meetings.[11]

Most interesting—and doubtless most telling with regard to Fard's own religious nature—were the theological resources Fard recommended to them. A veritable hodge-podge of religious ideas, the sources Fard recommended had no theological consistency, the only commonality being that Fard chose to use them to enhance his own teaching. For example, he saw no contradiction in using both fundamentalist and cultic source material. Thus, the "Moslems" were instructed to listen to the ultraconservative, hyperpatriotic Baptist radio preacher Frank Norris, and also to Judge Rutherford, a leading spokesman for the Watchtower Bible and Tract Society.[12] Ironically, neither Norris's Christian theology nor his political conservatism would have been beneficial to Fard. But Norris's conservative moral teachings probably reinforced the legendary spartan moral code of the Nation of Islam and Norris's Christian Dispensationalism undoubtedly gave the "Moslems" the kind of context suitable for the outrageous apocalypticism for which the Nation of Islam phenomenon is still known today.

Another irony of the Black Muslim movement is its apparent dependency—directly and indirectly—on the prevailing notion of the "fulfillment of biblical prophecy" made possible by modern fundamentalist Christian Dispensationalism. Dispensationalism (named for its division of redemptive history into seven distinct "dispensations," including the millennium) originated in England and is largely attributed to a nineteenth-century leader, John Nelson Darby, of the Plymouth Brethren movement. In the early twentieth century, Dispensationalism was further advanced in the United States through the popularity of the biblical study notes of Cyrus Ingerson Scofield, an ex-Confederate soldier, lawyer, and Bible teacher.[13] The premise of Dispensationalism is that the apocalyptic texts of the Bible, especially the book of Revelation, are to be interpreted literally and with the assumption of present-day and near-future fulfillment. Rather than focusing on the primary historical and redemptive themes of those writings, Dispensationalism at its best overreaches itself, its adherents constantly revising and reformulating their "prophetic calendar" with the passing of time in order to sustain their future and literal orientation. At worst, Dispensationalism has lent itself to a future mania that has given to religious culture a carte blanche for speculation, fantasy, and other forms of scriptural abuse so common in the presentations on "Bible prophecy" typified in fundamentalist television broadcasts like the "700 Club."

By the era in which the first Nation of Islam was born, the cultural

impact of Dispensationalism had undoubtedly provided a new theological genre for religion in the United States. With the burgeoning
"Bible school" movement (itself a reaction to liberal and intellectual
seminaries) and the popularity of Scofield's notes on biblical apocalyptic literature appended to the King James Bible, the age of Dispensationalism came to full flower at a time when fundamentalist Christians were also fighting the Lord's battles against theological liberal-
ism and evolutionary theory. Unfortunately, Dispensationalism
ushered in an obsessive futuristic orientation and a pessimistic, oth-
erworldly form of premillennialism that seems to have replaced the
more reasoned and optimistic postmillennialism of the Reformation
that had predominated in the United States up until the Civil War
era.[14]

The significance of this development with regard to the Nation of
Islam is that Fard's approach to the Bible was inevitably framed in this
new "prophetic fulfillment" genre, which in turn provided the Nation
of Islam a context for its own peculiar futuristic apocalypticism and
its convenient appropriation of biblical language in the name of in-
terpreting biblical "symbolism." As a religious voyeur on the fringes
of religion in the United States, Fard flourished in the climate created
by Dispensationalism: excising biblical terms and texts from their
original covenantal-historical context, Fard was imitating the techniques of many fundamentalist Christian Bible teachers—only outside the pale of orthodoxy. However, if the rise of Dispensationalism
was only an indirect influence, there were also direct sources of influence that had themselves blossomed in the new age of Christian theo-
futurism.

Not surprisingly, Fard found the "cryptic ambiguity" of the Watchtower Bible and Tract Society (the Jehovah's Witnesses) even more
appealing. The cult's method of "biblical" explanation permitted
multiple interpretations of the text—a practice that would become
key to the Black Muslim treatment of the Bible thereafter.[15] The
Watchtower was apparently a cult spin-off from the remote Christian
sect, the Seventh-Day Adventists (formed in 1863), which emphasized
the prophecy-oriented teachings of Ellen Gould White (who was herself influenced by the futuristic apocalypticism of William Miller).[16]

While Fard would undoubtedly have appreciated the Watchtower's denial of the divinity of Jesus Christ, what apparently attracted him was the Watchtower's apocalyptic teachings—its emphasis on the future and literal fulfillment of "biblical prophecy," especially pertaining to the great cosmic battle of Armageddon and the subsequent salvation of an elect 144,000 survivors who would inhabit the new earth. While Fard, like the Watchtower, did not futurize the millennium, he imitated its appropriation of the legendary thousand years as a literal period that marked the culmination of world history. Finally, Fard apparently seized the Watchtower's claim that the year 1914 had marked the end of the age, but that an extension had been granted until such a time as the divine mission could be accomplished through the organization. Of course, the "Moslems" were instructed that the teachings of Dispensational Christians and the Watchtower movement could not be accepted without Fard's explanation and interpretation. To his cultic curriculum of heresy, sectarian, and orthodox teachings, Fard eventually added the Qur'an. However, even though Fard introduced it as the ultimate authority, he first offered his associates an Arabic text, undoubtedly knowing they would remain dependent on him for interpretation. Though he eventually gave his closest assistant an English interpretation of the Qur'an, Fard hinted that he still had another revelatory canon besides the Bible and the Qur'an: "These are not the only books I have[;] but I have another book that I made myself."[17]

While the appropriation of biblical texts for heretical private interpretation is a problem as old as the church itself, the direct and indirect influence of the popular Dispensational method gave many sectarian, cultic, and orthodox religionists a kind of prophetic *lingua franca* that emphasized symbolic biblical language being literally fulfilled in contemporary or near-future contexts. Along with this came the double interpretation of texts and an increasingly sensational approach to biblical interpretation that adherents would claim was more "relevant" than traditional Protestant exegesis and preaching. To be sure, millennial fever and chiliastic chills had occurred as far back as the medieval and Reformation era, but Fard's peculiar treatment of the Bible was not informed by those older European movements. The supposed Eastern message he introduced as "Islam" to the black migrants of Detroit was more a rumor than the truth. The twisting theological roots of W. D. Fard were watered, quite ironically, by the swelling mainstream of the new apocalyptic movement that was already flowing through Christian churches, the fellowships of their dissenting brethren, and apostate competitors.

As Fard's influence grew and his organization solidified, he was challenged by competitors within the "Moslem" society of urban black America, including those who were either affiliated with or influenced by the Drew Ali Moorish movement. Furthermore, he was being observed and harassed by local police and federal agents determined to smother any black liberation movement in its infancy. Since Fard may have had links to West Coast radicals, or at least had left a trail for them to follow to Detroit,[18] his activities were clearly marked as subversive. However, while Fard's major worries involved divisive "Moslem" competitors and police harassment, he also found a third battlefront before him. The Nation of Islam's anti-Christian teachings were apparently not lost on the black clergy in Detroit, who may have also conveyed their disgust to white associates. To be sure, an element of jealousy may have provoked these ministers given Fard's unprecedented popularity, often manifested in large crowds competing for a place to stand and listen to "the savior of the race." Yet, even granting the inevitable eruption of jealousy, concern on the part of the Christian clergy regarding Fard's anti-Christian teachings was legitimate. On one occasion at least, some Christian ministers actually confronted Fard. Even before the eyes of his followers the clergymen were baffling Fard with their questions, especially when they demanded proofs about his prophecy. Fard hedged, avoiding their challenges by donning the guise of an omniscient messiah: "You think I do not understand what is going on in your mind; I can tell you just now what you think, what each individual here thinks and all what is going to happen in the future."[19] To no surprise, though Fard was apparently cornered and incapable of proving himself to the more knowledgeable leaders of the church, his followers were not dissuaded.

Police harassment and internal conflict ultimately undermined the Nation of Islam. After being targeted, probably unfairly, in the case of a bizarre cult murder in Detroit in 1932, Fard's career as a race messiah began to spiral downward. He had already begun to withdraw from public meetings of the Nation of Islam due to his "Moslem" competitors. As pressure from hostile law enforcement agents increased, Fard was repeatedly arrested for disturbing the peace. After three such arrests he was deported from Detroit in May 1933 and relocated to Chicago—where he and a loyal follower had already carried out some preliminary evangelism. However, the surveillance network quickly tagged Fard in his new location and police harassment began in the Windy City, culminating in Fard's imprisonment.[20]

After his release, Fard traveled around the United States and returned to see his followers in Chicago, bidding them farewell in February 1934. Playing the role of Christ to the very last moment, Fard declared: "Don't worry. I am with you; I will be back to you in the near future to lead you out of this hell." His followers heard from him again by correspondence, but Fard was apparently reported missing by June 1934. W. D. Fard's final departure was as mysterious as his arrival. Cloaked in the mantle of a peddler, Fard had increasingly transformed his image to a kind of modern version of Jesus Christ. When circumstances outside of his influence eventually forced him out of the black community, Fard nevertheless postured himself as a Christ figure, including the promise of an apocalyptic return in which he would deliver his black followers from oppression in the white man's world.

Fard never returned to his movement in the literal sense, but the divine persona he had begun to shape for himself was reintroduced by his most devoted follower, who enhanced the image of the mysterious "white" teacher into an icon of devotion that strangely paralleled the prevailing white image of Jesus Christ in the sacred art of most black Christian churches. Whether or not Fard had originally intended to fashion himself as a counter-Christ is unclear; perhaps he had not anticipated the extent to which he would thereafter be perceived as a kind of anti-Christ by the Christian community. At first,

Fard seems to have intended only to present himself as a mystic-teacher. To have presented himself as a prophet (as had Drew Ali) would have been heresy in Islamic terms (though not in Christian terms). "He did not teach us that he was a prophet," his greatest admirer later admitted. "We used to call him prophet."[21] Of course, his Christian-oriented followers were hardly aware of the Islamic doctrine of the cessation of prophethood with the climactic ministry of Muhammad ibn Abdullah. In their thinking, undoubtedly conditioned by the teachings of Christianity, prophethood remained an open-ended phenomenon. However, those who followed Fard the closest were looking for even more than a prophet in the Christian sense. Like Elijah Poole of Sandersville, Georgia, who had attached himself devotedly to Fard as his best preacher and supporter, those who placed their faith in the mysterious peddler-turned-messiah were looking for a *savior*.

To be sure, the salvation they sought was redemption from racism, but it was ultimately indivisible from spiritual redemption. The black believer in the white man's world has never drawn absolute lines between the redemption of his soul and the liberation of his humanity. Even the most devoted black Christian of that day would not have comfortably joined either side of the war that was raging in the white church between "social gospel" adherents and fundamentalists. All the more, men like Poole—who did not believe the Jesus of Christianity could save him—still persisted in looking for a Christ figure. When he finally stumbled on a reasonable approximation, it seems Poole's inclination to worship a divine incarnation had provided the shrewd and discerning Fard with a far better platform than he had originally intended to build. Ultimately, Fard was deified, enthroned upon a theological construct from which Jesus had already been toppled, in the mind of the man who would become Elijah Muhammad.

2

Reincarnating the Savior

Elijah Muhammad and the Deification of W. D. Fard

Before we ever suffered ourselves, Master W. Fard Muhammad, our God and Saviour, the Great Mahdi, Almighty God Allah in Person, Himself suffered persecution and rejection. All for you and for me!
— Elijah Muhammad, *Supreme Wisdom,* vol. 2

In the first couple of years, Elijah knew nothing about Islam. He took a simple Christian fundamentalist concept and stuck on a few Moslem names.
— Surveillance report, New York City Police Department Legal Bureau, 1960s

Even a harsh critic ought to judge Elijah Muhammad as a man of importance and, in a very real sense, greatness. His religious apostasy notwithstanding, the quintessential Black Muslim proclaimed a message that the United States deserved, and he built a kingdom that could only have found credence in a society where religion and religious leadership had failed—and failed miserably—to address the immoral and unjust treatment of African Americans. Indeed, some heresies are born simply because of a disingenuous determination to advance untruth at the expense of others. But other heresies, like that which was introduced by Elijah Muhammad, explode upon the body politic with a sense of *rightness*. The former are like computer viruses, which are engineered on purpose and only to destroy or disrupt. The latter are more like biological viruses which, while dangerous and destructive, seem to find their being in the very chemistry of nature. In other words, such heresies are more like "acts of God," appearing almost as divine judgments in their own right.

In the early 1960s, when the moral infrastructure of the second Nation of Islam had already waned, one discerning scholar nevertheless made a similar observation about the efficacy of the Black Muslims and their presence in the United States: "One wonders if the movement does not have prophet qualities, and is perhaps like the wicked Assyrian of the Bible sent as the 'rod of God's anger,' in this case to chastise America instead of ancient Israel for past injustices, doomed to go down afterwards in archaeological curiosity."[1] "Prophet qualities" may exist, even in a heretic, and therefore what Abraham Heschel once wrote concerning the inspired seers of Israel may be diminutively (and perhaps grudgingly) applied to the little man from Georgia who became "the Messenger of Allah to the Lost-Found Nation of Islam in North America":

> The prophet is a person, not a microphone.... He speaks from the perspective of God as perceived from the perspective of his own situation. We must seek to understand not only the views he expounded but also the attitudes he embodied: his own position, feeling, response—not only what he said but also what he lived; the private, the intimate dimension of the word, the subjective side of the message.[2]

Elijah Muhammad was born Elijah Poole on October 7, 1897, in Sandersville, Georgia,[3] a child of sharecroppers, a scion of the poverty of systemic oppression. Yet he was also born into a vivid religious environment, the son and the grandson of self-styled, "jackleg" preachers, and consequently spent a good deal of time in Baptist church services. Young Elijah's experience in the church was very encouraging to him, particularly since he was regarded as the "dear" of preachers and parishioners alike. Typically, the young Elijah was allowed to sit in the honored seat of the speaker, the "preacher set," during the services. This childhood experience of favor and recognition helped engender in the young Elijah a sense of calling and the belief that he was to be a great preacher some day. This sense was so strong within him that, even as a youth, what little education he had been able to obtain in the public school he saw only as a means to learn how to study the Bible. "When I was six or seven years old," Muhammad recalled in his first magazine interview, "I went to school for only one objective—to study the Bible, to learn to read it."

Yet if the church was a source of encouragement and the genesis of his desire to become a religious leader, the world seemed to work against Elijah at every turn. His basic schooling was interrupted by the family's need to send him to work. One of thirteen children, Elijah used to chop wood with his sister in the countryside and haul it into town for sale. Venturing into the small town of Cordele to sell the wood, young Elijah wore only "one rough garment" which had to last him the whole season.[4]

The poverty and dire social limitations that were part of Elijah's youth was status quo for all African American sharecroppers in the Southern states. Not only was poverty enforced by the economy of the racist South, but violence against blacks was unbridled and seemingly without conscience. By the time Elijah was an adolescent, over 1,100 black people were known to have been lynched. Violence of this nature is typified in the brutal murder of Will Stanley in 1915. Stanley, a murder suspect being held in jail at Temple, Texas, was forcibly removed by a mob numbering up to ten thousand whites. The mob burned Stanley alive, having shackled him in chains on a pyre of wooden boxes, and afterward hanged him in display. Unsatisfied by this carnage, the savages made picture postcards of Stanley's charred corpse and sold them for ten cents each. Not surprisingly, the governor of Texas claimed no official notice of Stanley's murder.[5] If such an outrage could be committed in public upon an untried, unconvicted suspect under the eyes of the law, there is no way to estimate how many other incidents of brutality and murder took place without public notice. And while incidents of racist murder were widespread throughout the South, they were also a dramatic part of Elijah's personal memory of youth.

As a boy, Elijah actually witnessed a lynching—the unfortunate victim's only crime supposedly having been to insult a white woman. Elijah never forgot the tragic scene:

That event had impressed me so much that I cannot get over it; I did never [sic] forget it, not until this day. It was terrible and horrible to see such things happening and all our grown men right there in the section allowing such things to happen. I returned to our house, which was about four miles away from the little town, grieving all the way. I wished I were a man so that I could try to do something about it. That scene hurt me very much.[6]

As he grew, Elijah's hurt only increased. He later witnessed the immediate aftermath of another lynching in Macon, Georgia. Apparently after that lynching the perpetrators had dragged the victim's corpse through the streets attached to the rear of a truck.

Elijah's experience of white racism became even more personal to him, particularly as he encountered vicious foremen and bosses working in the fields and sawmills. The most notable case was an elderly white man for whom Elijah worked in his late teens. The man paid Elijah only eight dollars per month for twelve-hour workdays. The man frequently forced his black workers to take beatings at gunpoint, and he threatened Elijah with such a beating. Rather than face the certain consequences of fighting an oppressive boss, Elijah quit the job despite his great need for the income. "That man was a very cruel white man, as all the devils are," Elijah recounted decades later. "This man was not an exception; they were all about the same."

With such a distressing environment in which to grow, Elijah Poole nevertheless cultivated his own sense of divine calling. He continued to pore over the pages of his Bible; his family was impressed by the fact that, despite the limitations of having only a fourth-grade education, Elijah tearfully persevered in his strenuous examination of the biblical text. It seems that Elijah's continued struggles over the Bible increasingly involved theology more than anything else. He later told Malcolm X that as a youth he had felt "the Bible's words were a locked door, that could be unlocked, if only he knew how." It appears that Elijah had rejected the teachings of the black Christian church long before he had ever heard W. D. Fard in Detroit. Elijah wanted to be a preacher, to be sure, but not like the Christian preachers he had often heard.[7] Apparently two significant factors became characteristic of Elijah's increasing inclination toward nonorthodox, nontraditional religion. First, it seems his own father had such inclinations, or at least had a view of biblical interpretation that could easily turn unorthodox: "My father, who was a preacher, told me that each man interprets the Bible according to his own fancy, and I asked him wasn't there one *right* interpretation?" His father's notion that biblical interpretation required no objective guidelines may have nurtured in young Elijah the sense that he could also somehow "unlock" the truths he sought. However, unlike his father with whom he would argue over biblical interpretation, Elijah seems to have initially shown a stronger inclination to disregard orthodoxy and the plain meaning of texts in favor of interpretations he imposed on the text. To be sure, Elijah was looking for "the right" interpretation. However, that interpretation was contingent only on whatever personal revelations he might realize. And so, with tears in his eyes and a burning desire to preach and teach, Elijah persevered in his quest for a key that would unlock the door of private revelation.

Second, early on Elijah was strongly "race conscious," a fact that his family recognized. Witnessing murder, the cold-hearted racism of white Southerners, and having heard the stories of slavery from his grandmother made a deep impression on the sensitive youth: "My grandmother used to sit down and tell me how the white people used to beat her sister when she was young and under slavery," he later recalled. "They were beating her until her legs swell [*sic*] enough and blood comes out of her skin; and I sit [*sic*] and listened to her telling me the sufferings of slavery until I fill [*sic*] my heart with griefs." Elijah seems to have responded to his grandmother's stories with a sense of religious mission, though he obviously realized the tremendous burden such a mission presented: "I used to tell her: 'My grandmother, when I get to be a man, if the Lord helps me I will try to get my people out of the grip of this white man because I believe that we will not be able to get along with peace under his government.' She says, 'I do not think either, son.'"[8] Elijah's race consciousness and his religious inclinations thus shaped his formative years, and his approach to white people was mild-mannered yet bold and uncompromising. In working at the sawmills, Elijah was both gentle and intrepid when he told his white foreman that he would rather be fired than cursed or abused with racial epithets.

Generally, his attitude earned him respect from whites and blacks, and among his own siblings he apparently held an authoritative role as well. Elijah's awkward relationship to the black Christian church continued throughout the rest of his time in the South, and probably grew toward coldness once he migrated North. Already married and the father of two children, Elijah moved to Detroit in April 1923 and found employment in the Chevrolet plant from 1923 through 1929. Apparently, Elijah brought his hunger for a religious alternative with him to Detroit. It is likely that the alternative Elijah was seeking was a race-oriented religion that recognized the advancement of black people and a judgment upon whites for their age-old cruelty. Elijah may have hoped to find this in the Masonic order, which he apparently joined in 1924.[9]

The black Masonic order had originally been formed as a parachurch group in the eighteenth century. The founders had been refused admission into the white colonial Masonic order and so obtained a charter from the Grand Lodge in England. By the era of the Civil War, however, the Masons and other "mutual aid societies" had largely separated from association with the church. In the cities—as would doubtless have been the case with the Detroit order that Elijah joined—the Masons had lost their religious character altogether and were dominated by middle-class men whose interest was largely in social and secular matters. Perhaps Elijah was attracted to the Masons for their secret, ritualistic, and racially exclusive identity and their elite image within the urban black community. The fact that this order was not affiliated with the Christian church was probably also a strong draw to Elijah who, despite his inclination to preach, could not "preach the Christian religion" because he felt it was simply incorrect.[10]

Still, Elijah was desperately seeking a role for himself as a preacher, as much as he was seeking a new gospel to preach: "I told my wife, when I was working on a job, that no matter how well I did, I wouldn't be satisfied until I was preaching. Sometimes the spirit in me to preach was so strong that I almost cried." Like many other African

American migrants, Elijah Poole came to Detroit with a desire to find a new life and upgrade the conditions in which he and his family had lived. Yet he had come with his own highly sensitive race consciousness and a unique religious hunger that included a personal sense of mission. His desire was to find a religious teaching that would save black people and give them a new vision that could supplant the white man's religious vision— which Elijah inevitably associated with slavery and oppression. It may be that Elijah was simply not insightful or clever enough to do what Drew Ali before him had done—invent a religious cult of his own. However, it seems more likely that his religious ideas, rooted in the Bible, prevented him from doing so. That is, perhaps it was inherent in Elijah Poole's religious vision to seek a divinely incarnated messiah, and to receive a promised savior whom he could then declare as the divine solution. Thus, when he met W. D. Fard in 1931, Elijah Poole believed he had finally found the savior of his anguished black people.

"I moved to Detroit because I thought the life might be better," Elijah recalled many years later, "but even there the first year I saw my people shot down right on the street without any justice whatsoever." He was dreadfully impressed by the irony that he had left the South to escape violence, only to find the same violence against blacks was going on "all the time," especially at the hands of the police. "The difference is that they do not hang them up to the trees [sic] but they kill them right here on the streets." What embittered Elijah even more about the murders he had witnessed in Detroit was that the injustice of the police was not greeted by any act "on our people's part to do anything or to help." These were the same feelings Elijah had felt as a youth when he witnessed a lynching in the South—he was doubly appalled by the fact that "all our grown men" had stood by and allowed the travesty to take place. Now in Detroit, Elijah's frustrations and bitterness began to overflow. He continued to read the Bible zealously, searching its pages with a curiosity that could not be subdued; and the more he read, the more he longed to be a preacher and a "corrector" of his people. At the same time, Elijah seemed to have been experiencing an inner drive to launch out on a preaching mission. Sharing a residence with his older brother in Hamtramck, a small black suburb of Detroit, Elijah was daily involved in Bible study and religious discussions. While he persevered in his belief that Christianity was wrong, within himself Elijah sensed a warning to reform himself and "be a better man" and likewise to start to preach. It was as if a signal had gone off within, announcing to Elijah Poole that he was about to find the answer to his deepest desire.

Elijah first heard W. D. Fard in 1931, about a year after Fard had entered the Detroit area. Elijah was introduced to Fard through his father, who had migrated northward with him. Elijah's father was apparently a friend of Abdul Mohammed, a follower of Fard (and an ex-Moorish American from the Noble Drew Ali movement), and urged his son to get information from him about Fard. Through Mohammed, Elijah and his brother were directed to Fard's meeting on Hasting Street, the main thoroughfare in black Detroit. Apparently Elijah liked what he heard, for he later returned to the meeting place to hear Fard again. After the next meeting, Elijah approached Fard and, it seems, the mixture of the two men wrought an immediate and strange chemistry of messianic delusion.

Elijah later recalled approaching the teacher to shake hands, and immediately declared to Fard that he knew his true identity. "He didn't have to tell me that he was Allah," Muhammad told *Ebony* magazine over thirty years after the incident. "I recognized him. And right there I told him that he was the one the world had been looking for to come [*sic*]." The sincerity of Muhammad's testimony, which seems to have been consistent whenever he told the story of his first encounter with Fard, clearly evidences a messianic hunger that no one, not even Jesus, had satisfied. "I was a student of the Bible," Muhammad told another journalist. "I recognized him to be the person the Bible predicted would come 2,000 years after Jesus' death. It came to me the first time I laid eyes on him."

Not surprisingly, Fard's first response to the approach of the little Georgian seems to have been cautious. According to Muhammad, Fard bowed his head closer to him, a posture which perhaps suggests Fard's sensitive, pastoral manner and his quiet apprehension over what the small, smooth-skinned man was about to say. "Yes, Brother,"

Fard said with a serious expression. He was probably relieved when Elijah's confrontation became an adoring confession of faith: "You are that one we read in the Bible that he would come in the last day under the name of Jesus." Perhaps Elijah was motivated by the model of messianic revelation in the Gospel of Matthew's account of Peter's confession at Caesarea Philippi. In that classic text, Peter was asked by Christ, "Who do you say that I am?"—to which Peter answered, "You are the Christ, the Son of the living God." Perhaps Elijah Poole had wished that Fard would make a similar request of him, but Fard had only bowed his head carefully, saying, "Yes, Brother." Yet Elijah was driven. Having declared his faith in Fard, he still wanted his new-found master's confirmation. "You are that one?" Elijah asked, his regal face with its high cheekbones pointed reverentially upward to Fard. "Here he looked at me very serious [sic] when I said that to him," Muhammad recalled. "'Yes, I am the one that you have been looking for the last two thousand years; I am the one.'" Having affirmed Elijah's confession, Fard casually ended the conversation. "But you go ahead now, brother, that is good." It seemed to Elijah that his messiah did not care if others had understood or believed what Elijah was saying. Still, this was the only spark needed to light a torch that in the decades to come would burn brightly in North America's urban community—a torch carried by the indefatigable Malcolm X.

In the next meeting, according to Elijah, Fard became bold about his identity, announcing that he was, in fact, "El-Mahdi," the Muslim term roughly equivalent to the Jewish—but not the Christian—concept of the messiah. To the Jew and the Muslim, the messiah is a mortal leader anointed by God (Allah) to accomplish some great redemptive purpose. However, unlike the Christian concept of Jesus Christ, neither Judaism nor Islam understands the messiah as sharing the divine nature. Fard followed the Muslim conceptualization by avoiding the "prophet" title. He also specifically announced that while he was "El-Mahdi," he was not Jesus Christ in person. Christ, Fard said, was killed and would never return. "But," Fard assured his amazed listeners, "I am his brother, I am the one you were expecting."

Interestingly, the one aspect of Muslim belief that Fard seemed to respect, the cessation of prophethood after Muhammad, was overlooked by the eager, adoring Elijah Poole. Elijah had rejected Jesus as being the divine incarnation, but the Christian construct of a God-man seems to have prevailed in his thinking, at least in those formative years of his religious teaching. Elijah "didn't know world religions or anything," his son recalled many years after this event. "He came from the South with no high school education, and he had no way of knowing what the Islamic world believed in or what it didn't believe in." Determined, as it were, to fit Fard into the sandals of Christ, Elijah thereafter cast him increasingly as incarnate deity, as a persecuted, suffering savior whose supreme anointing, like Jesus, was overlooked by the kingdoms of the world and understood only by the faithful. Indeed, though Elijah would undoubtedly become more informed as to the distinctives of Islamic "theology" in the years to come, he would never surrender his adoring view of W. D. Fard. The time would come when Elijah would found his own movement, rename it "The Nation of Islam," and set as its most sacred day the celebrated W. D. Fard's birthday.[11] "Savior's Day" would thereafter be recognized with an annual conference of all Elijah's followers—a celebration that for all intents and purposes was the Black Muslim Christmas.

3

The Advent of Elijah

The Birth of the Temple People Movement

Behold, I am going to send you Elijah the prophet before the
coming of the great and terrible day of the Lord. And he will
restore the hearts of the fathers to their children, and the
hearts of the children to their fathers, lest I come and smite the
land with a curse.   —Malachi 4:5–6

The followers, like Elijah, didn't know biblical meanings, and
misquoted biblical passages, as one who was sure the Bible
stated (in the book of Malachi) that a prophet named Elijah
Mohammed was to be sent (actually, the prophecy said only
Elijah would be sent).
                          —Hatim Sahib, "The Nation of Islam"

With the confirmation of his master, Elijah recalled, he
felt satisfied that he now had a message to spread among his people
in Detroit. He immediately began to advance the word about Fard,
evidencing the same kind of independent enthusiasm that Malcolm
X would later assume on his behalf in the same city. Not surprisingly,
Elijah's zeal got Fard's attention. One evening, when only Elijah's
wife, Clara, was present at the meeting, Fard openly asked for him.
When Clara approached Fard, he told her he would authorize her
husband as a preacher of "Islam." Elijah received the news with joy:
"I said to myself, 'Now, we really have something to teach, and it is
good.'"

Elijah's encounter with Fard and the assurance he felt regarding the latter's messianic identity was unparalleled in his life. Elijah continued to hold house meetings in Hamtramck, declaring, "This is the salvation that I was praying for; it came now to me in person." His mind was filled with messianic expectation and stoked with stories he had studied from "the lives of the prophets and their histories and their prophesying." Most amazing was Elijah's pious devotion and his apparent belief that Fard was not only his savior but his divine intercessor—a belief he demonstrated in childlike trust: "I used to go to my clothes closet and pray to Fard, who brought us the truth that I was longing to hear."[1]

As an official minister in the Nation of Islam, Elijah and Fard became quite close, the latter placing the eager neophyte in a position of apprenticeship. Apparently Fard badly needed a reliable follower with strong faith in him because he was locked in competition with two "Moslem" upstarts who had begun to pull away from the Nation of Islam (one of whom was the very man who had introduced Elijah to Fard). Besides the fact that Fard was busy repulsing critics and exploiters, he had to fortify himself against challenges from his own flock. When Elijah's commitment was absolutely clear, Fard announced to the rest of the membership that he had chosen Elijah and commissioned him to teach and make reports of what the other ministers were preaching. Elijah was thus selected as "Supreme Minister"—a choice that evoked the envy and jealousy of Fard's other ministers, some of whom were more articulate and better educated than Elijah. As in his childhood, Elijah was once again the "dear" of the congregation, privy to the seat of authority. As Fard's favorite follower, Elijah was given opportunities to preach. At first, Fard sat and encouraged him from the audience, but as challenges intensified and Fard began to withdraw, Elijah became a regular speaker on his own in the meetings. Elijah's new authority apparently allowed him to enhance the message according to his religious predisposition. Apparently drawing on his own Christian vocabulary at first, Elijah began to refer to Fard as a prophet. However, he also identified him as "Master" and even began to suggest that the followers refer to Fard as "Almighty God" because, as Elijah explained, his work was the work of God and not of a human being.[2]

Elijah's conversion to the Nation of Islam cannot be attributed to sheer naivete; he must have recognized many levels of opportunity in Fard's movement, including financial opportunity and race uplift-ment. On the other hand, because historians are generally uncom-fortable accepting religious experience as an independent motivation with its own priorities, it is equally problematic to suggest that "other more practical factors" were required before Elijah threw in his lot with W. D. Fard. Similarly, it is true that Fard and Elijah enjoyed a symbiotic relationship that mutually supplied the two men with the personal support they needed to achieve their respective goals as race-oriented religionists. On the other hand, the relationship be-tween Fard and Elijah was distinctly one-sided, with Elijah the wor-shiper and Fard the object of worship.

This religious dynamic reflects the essence of Elijah's conversion and commitment to Fard and it stands alone as the key to explaining Elijah's credulous embrace of Fard, however impractical it may seem to historians. All other factors taken into consideration, the defining feature of Elijah Poole's religious life was his own unique messianic void, the apostate spiritual hunger that gave him an appetite for the form of biblical religion but not for its essence. That Elijah was "sat-isfied" with Fard cannot be explained any more than the fact that he was never "satisfied" by the Christian message. Neither can his choice to follow Fard be seen merely as the working together of the right combination of supposedly practical factors. Ultimately, the unquan-tifiable factor of personal religious faith has a life of its own and should be recognized as distinct and overarching in any conversion story, including that of Elijah Poole.

Elijah Poole was not immediately dubbed Elijah Muhammad upon joining the Nation of Islam. Initially, Fard gave his eager assistant a different "original" surname, Karriem, as all his followers were sup-posedly being restored to their actual heritage and identity according to the omniscient spirit of Allah indwelling the master. However, it was not lost on the first scholarly observer of the Nation of Islam that Fard had failed to ascertain that Elijah and his two brothers were re-lated and had thus given each of the three Poole brothers a different "original" surname. When Fard was informed of his error he explained it away by claiming that he was divinely aware that the three Poole brothers actually had different fathers.[3]

Elijah Karriem, the devoted young preacher, advanced his master's message, traveling to Chicago where he extended his christologized view of Fard even further than he had in Detroit. Setting up in a rented hall on Wentworth Avenue, Elijah Karriem began to proclaim W. D. Fard not only as the savior of dark people, but as Allah incarnate. Fard was undoubtedly aware of this theological development but discouraged it only when it was tactically expedient. Indeed, when the master himself had come to preach in Chicago on one occasion he openly proclaimed, "I am God Himself." Thus, Fard had no apparent problem with his associate spreading what—in Islamic terms—was a supreme blasphemy, an irony considering Fard seems to have avoided the title of "prophet."[4] However, this theological incongruence reflects Fard's fundamental unorthodoxy. It is possible, of course, that Fard had some mystical rationale for accepting the "Allah" designation from Elijah, but even so it would be a mysticism too controversial for traditional Islam. On the other hand, Fard undoubtedly understood the implications to his ex-Christian followers in being referred to as "God in the flesh." Had he felt any true commitment to Islam, he would probably have renounced the "Allah" title immediately. Fard seems inevitably caught on the outside of the Islamic and Christian communities, a dilemma he has bequeathed to all those who have blessed his name ever since.

Had the movement's situation been different back in Detroit, Elijah might have successfully extended the Nation of Islam's territory while also expanding its kerygma from the proclamation of a quasi-Islamic teacher/messiah to that of a quasi-Christian god/messiah. However, the Nation of Islam collapsed with the blow of Fard's deportation in 1933. The promising new religious empire that had briefly peaked at eight thousand members in the Detroit area quickly fell apart without its Christ figure; Elijah groped for power, competing with those who had already been chewing on the hem of Fard's messianic garment. Even his own brother sought to upstage him, aligning himself with one of Fard's competitors in order to seize "the teachings."

After Fard's departure, Elijah headed what might be considered the loyalist camp within the crumbling Nation of Islam. So sharp were the controversies and contentions within the movement that it quickly fragmented into splinter groups. Elijah Karriem, who had been renamed Elijah Muhammad by Fard as part of his last-ditch endeavor to secure the movement prior to deportation (Fard also modified his own name, becoming Wallace Fard Muhammad), now led a small faction. This group called themselves "The Temple People," their name apparently expressing fidelity to their absent savior and their claim to the site of Fard's teachings. Moving his base out of Detroit because of intensified opposition and legal problems, Elijah Muhammad left a small group of loyalists at his Temple No. 1 and established a new base in Chicago, Illinois, in 1934. Chicago would thereafter remain the holy city of the Nation of Islam, ironically sharing that city's sacred space with the legacy of Drew Ali, whose movement Muhammad would eventually overshadow in the cultic world of "Islam." Meanwhile, many of Fard's "Moslems" returned to the Christian church, probably being intimidated by increasingly hostile intra-group clashes or being wary of involvement with a pariah movement that continued to draw police harassment. Perhaps some even reassessed the supposed superiority of Muhammad's master over the Jesus of the black church. A man who had employed hair dye and parlor tricks in order to enhance his divine mystique could hardly have fooled all the people all the time.

From 1935 to 1942, Elijah Muhammad led the Temple People in absentia. Driven to flight by his rivals, Muhammad took to the road, finding his way to Milwaukee and Madison, Wisconsin, and then to Washington, D.C. Nor had his followers in Chicago found it easy to establish themselves since landlords—probably under pressure from authorities—kept forcing them out of leases. Furthermore, Elijah's followers had proven to be more militant than the Nation of Islam in Detroit, as demonstrated in several clashes with police in 1935.[5]

By the time the United States had become involved in World War II, Elijah was already in the nation's capital, having established the fourth Temple People congregation in 1939. Preaching under the pseudonym of Mohammed Rasool, Elijah kept up his work until he was arrested by federal agents in 1942 on charges that he had incited his followers not to register for the military draft. Meanwhile back in Chicago the police closed down Temple No. 2 on the pretext that the Temple People were somehow affiliated with the Japanese. Largely due to the devotion of Clara Muhammad, however, the Chicago base persevered and eventually the Temple People purchased the site of a former animal hospital, which they would refurbish and dedicate to Fard.[6]

Muhammad ultimately served a prison sentence in the Federal Correction Institution at Milan, Michigan, from July 1943 to August 1946. Upon entering the institution, he was given a standard psychiatric evaluation in which he was judged schizophrenic because he claimed to have had visual and audible communication with "Allah."[7] It is perhaps understandable that a psychiatrist would greet these claims with such professional disbelief, yet they ought not to be dismissed without further consideration.

According to Muhammad's claim, he heard the voice of Allah—Fard—after circumstances had worsened for the Temple People in late 1934 and early 1935. At the time, Elijah said, "most of the followers" in the Nation of Islam had proven to be "hypocrites"—a bitter epithet he reserved for competitive opponents, and one he would later use to justify a deadly assault on Malcolm X. So intense was the opposition, and so treacherous that it involved his own brother, Elijah realized he had to flee "to save my own life." When "hypocrites" from Detroit apparently teamed up with those in Chicago, Elijah found it impossible to involve himself in any religious activities for fear of assassination. It was at this point, Elijah claimed, that he received his first warning from Allah to leave. After he fled to Milwaukee, according to Muhammad, not only did Allah urge him to flee once more, he also revealed the nine people "in a vision" who wished to kill him.

As Elijah Muhammad later reflected on his hiding period, the memory of these revelations from Fard served as the framework for solidifying his convictions about the divine nature of his master. As one scholar noted concerning his interviews with Muhammad:

> He used to tell the writer that in his hiding period (1935–1942) he was hearing the voice of Fard, the voice that he knows, warning him and directing him to save his life from the enemies who were seeking him.

He told the writer once that when he read the Koran after the departure of Fard he found the validity of the deity of Mr. W. D. Fard himself. "At that time I realized his intention why he was asking me insis-
tently to read the Koran. It was just to know who he was."[8]

Elijah Muhammad apparently made reference to his hiding-period
revelations more than once, and it is probably because his flight was
not only a stressful period of peril but also an intensely spiritual trek
in which he may have entertained primal experiences that seemed to
confirm his mission and prompted him to persevere in the midst of
tribulation. Of course, the cynic might easily dismiss Muhammad's
claims, suggesting that either Muhammad fabricated these revelations or that he stylized actual conversations with Fard conducted either in person or by telephone. Yet Fard seems to have completely dis-
appeared by this time, and had he been so accessible to Muhammad
one would expect other evidence of Fard's continued availability to
the cult. On the other hand, if these ostensible revelations were actual
fabrications which Elijah used to enhance his role, why would he
limit them to the hiding period? Such claims would certainly have
also enhanced his prison experience, and even his later career as the
Black Muslim leader. The answer, if indeed it is possible to speak of
an answer with regard to primal experience, may lie closer to the
realm of belief than fact.

It was a vision that later sealed Malcolm X's faith in Elijah Muhammad; is it possible that Muhammad himself was drawing on a similar
vein of primal religious experience, and that his life-long quest for
spiritual fulfillment had actually culminated during the hiding period?[9] In conjunction with this period, Elijah also pointed out that
"when Fard left he gave me a list of 150 books to read. When I began
to read I have detected, specially after reading Koran carefully, that
Fard was Allah himself incarnated. The more I read the more I become sure about this fact, especially that his name has been mentioned in the Bible and the time of his coming has been assigned, but
the devil has concealed him under another name."[10] Like Malcolm X's
time in prison, Muhammad's hiding period was a stressful experience
enhanced by conversion and complemented by intensive study. In
Muhammad's case, during his flight he was completing the recom-

mended readings on Fard's list, along with further study of the Qur'an and the Bible. The primal experiences of which Muhammad later spoke were complementary to his crisis and study, perhaps acting like the glue that held together his entire religious scenario. Indeed, while much of the study of Fard's reading list was completed in the Congressional Library in Washington, D.C., Muhammad found his own subsequent presentations strengthened and affirmed when he made brief speaking forays into other cities, such as Newark, Baltimore, Pittsburgh, and Cleveland.

A key to understanding Muhammad's primal experiences during the hiding period may perhaps be found reflectively in Malcolm X's later conversion story and in his preferred motif, the conversion of the Apostle Paul. For Malcolm, the Apostle Paul's conversion story gave him a basis for explaining something of his own sense of transformation at the time he placed his faith in Muhammad. Is it possible that, over a decade earlier, Muhammad was also configuring his own spiritual drama according to a similar motif? Since we may assume that, by this time, Muhammad was drawing from biblical and Qur'anic themes, he probably perceived himself as a kind of Prophet Muhammad and an Apostle Paul. Perhaps his experience of danger, flight, and extreme sacrifice in the cause of W. D. Fard gave the fleeing Elijah Muhammad a sense of continuity with the historical Muhammad and the great Christian missionary apostle.

A student of Muhammad's movement later observed that besides identifying Fard with Allah, the Temple People placed Muhammad on the level of a prophet and actually referred to him "reverently as the messenger or the Apostle Elijah Mohammed."[11] He also noted that the "basic prayer" of Muhammad's organization went like this:

> Say He Allah is one; Allah is He of whom nothing is independent but upon whom we all depend. He begets not nor is he begotten. And I bear witness that nothing deserves to be worshipped beside Allah. And I bear witness that Mr. Elijah Mohammed is his servant and apostle.[12]

Besides their obvious imitation of an Islamic confession, these developments, observed less than five years after Muhammad was released from the federal penitentiary, reflect a solidification of

Muhammad's experience in the rubric and worship of the movement thereafter. While "apostle" is a term that can be used in both the Christian and the Islamic contexts with reference to God's messenger, it is possible that Muhammad found in the visions and revelations of men like Peter and Paul a basis for constructing his own sense of divine leading, an experience that would later serve to mediate Fard's authority through him to the rest of the Temple People movement.

Of course, ultimately, Muhammad's revelatory voices and visions during the hiding period are a mystery. However, it is clear they substantiated his own calling as an apostle and consequently enhanced his personal study and presentation. The historian, therefore, understates the impact of Muhammad's years of flight if he attributes to them only heightened "feelings of persecution and sacrifice." It seems likely that in this period, Elijah Muhammad not only endured the flames of persecution and found himself stronger for it in terms of psychology and leadership, but was spiritually transformed from a struggling substitute to a superb visionary interpretor of the arcane. It is likely that this spiritual experience lent itself to what one scholar perceived was Muhammad's status as the "intellectual of the movement." It also may help to explain how the sons of Earl and Louise Little, especially the discerning young seeker named Malcolm, might be attracted to "the Messenger of Allah." His devotion to black people, empowered by a spiritually transformative experience, endowed Muhammad with an authority that secular critics probably failed to discern, being distracted by Muhammad's obvious lack of formal training and his relatively unimpressive physical presence. Years later, one of Muhammad's attorneys, who never joined the organization, reflected this sentiment in an interview. To him, Elijah Muhammad was a "very religious man" in whose company he sensed a "special presence" he had not known in any other person. Likewise, perhaps the most sincere attestation of Muhammad's transformation may be seen through the eyes of one of his own progeny, who remembered his grandfather's bearing and actions as "reverential."[13]

After emerging from prison in 1946, Muhammad appeared to be

less of an activist and more of an administrator. New economic programs and strategies replaced overt confrontation with authorities; a business mind seems to have succeeded the prevailing underground mentality of the Temple People movement. According to Muhammad's son, Elijah's post-prison period marked the beginning of an era of "new vision" in which the followers were encouraged to cultivate a positive image in the community, utilize modern technology (like the newly marketed television), and open businesses that would serve "Muslims" and Christians alike. At the same time, Muhammad either seized or appropriated all of Fard's publications and instructional materials from the followers and became the sole dispenser and interpreter of the Fard legacy.

A survivor, Elijah Muhammad had already endured hardship, opposition, and imprisonment. However, his ability to reemerge on the scene, assert his influence, and seize the lion's share of black "Islam" suggests Muhammad had not only grown intellectually but had framed the historical Fard within a theology he had constructed and enforced within the movement. To underscore his triumph, Elijah assumed Fard's themes, including the problem of the Bible—the fact that the very book containing the sacred stories upon which he depended was also a book laden with distortions and symbols prepared by "King James the Virgin" (perhaps a corruption or a derision of the "King James Version"), in which all references to "dark people" had supposedly been substituted by "the Jews."

And just as Fard had used the Bible to vindicate his claims, Elijah Muhammad enlisted the same text to prove his own special role as the "Messenger of Allah." Declaring himself the fulfillment of the prophecy of the Hebrew seer Malachi concerning the return of Elijah, or purporting himself to be the one who Moses predicted would be raised up from among the people (Deuteronomy 18), Elijah Muhammad now laid claim to a most sacred status in the history of the world.[14]

Not surprisingly, sometime after he came out of prison, Elijah Muhammad also changed the name of his movement to "The Nation of Islam." None would thereafter doubt his apostolic succession, and even outsiders would come to believe that Elijah Muhammad's Nation of Islam was one and the same movement that had begun in the urban wilderness of Detroit in 1930. Yet, if Muhammad had slain his thousands, a young man was rising in the ranks of Allah who would slay his ten thousands—his choicest weapon the Bible, his target the "white man's religion," Christianity.

4

Among the Living and the Dead
The Gospel According to Elijah Muhammad

Why do you seek the living One among the dead?
— Luke 24:5

[I]t is my duty to awaken them from [the Bible], because it is
surely the graveyard of my people.
— Elijah Muhammad, *The Supreme Wisdom*, vol. 2

And he had his dwelling among the tombs. And no one was
able to bind him anymore, even with a chain.   — Mark 5:3

Elijah Muhammad went far beyond previous offensives
against white Christianity, attacking also "integrationist Negro Christianity." Yet Muhammad's cut went still deeper. It "was based on more
than the ethical failure of white and Negro Christians; it was also
based on a theological critique of orthodox Christianity"[1] intended
to appeal to blacks who were responsive (or perhaps vulnerable) to
questions about the integrity of biblical doctrine.

With few exceptions, most discussions about Elijah Muhammad's attacks on Christianity have been centered on the race
mythology of the Nation of Islam, just as today's coverage of Louis
Farrakhan's Nation of Islam prompts heated discussion on race issues, including black-Jewish relations. As far as the public is concerned, the Black Muslim campaign has been interpreted primarily
by the media, not the clergy—though it would seem neither have

ever really taken the Nation of Islam's *religious* presence seriously. Typically, white liberal narcissism has led social critics into conflict with the Nation of Islam over integration—the real agenda of the former apparently being to defend the dignity of white goodwill before the scornful Black Muslims. Not surprisingly, the other half of the battle, which concerns the theological integrity of the Nation of Islam's critique, has rarely been engaged let alone mapped out. The general lack of conviction shown by Christian clergymen in contending for the Faith—either *mano a mano* or tête-à-tête—has allowed the Black Muslims considerable leeway in launching their broadsides, some of which were actually quite absurd. With notable exception here and there, most of the negative retorts from churchmen were probably personal reactions to assaults on the clergy and culture of the black church rather than exegetically reasoned theological counterattacks. As a result, the public has been far more aware of "white devils" and "the mother ship"(the latter of which, even today, Louis Farrakhan believes is hovering above the United States) than the Nation of Islam's abuse, denial, or perversion of Christian doctrine.[2]

Despite his lack of formal training, Elijah Muhammad was a prolific writer and used newspaper columns and, eventually, his own publications to advance the teachings of the Nation of Islam. While he had initiated a publication, *The Final Call to Islam*, in the early days, Muhammad's Nation of Islam apparently had no official paper until Malcolm X started *Mr. Muhammad Speaks* in 1960. Malcolm apparently tried a number of other publication endeavors for the Nation of Islam, but none of them were successful except the New York-based *Muhammad Speaks* (though it was later transferred to Chicago when Malcolm's place in the movement was declining).[3] Initially, prominent black newspapers like the *Pittsburgh Courier* and the *Amsterdam News* ran Muhammad's columns. Despite the predominant Christian readership of these and other black publications, they featured his controversial writings, apparently because Muhammad's column sold papers. Only when *Muhammad Speaks* emerged as competition did the black press's enthusiasm for Muhammad lessen. However, other black papers continued to carry his column while

Muhammad Speaks was advanced throughout the Nation of Islam's growing network of temples (called mosques after 1960) from coast to coast.

Elijah Muhammad's presentations on Christianity invariably negated orthodox teachings. Often, Muhammad's comments on Christian beliefs were characterized by outright gainsaying and simple (sometimes simplistic) contradiction that was intended to disprove the reasonableness of the church's message. However, following Fard's example, Muhammad also utilized his authority to advance apocryphal stories featuring biblical names and characters. In so doing, he placed his droll innovations over against the Bible, claiming his accounts were revealed to him by Allah, that is, W. D. Fard. In one speech given before the Nation of Islam, Muhammad made a claim to authority clearly comparable to that of the New Testament apostles: "I was in the presence of God for over three years, and I received what I am teaching you directly from His Mouth." Supposedly outdoing even Mecca's Muhammad, whom Muslims believe had received his revelations from the angel Gabriel, Elijah Muhammad declared that he "did not receive this gospel from a paper, nor a book, nor from a vision, nor from an angel, but directly from the Mouth of Almighty God Himself."[4] This claim to apostolic authority was an inherent Christian construct that belied Muhammad's apostate character. In a very real sense, then, Muhammad was both Peter and Paul to his followers—the former because he spent a three-year apprenticeship under his master's ministry, the latter because, unlike the founder of traditional Islam, the apostle of black "Islam" did not receive his message from an angel but claimed direct access to the wisdom of God incarnate. The notion that Elijah Muhammad's teachings represented the inspired, inerrant word of God thus gave him license to negate established canon and offer new renditions of Bible stories according to his judgments.

But the Bible continued to present a problem to Muhammad, just as it had to Fard and his Nation of Islam. While Muhammad demonstrated a fundamental dependence on the Bible, he constantly maligned it as a book poisoned, skewed, and perverted by white people. This contradiction, however, did not prevent him from skillfully using it to advance his message—though his claim that he used it so much because blacks "read no Scripture other than that" probably veiled his own predilection for the Bible.[5] Mindful of this problem, Muhammad periodically addressed the topic by demonstrating the supposed unreliability of the Hebrew and Christian scriptures.

To do so, Muhammad had to create the illusion of gross textual contamination—a claim similar to the expedient charge employed by traditional Muslims in their attempt to replace the Bible with the Qur'an. However, Muhammad's focus invariably targeted the King James Bible, the overwhelming favorite among Protestant Christians until recent years. By attacking the veracity of the King James version of the Bible, not only was Muhammad calling into question the heretofore unquestionable, but he was conveniently evading the challenge of proving his charges against the impressive corpus of thousands of surviving ancient Greek manuscripts (in whole or part) of the New Testament. "You must remember," Muhammad warned the readers of his syndicated column, "that according to the preface of the Bible, under the authorized version of King James, it has been 346 years, and you have only been permitted to read the Bible for the past 90 years." Muhammad's reference, of course, was to the prohibition of black slaves from reading, especially the Bible, though his gross generalization overlooks the fact that many African Americans had been reading the Bible far longer. "The white man, our slavemasters and enemies, had the Bible over one hundred fifty years before we were allowed to read the book."[6] The significance of this disadvantage, according to Muhammad, was that in the time the Bible was dominated by white slave masters it was tampered with to the extent that it is highly unreliable. In another article, Muhammad wrote:

> The Bible is my poor people's graveyard. The Holy Qur'an would resurrect them if they would study its teachings, with someone to teach its meanings. . . . [The Bible] is a "fixed Book" in which the truth has been added in and taken out of [sic] by the devils, the slavemasters of my people. It is revised every few years, and some of the filthy readings in it cannot be read in public by any decent person without feeling ashamed.[7]

Obviously, Muhammad's charge was multifaceted. He not only pre-scribed the Qur'an over the Bible (though hinting at his exclusive ability to interpret both), but propounded the notion that the bibli-cal text was excessively and frequently manipulated by white people to the detriment of blacks. Obviously, here he was not referring to the historic manipulation of the Bible by preachers on plantations dur-ing slavery, in which the skewed "servants obey your masters" theme was constantly taught. Rather, Muhammad's claim that the Bible was periodically "fixed" was his way of casting aspersions on the doctrines of the Bible itself. In speaking of revisions "every few years," it seems Muhammad was alluding to the periodic release of new English translations of the Bible in part or in whole, such as the *Revised Stan-dard Version* (1952), Phillips' *New Testament in Modern English* (1958), the *Berkeley Version in Modern English* (1959), and the *New American Standard*, New Testament (1960). Though Muhammad would have been hard-pressed to demonstrate that contemporary English trans-lations of Greek and Hebrew texts were actually corrupted, his con-descending and rough-handed treatment of the Bible went unchal-lenged, perhaps because those who took him the most seriously would likely not have known better.

Indeed, in one column, titled "The Bible and the Holy Qur'an," Muhammad sniped, using the Bible to justify his teachings while con-demning it because some of its frank narratives contained graphic subject matter. However, his criticisms of the text, like his attacks on Christian doctrine, were petty and simplistic: "The Bible is dedicated to King James and not to God"; "If the Bible is the word of God, He should be the One speaking . . . not His Prophet"; "Could Moses have known the Angel to be of the Lord, since he had not seen or met ei-ther one before?" In short, Muhammad contended that without his personal intercession as interpreter and guide, giving African Ameri-cans the Bible was "like throwing a rattlesnake in the lap of a baby."[8]

In practice, Muhammad and his Muslims used the Bible as a per-sonal repertoire of proof texts. Muhammad taught his ministers that the Bible was a book of symbols, parables, and prophecies that per-tained to the African American community and its history of oppres-sion in North America,[9] overlooking and even negating the primary historical contexts of the scriptures. Drawing on the cultural current of the Dispensational era, Muhammad—like Fard before him—excised biblical texts in the name of "prophecy," applying them to the racial situation in the United States and making the end of the world into an imminent black apocalypse that would consume the white man's world system.

In so doing, the various literary forms and themes of the Bible were essentially flattened into one continuous layer of racial discourse. For instance, the parable of the rich man and Lazarus (Luke 16:19–31), which Christ clearly intended as a commentary on the religious leaders of his day, became a representation of the psychology of racial oppression. "You are the real 'Lazarus,'" Muhammad declared in one of his columns, "charmed by the riches of the slave masters, and are too lazy to go for self!"[10] Far from a homiletic application, Muhammad actually maintained that his interpretations of the Bible were the original intent of the biblical writers, though these intentions were either hidden or destroyed by the "fixing" of whites.

Certainly, it was easy work for Muhammad to hijack Ezekiel's famous apocalyptic wheel (Ezekiel 10) and force upon it W. D. Fard's mythical "mother plane" story. "The vision of Ezekiel's wheel in a wheel is true if carefully understood," Muhammad wrote in a column sensationally titled "Battle in the Sky." Rather than being a representation of the eternal and sovereign God, the "Great Wheel" became "a plane made like a wheel . . . a masterpiece of mechanics." Thus, Ezekiel's ancient vision not only entailed the future from a twentieth-century perspective (also a keynote of Christian Dispensational abuse), but was a specific description of Fard's "mother plane," which Muhammad described as being one-half mile by one-half mile in size, "the largest mechanical man-made object in the sky . . . a small human planet" designed to destroy the white world. Muhammad claimed this awesome ship was equipped to stay outside of "the earth's gravity" for as long as one year, and held fifteen hundred "bombing planes" whose missiles could drill themselves one mile into the earth before explosion. This supposedly invincible apocalyptic war ship of Allah, Muhammad wrote, would devastate anyone who sought to oppose it. "[D]o not think of trying to attack it," he concluded dramatically. "That would be suicide." In another column, Muhammad claimed the "mother plane" had taken twenty years to build, and that it had been foretold in the writings of the prophet Isaiah (14:13–14); however the text he cited said nothing about a flying vessel and was actually a prophecy made by the Hebrew seer against an ancient Babylonian ruler.[11]

If Muhammad ran roughshod over individual texts and themes in the Bible, he was even more determined to trample on the essentials of Christian doctrine. Like the Muslim world of which he claimed to be a part, Muhammad and the Nation of Islam rejected Christian Trinitarianism and other doctrines that pertained to the divine nature of Jesus Christ, his atonement, and resurrection. However, while Muslims premised their dissent from an alternative canon, the Black Muslims were far more inclined to engage in denials based on claims of logic and science, along with biblical gainsaying.

Like his mentor W. D. Fard, Muhammad demeaned the Christian conception of the divine Spirit as a "Mystery," an epithet that suggested irrationality. Like Fard, Muhammad premised his arguments against Christianity with a claim to scientific and mathematical reason. Indeed, much of the cult's mathematical and scientific language was mere rhetoric that gave naive and unschooled followers the notion that "Islam" was not only religiously superior but also scientifically reliable. From the onset, Fard's myth of the genesis of creation and the white and black races was filled with references to primordial "scientists," planetary bodies, and other terms that gave his message a shell of sophistication, as did the movement's catechism with its extravagant numerology. Not surprisingly, Muhammad appropriated the same pseudo-scientific rubric as an essential part of his presentation.

As the Messenger, Elijah Muhammad claimed to have received data, "scientific knowledge of the world" regarding "the size of oceans, the weights and ages of the planets and so on," which the Black Muslim leader claimed to interpret in their "full meaning." Indeed, during a Savior's Day convocation, Muhammad stopped speaking in the middle of a sermon, apparently meditating in profound quietness for three minutes while his audience waited in patient reverence. One observer was surprised at the enthusiasm of the audience when Muhammad finally blurted out: "The waves of the ocean do not come to us, they go to the moon." In fact, he was amazed at how un-critically the Black Muslims accepted the utterance of such a "non-sensical statement" from their leader.[12] However, the statement was apropos of Elijah Muhammad's peculiar blend of religious and scien-tific terminology.

As for the Trinity, Muhammad saw it as sort of an incorrect math problem—God divided into thirds, which was "contrary to both na-ture and mathematics" since "the law of mathematics will not allow us to put 3 into 1." Of course, objections of this nature are similar to monotheistic critics of Christianity in general, who also object to the Trinitarian notion. What peculiarly distinguished Muhammad's cri-tique, however, was a thesis essentially premised on a human arche-type. In other words, however much the Christian may differ with the Jewish or Muslim objection to Trinitarianism, the debate issuing from it is one based *on high*—that is, one that assumes a transcen-dent, original, eternal, and divine Spirit. Jewish and Muslim critics may see the Christian Trinity as a multiplicity of gods, though the most sensitive among them will recognize the unique context (indeed the "Jewishness") of its origin, which Christian theism shares with Ju-daism and Islam, and which stands in contrast to the sheer polythe-ism of non-Abramic religions. Of course, the Christian believes Abramic opponents of Trinitarianism to be rigidly unitarian (and sometimes reactionary). An irreconcilable conflict, to be sure, but at its best it remains a debate within a shared tradition.

For Elijah Muhammad, however, Trinitarianism was not merely objectionable to "Islam," it was nonscientific and nonmathematical. Even more, it was unnatural. According to Muhammad, it would be impossible for a spiritual entity to interact with the natural realm, and thus the idea that a spirit God could have any tangible manifes-tation in the world was rejected—a problem not only for Christian Trinitarianism, but even for the theophanic appearances of God in the Hebrew scriptures. The "Mystery God of the Jews and Christians," as Muhammad called the God of the Bible, was a contradiction in terms. Muhammad wrote that such a Spirit could not make a human reflect the divine image because such a Spirit would not have traits and behaviors like humans. Neither could a Mystery God send a prophet to represent himself, nor would a nonmaterial God get pleasure from a material universe.[13] As to the spiritual nature of God, Elijah Muhammad had to contend with many attesting Hebrew and Christian scriptures, all of which he conveniently ignored, except for one particular quotation by Jesus. But the fact that Jesus himself had said God was a Spirit could be easily brushed aside by Muhammad on the grounds that Jesus was only a prophet, and his words had not come "from the mouth of God."[14] Of course, Muhammad should have realized that all the Abramic religions viewed the word of a true prophet as the very word of God; the Muslim world in particular would take exception to his rationale, since prophethood is Islam's central redemptive construct, not the messiah.

In reality, then, Muhammad's problem with Trinitarianism was rooted in a more complex stratum of theological opposition toward Christianity than either Islam or Judaism. At heart, Muhammad's gospel denied not just the Christian conception of divinity, but the shared beliefs of Judaism, Christianity, and Islam regarding God as a personal and transcendent Spirit who both communicated and interacted with humanity by condescension. In a very real sense, then, to say that Elijah Muhammad used a Christian construct to present W. D. Fard as "God in the flesh" is not wholly accurate. For Muhammad, divinity and humanity were one, not in an incarnational sense but in a "natural" sense. "God is a man, a flesh and blood being," Muhammad declared elsewhere. "Why do we call God a Divine Being? Because He is a being like we but His wisdom, power, and other capabilities and attributes are supreme . . . making Him the Highest Power." No wonder that Muhammad rejected Christian incarnational theory so stridently. "Our nature rebels against such a belief of God being a mystery," Muhammad wrote. Without a wife, God could not have a son; and being a "Holy Ghost," he concluded, God could not take a wife since such a Mystery was not "something in reality."

If Muhammad had "natural" reasons to oppose the idea of Christ's divine incarnation, he also attempted a moral repudiation of the Christian doctrine. In a speech delivered in Atlanta, Georgia, in 1961,

Muhammad explained that since the Mystery God of the Christians had "overpowered" Mary in a sexual manner, not being married to the Virgin made it an adulterous act—because "when a man is not married to a woman and he commits such a sinful act it is called adultery." The incarnate Son of God thus being produced "out of wedlock," Muhammad concluded, would open "the gateway of adultery to the entire world," encouraging "adultery and other indecent acts." Furthermore, in upholding the doctrine of divine incarnation, Muhammad declared, Christians were actually charging God with adultery.[15]

Muhammad's speech was telling on two levels. Theologically, his contention clearly reflected his natural view of God as a man. Unlike traditional Muslims, of course, Elijah Muhammad believed Jesus was the literal son of Joseph, as W. D. Fard had taught. Rather than seeing the birth of Jesus as a biological miracle (which he considered impossible), Muhammad reckoned the bastardy of Jesus as the only natural explanation for his birth—despite the fact that the Qur'an, which Muhammad claimed to uplift, taught that the birth was indeed miraculous.[16] The deeper level of Muhammad's tactless assault on incarnational theology is hinted at in his reference to the overpowering of the Virgin Mary as being a case of adultery. For if, as Muhammad himself contended, neither the Mystery God nor the Virgin were actually married, no adultery could have taken place. Even allowing Muhammad's bizarre contention to stand, the overpowering of Mary would have constituted an act of fornication, not adultery.

Muhammad's sexual interpretation of an event that was not so presented in biblical terms is interesting for a man who had railed against so much indecency in the Bible. Indeed, while Muhammad chose to use the term "overpower" with respect to the Christian story of the immaculate conception, the actual biblical term used is "overshadow"—a strictly spiritual term alluding to the overshadowing presence of the Glory Cloud that appears in the Hebrew scriptures.[17] Not only did Muhammad portray the immaculate conception as a case of adultery but he inadvertently suggested that it was an act of a stronger man overpowering a younger, weaker woman. Muhammad was clearly preaching more than Black Muslim doctrine; he was making a veiled commentary on his own life, and imputing it to a God—and a moral code—he himself had forsaken. As Malcolm X later discovered to his horror, Elijah Muhammad's predilection for young women had been vigorously exercised in the Messenger's private offices—including even the seduction of one of his own relatives. Though these young victims have since been recast by Louis Farrakhan as Muhammad's wives, it is clear they were neither legal nor ceremonial spouses at the time the seductions took place. Indeed, if anyone had opened the gateway to adultery to the world of the Black Muslims, it was Elijah Muhammad himself.[18]

Muhammad's adulterous affairs were not simply based on the quest for carnal pleasures, though understanding his immorality should not be limited to social and psychological factors. One observer states that Muhammad's adulteries provided him release from accumulated pressures; renewed his sense of power; kindled an edifying love for his illegitimately born children; provided an invigoration that countered his fear of mortality; and demonstrated that Muhammad himself fell victim to the indulgences of his prosperous family, whose material abuses at the expense of the faithful gave him a rationale for testing other boundaries.[19]

While these explanations (some of which sound suspiciously like apologia) have validity, they are baseless without a spiritual interpretation—an interpretation that historians are often unwilling to venture upon lest they be accused of losing their professional objectivity. However, the ultimate debauchery of Muhammad's sexual abuses was a result of the entangling of his personal moral and spiritual dilemma with his disingenuous religious teachings and practices. A sexual indiscretion or dissonant practice of sexual misbehavior by a clergyman is not really at the basis of Muhammad's case. Many clergymen succumb to moral lapses, some repeatedly—most notable in this context being Muhammad's political counterpart, Martin Luther King, Jr. Yet Muhammad's abuses were not mere lapses, nor were they even the ongoing adventures of a moral hypocrite caught in a trap of his own lust. Muhammad's adulteries were fundamental to the religious totalitarianism of his teachings—teachings that inflated him to godlike proportions and required his followers to subject themselves to his directives. In other words, Muhammad had made *religious captives* out of his young victims before he overpowered them as sexual captives. Before he could disrobe and penetrate them physically, Muhammad had to strip away the religious and spiritual garb of mind and heart, penetrating their personal morality and spirituality with the claim of his access to the divine. According to one of Malcolm's close followers, one of Muhammad's victims was told to undress and yield herself to him in order that she might help him build his Nation in half the time it would take otherwise. One of the young women recounted that one night while she was working in the office, Muhammad entered the room, locked the door, and forced her down on the floor for sexual relations. Despite his fragile frame, the Messenger was able to overpower these unfortunate young believers because of the spiritual weakness resulting from his demagogic teachings.[20] Muhammad's sexual abuses may or may not have been statutory rapes, but they were clearly acts of religious exploitation.

It is likewise the case that Muhammad's behavior reveals the suffering and decline of his own spirituality, culminating in the duplicity with which he approached his young "secretaries." However, rather than attributing his family's growing material lust as the context for the adulteries, it is more likely that during his post-prison years, when the Temple People movement began to outgrow its earlier form and became the new Nation of Islam, Muhammad gradually came face to face with his own religious dilemma. Apparently the more his knowledge of traditional Islam increased, the more Muhammad suppressed the problematic nature of his own teachings and perhaps even doubts about the viability of Islam as a religious answer to black people—all the while his spiritual life suffering for it, perhaps the way Oscar Wilde's Dorian Gray remained attractive while his portrait became increasingly hideous and scarred.

In the last speech Malcolm X would make to his Organization of Afro-American Unity in February 1965, he found occasion to mention Elijah Muhammad's religious decline. In highlighting the moral and spiritual decay of the Nation of Islam, Malcolm said that up through 1960, "just before Elijah Muhammad went to the East, there was not a better organization among Black people in this country than the Muslim movement." Unfortunately, however, when Muhammad made his little-known trip to the Muslim world in late 1959 and early 1960, something seemed—at least to Malcolm X—to have shifted in the life of the Messenger. In retrospect, Malcolm said, Muhammad began to change, to become mercenary, his focus especially turning to wealth and girls.

Even allowing for some retrospective stylization—since Malcolm probably should have recognized that Muhammad's decline had begun much earlier—his point is vital.[21] Simply put, in the early days of the Temple People movement, and even after Muhammad renamed the organization after Fard's Nation of Islam, the Messenger had been largely uneducated regarding traditional Islam. In the post-prison years, however, growth (largely engendered by Malcolm's contributions) brought Muhammad increasingly in contact with traditional Muslims. Early on, Elijah had apparently been able to dismiss the threat of orthodoxy with ease—such as the case of one traditional Muslim who taught in the University of Islam grade school in Chicago, and who attempted to introduce Qur'anic Islam to the followers. Muhammad fired the teacher,[22] temporarily repulsing what was inevitable—his own failure to meet the standards of the Muslim community worldwide.

Eventually, Muhammad's increasing notoriety and representation by Malcolm X brought "the Messenger of Allah" into contact with those who represented the Allah of the Qur'an. Apart from those who criticized the movement, the Muslims who befriended it were perhaps the most dangerous to Muhammad's continued religious comfort. As Malcolm's oratory and interaction virtually reached across the ocean to the Muslim world, Muhammad was undoubtedly being drawn toward the inevitable challenge: would he alter his teachings in favor of traditional Islam as his Sunni Muslim allies apparently hoped he would? When one of his own sons, Akbar, went to live and study Islam in Cairo, Muhammad became even more entangled in the dilemma of his own religious duplicity. How long could he pretend unity with the Muslim world and also claim that his version of "Islam" was suited to the peculiar needs of the black community when his own sons were sincerely advancing in the religion of the Qur'an?

The moral turning point became apparent when Muhammad himself was invited to the Muslim world. Malcolm X had preceded him as his emissary in the summer of 1959, and Muhammad finally embarked at the very end of the same year. Clearly, Muhammad's sojourn served as the Muslim world's opportunity to court the Nation of Islam. While Egypt's president Gamal Abdel Nasser and others probably hoped to gain in Muhammad a political ally in the United States, Muslim leaders undoubtedly hoped to gain a religious advocate as well. Indeed, Muhammad probably had revelations similar to those of Malcolm X in 1964—but rather than acknowledging that the Muslim world was multicolored, the leader of the Nation of Islam suppressed the truth about that world. Perhaps Elijah Muhammad also came to see that the Muslim world in Africa was not so ideal as he had believed it was. As his historian notes, Elijah Muhammad's idealized image of the land "had been eroded by African realities." Muhammad visited Mecca and made the traditional Muslim pilgrimage, though not having gone in the hajj season, he made only the minor hajj, or *umra*. The importance of this pilgrimage has probably been exaggerated by his biographer, who suggests that Muhammad was afterward "recognized as a true Muslim by the custodians of Islam's holiest city."[23]

Muhammad's case was clearly exceptional. He was admitted for political reasons and, like Malcolm X after him, was the recipient of special treatment that his gracious Muslim hosts probably hoped would result in an advantageous harvest for Islam back in the United States. In actuality, Muhammad was a guest, his pilgrimage more a token gesture that enabled him to evade cross-examination by Muslim authorities while also being able to boast of having made the pilgrimage. Ultimately, though, Muhammad was probably as big a disappointment to the Muslim world as the Muslim world was a disappointment to him. He never subscribed to the traditions and teachings of the Muslim community, a conversion he left for his sons to carry out. Nor did he ever return to complete the required hajj in its proper season (it is therefore inaccurate for his biographer to refer to him as "El-hajj Elijah Muhammad"). As Malcolm X, El Hajj Malik Shabazz, later wrote to Alex Haley from the Muslim Holy World:

"Mr[.] Muhammad and two of his sons made what is known as 'Omra' (the pilgrimage or '*visit*' to Mecca outside of the *Hajj season*). I think I'm the first *American born Negro* to make the actual Hajj." Malcolm's comments are not so much about one-upmanship as they are intended to emphasize the authenticity of his pilgrimage over the "Muslim" claims of Elijah Muhammad—claims he had formerly helped to advance.[24]

In turn, the Muslim world apparently looked in different directions for a new advocate when Muhammad proved unfaithful. Momentarily taking heart in Malcolm's break with the Nation of Islam in 1964, perhaps they hoped to find in the ex-Black Muslim firebrand an evangelist they could manipulate. Of course, Malcolm was cooperative and sincere—far more sincere than Elijah Muhammad had proven. But in the end Malcolm, too, would disappoint them by adhering to the black struggle while also turning his insightful lens of criticism upon their world—a courageously moral act that Muhammad had neither the guts nor the gumption to perform.[25] Instead, Muhammad packed his pilgrim's bag and returned to Chicago in early 1960, his tentative Muslim credentials in tow. However, as Malcolm X observed, Muhammad returned to Chicago with more interest in reaping a harvest of wealth and sexual pleasure than in either proving or improving his standing in the Muslim world. At the same time, Muhammad's provincialism and prejudice prevented building substantial relations with blacks outside the United States, like Caribbeans and continental Africans. Several years before making his journey to Mecca, Muhammad virtually summarized his actual posture toward Islam and Christianity in a column where he discussed the sacred stone of the Ka'ba, Islam's holiest site: "Oh, that you would only understand the Scriptures. The Christians think the stone was Jesus. The Muslims think that it represents Muhammad 1,370 years ago. . . . There certainly is a surprise in store for both worlds (Islam and Christianity) in the revealing of the last One."[26] The "last One" was an allusion to himself, since Muhammad claimed to be Allah's last messenger. However, the only "surprise" was reserved for sincere followers like Malcolm X, who later discovered that they believed in Muhammad more than he did himself.

Given the limitations of the pilgrimage and his refusal to conform to the standards of the Muslim community, Elijah Muhammad and his Nation of Islam increasingly devolved in a religious and spiritual malaise. Without the authenticity that could be granted by the Muslim world, Muhammad could not go forward, and having abused the Christian conception of atonement and redemption, neither could he return to the integrity of the church. Without a redemptive paradigm, Elijah Muhammad thereafter began to back away from his public role as a religious figure, instead emphasizing organizational and community issues.

The broadening acceptance Muhammad enjoyed in the last decade of his life (1965–75) marked the extent to which he had opted for civic safety—which he could only have attained by surrendering his aggressive religious approach.

Caught between orthodox Christianity and traditional Islam, Elijah Muhammad had neither Jesus Christ nor Prophet Muhammad—though in characteristic pretense he claimed harmony with both. Unlike Malcolm X, Muhammad was no more interested in teaching his followers Sunni Islam than he was in the liberation of colonial Africa. His innocence had gone, having slowly dissipated until finally—in the light and heat of Mecca—it had vanished altogether. Now, the only innocence Elijah Muhammad sought was back home, in the tender, trusting embraces of the young women who believed that Allah would be well pleased with their surrender.

PART II

X and the Cross

Malcolm, the Nation of Islam, and Christianity

The White man, someone told me, discovered the Cross by way of the Bible, but the Black man discovered the Bible by way of the Cross.

—James Baldwin, *The Evidence of Things Not Seen*

A bitter place! Death could scarce be bitterer. But if I would show the good that came of it I must talk about things other than the good. —Dante Alighieri, *Inferno, Canto* 1:7

5

Faith of Our Fathers— and Our Mothers

The Little Family, Marcus Garvey, and Christianity

Faith of our fathers, holy faith
We will be true to thee till death!
—"Faith of Our Fathers," hymn, lyrics by
Frederick W. Faber, early 1900s

The Black Man has a greater claim to the Cross than other men. If it is a symbol of Christ's triumph, then the Negro should share in the triumph because Simon the Cyrenian bore the Cross. Simon the Cyrenian shared in the original triumph.
—Marcus Garvey, *The Course of African Philosophy* (1937)

"My father, the Reverend Earl Little," Malcolm X would write through the pen of his amanuensis, "was a Baptist minister." Malcolm's characterization of his clergyman father as a "dedicated organizer" for the Marcus Garvey movement, the Universal Negro Improvement Association (UNIA),[1] has been popularized in countless reiterations of *The Autobiography of Malcolm X* and, more recently, in Spike Lee's film adaptation of a screenplay largely premised on the *Autobiography*. Malcolm's early memory of his father "doing free-lance Christian preaching in local Negro Baptist churches" while devoting the rest of the week "to spreading the word of Marcus Garvey" has been generally accepted as a historically factual description. However, it is in reality a stylization that reflects Malcolm's inaccurate childhood perceptions and perhaps even a later need to separate his father's religious duties from his race work on behalf of the UNIA.

Malcolm remembered his father as an itinerant clergyman with no regular church of his own, a perpetual visiting preacher whose demonstrative oratory inflamed his black audiences. Malcolm recalled his father leaping and jumping in the pulpit, his resonant voice igniting the worship and praise of his listeners. He also remembered a particular sermon his father preached about a "little black train," which Malcolm later connected to Garvey's African redemptionist theme, "Black Train Homeward." Malcolm called this his father's favorite sermon, but it may simply have been the only theme Malcolm himself remembered because of the appeal of trains to his young mind. Certainly, Malcolm acknowledged he had little memory of his father's funeral service, though his remembrance of that event is at once trivial and significant.

Malcolm vividly recalled how, during the funeral service, a large fly descended on the face of his deceased father and his eldest brother, Wilfred, instantly sprang from his chair to brush it away. Malcolm's boyish attention was understandably focused on the irreverent intrusion of the flying pest and he was far more conscious of it—as he was also of the tears flowing down his older brother's face—than he was, for instance, of the issues surrounding his father's unpopular career, his tragic death, or even the conversation of the guests at the funeral. However, his young mind did prove perceptive in wondering why the funeral service of a preacher was being conducted in a funeral parlor instead of a church. An awareness of the limitations of Malcolm's early observations and recollections is therefore the first factor for critically reading the childhood narrative in *The Autobiography of Malcolm X*, and it is especially key in discussing his father as a religious figure.

The second factor, which overarches almost the entire autobiography, is the initial purpose and motivation behind the writing itself. Malcolm's autobiography was the brainchild of a magazine producer, who in turn prompted journalist Alex Haley to approach Malcolm with a proposition for the work. Malcolm's response was guarded and he consented to the project only after it was approved by Elijah Muhammad—which, given the way things turned out between Muhammad and Malcolm X, was an ironic opportunity for the latter to make a literary contribution that would overshadow Muhammad for the rest of his life. At the time, of course, Malcolm undoubtedly saw the opportunity to tell his story as a means of advocating on behalf of Muhammad; however, it was also a means of demonstrating his fidelity to the elder at a time when Black Muslim opponents were endeavoring to alienate him from the movement. Malcolm's autobiography was thus undertaken by Malcolm quite consciously as an evangelistic tool, and Haley's memory of the early days of the project attest to Malcolm's inflexible propagandistic bent. Haley recalled that at the end of their first month of work together, his notebook "contained almost nothing but Black Muslim philosophy, praise of Mr. Muhammad, and the 'evils' of 'the white devil.'" Haley and Malcolm eventually found a more positive way of fulfilling their respective literary agendas but only after Haley almost decided to quit the project. Ultimately, however, Haley's creativity overcame his subject's rigidity and Malcolm himself finally opened up, not surprisingly, when Haley broached the subject of his mother.[2]

Nevertheless, the religious devotion of Malcolm X to Elijah Muhammad and his earnest desire to advance the cause of the Nation of Islam gave form to *The Autobiography of Malcolm X* in ways religious and political, especially Malcolm's childhood narrative. Taken into consideration, the limitations of his childhood memories and his Black Muslim stylizations are quite helpful in reflecting on Malcolm's religious roots vis-à-vis Christianity.

Malcolm's father was never a Christian minister though he did involve himself in spiritual matters and was certainly a guest speaker in the pulpits of pastors who were sympathetic to the UNIA. Malcolm remembered one of these special occasions when his father was invited by a sympathetic pastor to preach—unusual, considering the fact that most black ministers found Earl Little and his Garveyite message quite threatening. On this particular Sunday, Little was quite effective at stirring up his audience, and young Malcolm watched wide-eyed while people jumped and shouted and his preacher father trumpeted the old-time religion.

Contrary to Malcolm's belief that his activist father made a living as an itinerant preacher who did odd jobs on the side, Earl Little actually made his living by doing skilled work and—in practicing the living gospel of black economic independence—raised his own foods for consumption and marketing. Little's independent economic status not only allowed him and his wife, Louise, to carry on efforts on behalf of the UNIA but protected them from the inevitable interference that would have resulted had he been dependent on white employers. Of course, given the fact that Earl died when Malcolm was still quite young, it is largely due to Louise's devotion to the cause that Malcolm and his siblings were subsequently exposed to Garveyism. However, one must wonder if Malcolm X, writing on behalf of the Nation of Islam, retrospectively found his parents' activist heritage troubling in one sense. While he was certainly proud of their Garveyism, Malcolm may have been quite inconvenienced by their involvement with a movement that was dominated by a Christian philosophy.

While it would be quite inaccurate to refer to Marcus Garvey as either a fundamentalist or a traditional black Christian, it is clear that he expressed no objection to the theological constructs of biblical Christianity and clearly established an orthodox approach to the faith on behalf of his followers. In one case, Garvey even sought to support Trinitarian doctrine and advocated an interpretation of Christ's death that seems to have included a view of the cross as a model of moral obedience and as an atoning sacrifice. Indeed, though the UNIA maintained a philosophy of religious tolerance for the sake of the unity of its Christian and Muslim followers, many of its leading activists were Christians and often Christian clergy. Of course, Garvey may have taken an orthodox posture on behalf of many of his followers who were Christians, since he is said to have personally made no ultimate differentiation between Christianity and other religions.[3] But it is significant that he saw no fundamental whiteness in Christian theology as did W. D. Fard and Elijah Muhammad, and attacked neither black Christianity nor the Christian church as did the Black Muslims. Indeed, Garvey declared: "I would rather stand alone and be framed for the prison a thousand times, than deny the [black] religion of my mother—mark you, not the [white] religion—the religion that taught me to be honest and fair to all my fellow men."[4]

UNIA meetings generally carried over many aspects from the church. Sunday evening meetings especially included hymn singing, recitation of scripture and the Lord's Prayer, formal prayer, a sermon or comments by the division chaplain, and then, finally, organizational business. Christian holidays were also observed, but with a Garveyite interpretation (most certainly, this would entail a black Madonna and Child at Christmastime). It is possible that these religious duties comprised much of what Malcolm remembered as his father's preaching activities. This is clear, for instance, in one report concerning the Milwaukee, Wisconsin, division of the UNIA, published in the Garvey paper around the time Malcolm was two years old: "Our religious services, which are held at 11 o'clock Sunday mornings, are making wonderful progress under the leadership of Elder E. Little and are quite an asset to the division." Interestingly, one can also imagine Malcolm as an infant, being dedicated by the chaplain of their UNIA division in keeping with the organization's quasi-Christian imitation of infant baptism.

While Garvey is known for his sympathies toward Islam and his association with Ahmadiyya Muslims, the greater influence of Christianity on the UNIA is typified by Bishop George Alexander McGuire, who served for a time as the UNIA's Chaplain-General and prepared the organization's "Universal Negro Ritual" and "Universal Negro Catechism." While McGuire was eventually obligated to leave the UNIA because he had founded his own African Orthodox Church, his separation was relatively brief and his impact upon the movement was significant, eventuating in his return in an honorary position.[5]

To what extent Earl Little's religious ideas either differed from or resembled the theological ideas of men like Garvey and McGuire is not clear. A Southern-born man, whom Malcolm characterized as a "real Georgia Negro," Earl Little was undoubtedly acquainted with the same religious experience as Elijah Muhammad, though the former had chosen to embrace the cross instead of curse it. He undoubtedly held a high view of the Bible and would have used it exhaustively in styling his Garveyite-Christian appeals. Little is repeatedly referred to as "Elder" within the UNIA's publication, suggesting that he did aspire to spiritual endeavors within the movement and was apparently as capable at edifying black folks as he was scaring white folks with his bold Garveyite pronouncements. "My father was a race man," Malcolm told a reporter many years later, "a Garveyite—a little too outspoken for Lansing, Michigan, where we moved when I was a child."

As a Black Muslim, however, Malcolm X could not honor Christianity, not even the Christianity of Garvey. Though Elijah Muhammad himself openly admired Garvey, he somewhat disingenuously referred to him and Drew Ali as "fine Muslims." To be sure, this may have been a salutary remark but it also hints at the Nation of Islam's contempt for Christianity and the movement's basic unwillingness to recognize any good in it. Though Malcolm X personally defended Garvey to the extent that he openly criticized the popular black leader A. Philip Randolph for his early opposition to the UNIA,[6] it seems that even Malcolm could not acknowledge the viability of Garvey's Christianity as a religio-political tool against white oppression—even when it came to his own parents.

In a sermon in late 1962 in New York's Temple No. 7, Malcolm provided an interesting illustration during one of his remarkable polemics against Christianity, in which he used his own parents as examples of "Negroes" who "desire to be white."

> My mother was a Christian and my father was a Christian and I used to hear them when I was a little child sing the song "Wash Me White As Snow." My father was a black man and my mother was a black woman, but yet the songs that they sang in their church were designed to fill their hearts with the desire to be white.[7]

About a month later, in January 1963, Malcolm made a similar comment when addressing students at Michigan State University on the subject of "the twentieth-century Uncle Tom."

> He's not interested in any religion of his own. He believes in a white Jesus, white Mary, white angels, and he's trying to get to a white heaven. When you listen to him in his church singing, he sings a song,

I think they call it, "Wash me white as snow." He wants to be—he wants to be turned white so he can go to heaven with a white man.[8]

Admittedly, while Malcolm made no direct reference to his parents' being "Uncle Toms," his remarks suggest the inflexible, hypercritical religious posture of the Nation of Islam that could not interpret Christianity, even with regard to spiritual symbolism, in anything but racial terms. Earl and Louise Little would perhaps have been offended by Malcolm's remark, not only because it suggested their racial identities may not have been entirely intact, but because it was simply unfair. The use of spiritual allegory regarding the cleansing of sins and the theme of whiteness as being symbolic of purity and forgiveness is as ancient as the church itself and predates modern racial thinking.

Antagonists of Christianity like the Black Muslims have found an easy and convenient target in the spiritual language of whiteness that is often linked to Christian redemptive discourse. However, a critical retrospective will discern that the modern European concepts, like "white = good" and "black = evil," are not rooted in biblical language but in other Eastern philosophical and cultic influences that contaminated not only European Christendom but, to a lesser extent, also the Muslim world. Indeed, the extravagant use of color-oriented allegory by Christians in the postapostolic era evidences non-Christian influences like astrology, alchemy, and Gnosticism as opposed to biblical theology and anthropology.

Furthermore, the biblical concept of spiritual purity is actually bound up with the idea of washing, not whiteness, and it is this point that the Nation of Islam has consistently overlooked in its diatribes. So poised to react to any reference to color, the Black Muslims—who wouldn't even eat white bread—could not differentiate the profoundly spiritual language of the Bible from the skewed racial religion of modern white Christendom. This religious prejudice not only militated against the Nation of Islam recognizing even the most equitable endeavors among Christians, but reinforced the tendency of its spokesmen to authenticate the movement's spurious religious message by engaging in a constant barrage of what one scholar called "evidence by ridicule."[9] In other words, following Elijah Muhammad's example, ministers like Malcolm X found an essential tactic in focusing on things that could be generalized, inflated, or simply taken out of context to the detriment of Christianity itself. This is not to suggest that the race critique of the Nation of Islam was without substance or even brilliance. To the extent that the Nation of Islam presented an authentic criticism of white Christianity and the foibles of black Christians who followed it, its voice was not only sane but oftentimes prophetic. However, when it engaged in opportunistic religious skullduggery, such as harping on the lyrics of hymns or decontextualizing biblical passages, it revealed the ugly underside of its own cultic nature.

In contrast, given the humanitarianism that actually underlay Garvey's bold Africentric religious ideas, the UNIA was never so ideologically constricted.[10] Undoubtedly, Earl and Louise Little had no difficulty singing Christian hymns like "Wash Me White as Snow" or even "Onward Christian Soldiers," not only because they understood the spiritual formations upon which those words were based but because they were far more secure in their racial identities than Malcolm X and the Black Muslims would grant them given their identification with the largely Christian UNIA.

Even allowing for some color ambiguity in their thinking as parents, it is probably the case that Malcolm's autobiographical reflections were far more useful to the Nation of Islam than they were as a wholistic portrait of Earl and Louise Little. Malcolm recalled his father as a strict man who set many household rules and who punished his children "almost savagely" when they broke them. Malcolm goes on to suggest, however, that he was spared these brutal beatings, probably because he was the lightest in complexion among the children. According to Malcolm X, Earl Little "was subconsciously so afflicted with the white man's brainwashing of Negroes that he inclined to favor the light ones"—an irony that even Malcolm recognized since he considered his father to be thoroughly anti-white. Malcolm said another reason he felt his father favored him was because Earl apparently took him to Garveyite house meetings, where people acted "intense, intelligent, and down to earth"—traits Malcolm would emphasize in his own ministry years later. In contrast to the favoritism Malcolm sensed from his father, he also recalled how it was his mother who gave him most of his "whippings."[11]

Here Malcolm is clearly reading his childhood memories through a Black Muslim lens. Malcolm was quite young when his father was alive, and this may account for the fact that he was spared harsh discipline. Perhaps Earl *did* take to Malcolm as his favorite, though it is simplistic to attribute this favor to mere skin tone. Years later, Wilfred Little recalled how his famous brother reminded him of their father:

> [M]any times when I would observe Malcolm . . . I was seeing a repetition of what my father had been doing in the Marcus Garvey movement, and Malcolm was doing the same thing in the Nation of Islam. And I don't think he was aware of it himself how the influence of—because he was too young when my father was doing this, to consciously be aware that he was doing the same thing.[12]

It is possible that Malcolm's father sensed an affinity with his young son that went deeper than intellect or physical traits. Malcolm remembered liking those intimate Garveyite home meetings much better than the typical religious services of the black church. When he was with his father in those house groups, even as a young boy, he seemed to absorb the atmosphere of intensity and intelligence that apparently characterized his father's discourse with other Garveyites. "It made me feel the same way." If Malcolm was happy in such an environment it is possible that Earl sensed it and that his feelings of favoritism, if indeed they existed, were rooted in a spiritual bond that existed between father and son—a bond that commonly exists between a parent and a particular child, often defying simple explanation. This may be speculation but it is, at least, no less reasonable than one psychoanalytic attempt to drop Earl and his young son into the depths of an Oedipal struggle, wherein Malcolm is seen to have been "jealous of his father's power and sexual prerogatives." Such an artificial, ideologically self-serving model fits more like a yoke than a framework for understanding Earl and his son, and quite predictably it skews the spiritual elements of Malcolm's legacy in the name of secular psychoanalysis.

Malcolm wrote that most of his whippings were given by his

mother, but even this may not reinforce his notions of parental color preference as much as his narrative leads us to believe. Given the fact that Malcolm was only six at the time of his father's death, it is reasonable that he received most of his childhood discipline from his mother. According to his narrative, Malcolm's behavior went sour after his father's death, when he and his brother Philbert became especially mischievous and unbridled. Their childish rebellion took place in the context of what Malcolm called the "psychological deterioration" of their "family circle," during which Louise Little's personal and economic circumstances worsened. It is likely that the many whippings Malcolm remembered were from the period which preceded the tragic breakup of the family by state welfare agents.[13] With his father gone and his mother desperately seeking to keep the family afloat on her own, it is hard to chalk up her harsh discipline, as Malcolm did, to personal color preference:

> Thinking about it now, I feel definitely that just as my father favored me for being lighter than the other children, my mother gave me more hell for the same reason. She was very light herself but she favored the ones who were darker. . . . She went out of her way never to let me become afflicted with a sense of color-superiority. I am sure she treated me this way partly because of how she came to be light herself.[14]

Not to rule out his race instincts entirely, but it is nevertheless probable that Malcolm was imputing to his mother a prejudice that fit the Nation of Islam's reading of Christian blacks, a reading quite inappropriate with regard to Louise Little, and for more than one reason. Certainly, if his mother dispensed "hell" upon young Malcolm, it was more likely because he deserved it. "Malcolm was always the most rebellious of us," remembers his eldest brother Wilfred in discussing the times the children were sent out to do yard work. "As he got older and became more independent, he'd find some excuse to go back to the house for something, and we wouldn't see him again. He'd go and get with his friends in the city." What does seem to be authentic in Malcolm's remembrance is the sensitivity of Louise Little to color preferences practiced by many African Americans, and her determination to keep her light-skinned son from adopting an attitude of superiority.

Louise Little was born and reared on the Caribbean island of Grenada and her thoughts on race, like her thoughts on religion, were significantly different than those of her black American associates and neighbors. While Earl Little was markedly different by virtue of his convictions as a "race man" and his involvement with the Garvey movement, Louise's orientation was Caribbean, not North American. The reigning absolute of "either black or white" in the United States was something that Louise had to learn. Despite her light skin and her ability to have passed for a white woman, Louise apparently held strong convictions about her mixed-race heritage. When she lived in Grenada she saw herself as a Creole woman in a society of "infinite gradations of class, color, caste, and status." She emigrated to North America in 1917 and met Earl Little at a Garveyite convention in Montreal, marrying him in 1919—after which she undoubtedly received her first lessons on race in the United States. A childhood friend in Grenada later remembered the first letter she received from Louise up in "Yankeeland." "She said that over there, she had to make a choice between being Black or white."[15]

If Louise Little made a choice regarding race, she apparently never felt compelled to do so regarding religion. As I have observed elsewhere, Louise Little's religious orientation was quite different from most African Americans. Her personal brand of theism tended toward eclecticism, and she determinedly trained her children in the same conviction. As Wilfred Little recalled, "We were always taught by our mother not to give ourselves to any religion, but to always believe in God, and practice it in a spiritual way, not in a religious way." Apparently, one of the reasons she emphasized individual spirituality over religious affiliation was to undercut the tendency for people to be involved in religious and denominational rivalries. "She said when you get hung up in religions . . . you see everything in relationship to that religion, and everybody else that's not that is wrong, or it makes you see them differently." Her resolve, then, was to teach Wilfred, Malcolm, and her other children that one's personal relationship with God cannot be defined by a church or by any other person but the individual. "But she believed that you should believe in God, and establish your own spiritual relation with God, and be true to that."[16]

It may be that Louise's feelings about religion were inspired by Marcus Garvey's teachings, though her tendency toward eclectic religion went deeper than the influence of her hero. Nevertheless, it is probably no coincidence that Garvey's ideas about religious life focused on the same private, individual experience that Louise emphasized: "You can worship God by yourself. You are responsible to God by yourself. You have to live your own soul before God. . . . In your soul [lies] relationship with God. Therefore, always worship with your own heart, soul and mind when you want to commune with God."[17]

Garvey encouraged his followers to make their hearts, souls, or minds "your altar," and he admonished them with a poem so titled:

My Altar
I've built a sacred place all mine,
To worship God, who is Divine,
I go there every day, in thought,
Right to my own, dear sacred heart—
MY ALTAR.

No one can change me in my mood,
For I do live on God's sweet food,
He feeds me everyday, with love,
While angels look at it above—
MY ALTAR.

When all the world goes wrong without,
I never hold one single doubt,
For I do find a great relief,
When I do trust my own belief—
MY ALTAR.[18]

If, indeed, Garveyism can be said to have had a religious distinction apart from its race critique and consciousness, it was perhaps the flexibility and individuality of Garvey's religious attitude and his aversion to denominational conflict. Thus, as long as George Alexander McGuire envisioned the UNIA as an inclusive black ecumenical institution, his work alongside Garvey was secure. When, however,

McGuire was consecrated bishop in his own African Orthodox Church in 1921, he was obliged to resign his position as chaplain-general of the UNIA. Garvey did not want his followers to be forced into choosing between their own denominations and what McGuire apparently hoped would be the UNIA's church. While the UNIA's *Negro World* offered congratulations to McGuire, who had been consecrated by a functionary of the Russian Orthodox Church, it was clear that he could not remain a religious officer in the movement. Though the African Orthodox Church would thereafter be closely associated with the UNIA, Garvey never compromised his commitment to the ecumenism of black-led religious groups under his banner. Ecclesiastical politics aside, however, the spirit of the UNIA, reflecting the conciliatory religious attitude of Garvey himself, promoted inclusiveness—a trait which seems to have flourished in the Little home in particular. As a reporter for the UNIA's *Negro World*, Louise Little undoubtedly embraced Garvey's sentiments within her heart.[19]

In one sense, it was Garvey who brought Earl and Louise together in marital union, not only because they had met at a UNIA convention but because they bonded at a point of commitment to the movement. For all of their conflicts and problems, the Littles were a UNIA family, sharing a deep-rooted belief in Garvey's vision. Interestingly, however, it seems that Louise Little ultimately defined the religiosity of the household, not only because she was left with the rearing of the children after Earl's death, but because her Garveyite–West Indian spirituality dominated the lives of the children instead of the traditional Bible-preaching orientation that would likely have defined Earl Little's approach to religion.

Following Garvey's admonitions to "never stop learning" and "master the language of your country," Louise—whose Anglican school training far exceeded her husband's elementary level schooling—kept issues of the UNIA's *Negro World* and a dictionary ready for use for the children's homework assignments. "[W]hen we mispronounced a word my mother made us look it up and learn both to spell and to pronounce it correctly," Wilfred remembered. This brief vignette adds an insightful dimension to the prison narrative in *The Autobiography of Malcolm X*, where he—supposedly ignorant and illiterate—began a process of self-education that came to fulness in the service of Elijah Muhammad. Granted, *The Autobiography* does not mask the fact that Malcolm's initial inspiration in prison came from "Bimbi," the prisoner-philosopher. But what Malcolm does not explain is that from the onset *he already knew how* to hone his intellect: "I saw that the best thing I could do was to get hold of a dictionary— to study, to learn some words." Of course, if Malcolm reached for the dictionary in prison it was because he had seen his mother and elder brother Wilfred using it many times, and had already internalized its great value for learning and the art of communication.

Besides the Garvey paper and the dictionary, Louise read *The West Indian*, the weekly publication of her countryman T. Albert Marryshow. In the 1920s, Marryshow led the vanguard for the West Indian Federation, demanding that the Crown Colony government of Grenada be removed and replaced with an elected government. Marryshow's slogan, "The West Indies Must Be West Indian," was as familiar in the Little household as was Garvey's famous cry, "Africa for Africans at home and abroad."[20] The subsequent campaign in her native Grenada to rid that island nation of Crown-nominated and *ex officio* representatives was very likely a topic that Wilfred and the other Little children not only heard about, but read about under the tutelage of their demanding mother. As Wilfred recalled:

> Every day when we came home from school, my mother would sit us down and have us read aloud passages from Marryshow's paper[,] *The West Indian*. . . . By reading that Marryshow paper day after day, we developed reading and writing skills superior to those of our white classmates. By reading Garvey's paper and Marryshow's paper, we got an education in international affairs and learned what Black people were doing for their own betterment all over the world.[21]

Just as Garvey's example and teachings gave Louise a framework for educating her children, it was actually the UNIA—not the black Christian church—that provided them a context for religious education. Despite the prevalence of Christianity in Garvey's constituency, and even more among the masses of African Americans, "The Aims and Objectives of the UNIA" officially promoted "a conscientious spiritual worship among the native tribes of Africa." In other words, black people were not necessarily to be evangelized with Christianity, but throughout Africa and the black diaspora people were to be nurtured with a wholesome spirituality in keeping with whatever religion they preferred: "Considering that there are so many different religious thoughts, the Negro should be brought under the influence of one system of religion and the belief in one God. An honest effort should be made to instruct him in his particular desires and not to exploit him by teaching him different religions."[22] In Louise's case, she seems to have preferred Garvey's ideal of personal religion, not Christianity. Like Garvey, Louise obviously valued Christianity, and perhaps it was the most significant element of her personal religion. However, as she applied it, her Garveyite religious context also incorporated Christian-sectarian and cultic elements into the family faith. Indeed, Louise taught her children to appropriate their experiences in various religious communities as tools in constructing their own altars of faith. "[W]e went to all of [*the churches*]," Wilfred recalled. "We went to the Methodists, and we'd observe theirs; so that we could get a feel for all of it." However, no matter which of the whole array of Christian churches they visited, Louise always issued one caveat. "[S]he always cautioned us—don't ever get so caught up in it that you think you're that [*religion*]—'You just understand God and try to establish your relationship with God, and be true to that.'"

Louise apparently had a religious strategy in bringing her children to various Christian churches. From mainline denominations like Baptists and Methodists she perhaps drew the core teachings of what is commonly referred to as the Judeo-Christian heritage. Wilfred noted that learning the Golden Rule and the Ten Commandments was essential to their religious education. In contrast, the Seventh-Day Adventist movement, a Christian sect with exclusive tendencies, provided Louise with the dietary regulations she found attractive. The fact that Louise took to dietary restrictions was likely an expression of what today might be considered a *holistic* belief system. In *The Autobiography*, Malcolm recalls that Earl and Louise locked horns over issues of this nature: "One cause of friction was that she had strong ideas about what she wouldn't eat—and didn't want *us* to

eat—including pork and rabbit, both of which my father loved dearly
... he believed in eating plenty of what we in Harlem today call 'soul
food.'" While this conflict proved more of a domestic spat than an ongoing religious conflict, it nevertheless pertained to religious conviction, one which also entailed setting the standard for the children's
lifestyle—the standard of Louise apparently having prevailed in the
household.[23]

If Malcolm's recollection is correct, after his father's tragic death
the Seventh-Day Adventists began to show an interest of their own in
the Little family. Some nearby Adventist neighbors began to visit for
lengthy discussions, leaving "booklets and leaflets and magazines" for
Louise and Wilfred to read. For a time she took solace in the Adventist community, not only in their emulation of the Mosaic dietary law
but also their future-oriented apocalyptic teachings. Malcolm remembered that the "Adventists felt that we were living at the end of
time, that the world was coming to an end." Interestingly, these religious issues prevailed despite the fact that "ninety-nine percent" of
her Adventist friends were whites—perhaps an aspect that had likewise disturbed Earl, and which had kept Louise distanced from the
Adventists until after his death.[24] In retrospect it is also interesting
that Malcolm X could acknowledge that these particular Christians
"were the friendliest white people I had ever seen" despite their unusual odor and bland cooking. (Years later, when he was inducted
into the Nation of Islam, he conveniently omitted his mother's caring
white Christian friends from the otherwise long list of de facto "white
devils" which served to justify his conversion.)

While Louise seems to have been most at home with the Adventists, she was not restrained from sampling other spiritual cups, including that of the Pentecostal church. Wilfred recalled that "she even
took us to the Church of God [in Christ], the ones that do all this
jumping and shouting and hollering—she took us there—it was just
like going to the show. . . . We would go and watch these people jump
up and down and dance and carry on and shout and fall out and all
that kind of stuff." After Louise's emotional condition had deterio-
rated due to domestic and financial crises and Malcolm was placed in
the care of a local Christian family, he found himself totally immersed

in the Pentecostal context, an experience that seemed as strange to him as it had to Wilfred. These "sanctified Holy Rollers . . . jumped even higher and shouted even louder than the Baptists I had known." Malcolm continued: "They sang at the top of their lungs, and swayed back and forth and cried and moaned and beat on tambourines and chanted. It was spooky, with ghosts and spirituals and 'ha'nts' seeming to be in the very atmosphere when finally we all came out of the church, going back home."[25] The people that Malcolm described with the less than flattering term "sanctified Holy Rollers" were actually first-generation African American Pentecostalists, a movement born out of the older Holiness tradition of Protestantism in the United States around 1906. Its distinctive practice, speaking in tongues as a sign of the "baptism of the Holy Spirit" (an innovation based on the older "second blessing" idea of the Holiness groups), was also accompanied by other ecstatic behaviors like prophesying aloud, falling backwards (being "slain in the Spirit"), or rolling around on the floor. While the movement originated among both whites and blacks, it was largely mediated through black clergy, whose Africanity ultimately shaped the movement much the same as black musicians had taken traditional American music and produced jazz. Indeed, Pentecostalism and jazz have proven to be global movements whose respective influences have spread an element of Africanity worldwide. Of course, the public greeted the initial wave of Pentecostalism with a cynicism largely influenced by white racism. ("The leaders of this strange movement are for the most part Negroes," one New York City newspaper commented in 1906.)[26] Racism would eventuate in the segregation of the Pentecostal movement; the "sanctified Holy Roller" church in which Malcolm sat as a boy was undoubtedly one of a myriad of black Pentecostal congregations abandoned by their hypocritical white counterparts, whose spiritual empowerment was apparently ineffective when it came to the status quo of white religion in the United States.

It is interesting, of course, that Louise thought to expose her children to the burgeoning Pentecostal movement. Judging from her preferred associations as well as the reactions of Wilfred and Malcolm, Louise Little probably did not identify with the Holy Rollers, though she thought them significant enough to visit and understand. If any-thing, the Pentecostal movement, with its exuberant worship, glosso-lalia, prophesying, and other high-profile spiritual activities may have been reminiscent of some aspects of Caribbean spiritualism, particu-larly in the openness of followers to the reality of the spirit realm. That young Malcolm saw the Pentecostal movement as "spooky, with ghosts and spirituals and 'ha'nts,'" may suggest his own sense of his mother's feelings about such churches—that the worship and ecsta-tic behavior provided a context for ascertaining the invisible world of the spirit. Wilfred definitely recalled that his mother's spirituality had been influenced by her early experiences among the native Caribe people in Grenada. According to one of her childhood friends, Louise was reared by her grandmother until the latter died and left her with an aunt. While staying with her aunt, Louise had Caribe neighbors, and, apparently, her association with them may have afforded her op-portunities to explore Amerindian spiritualism.[27]

While the high profile spirituality of the black Pentecostal church may have held some interest for Louise, its dogma was probably too rigid to draw her in closely. Resistant even to the whole of the Adven-tist teachings, Louise moved easily from sects to churches, selectively appropriating what she felt were the essentials but nevertheless re-mained opened to further exploration. It seems Louise even read Watchtower Bible and Tract Society materials because of her interest in their futuristic teachings. It may also have been through the Watch-tower's influence that Louise found a religious basis to dissent from Christian orthodoxy, though it is not clear at what point she deter-mined to reject Trinitarian doctrine. Whether or not she came to this conclusion before she married Earl in 1919, by the time she was rear-ing her children she taught them that Jesus was no more or less than the rest of the prophets. "All of them had received divine inspiration according to their level of consciousness,"[28] Wilfred recalled in dis-cussing what Louise had taught him and his siblings. This may have been a point over which she differed with Earl, but if it was it would seem that her influence prevailed in this matter as well. Certainly, Malcolm acknowledged in his autobiography that he had never be-lieved in Christ's divinity, although he leaves the impression this was an unusual opinion, especially for the son of a Christian minister. Of course, since Malcolm never embraced doctrinal Christianity, his religious orientation was "Christian" only in the sense that he was familiar with a diversity of Protestant churches, sects, and new religions. In the years to come, Malcolm X would speak disdainfully of his "Christian" background and attribute to it his worst sins and behaviors. This would serve the interests of the Nation of Islam by reinforcing its assaults on the church. However, unlike his beloved mentor, Elijah Muhammad, Malcolm was never an apostate. His relationship with the church was strangely familiar yet mediated through the religious interpretations of his unusually dynamic and eclectic mother.

In a very real sense it was the religious heritage of his mother which cleared the way for Malcolm X to embrace an alternative monotheistic tradition. That Malcolm was attracted to Islam because it was centered in the world of color is quite evident in his own narrative. What is not so evident but is still fundamental to his attitude toward Christianity is the fact that Malcolm was greatly unencumbered insofar as religious devotion is concerned because of his marginal orientation. Malcolm ultimately passed through Muhammad's cult and into traditional Islam. However, even in this last, most important phase of his religious life Malcolm seems to have overlooked the possibility that it was his mother's influence that had actually helped him to that point.

In what appears to be a later emendation in *The Autobiography*, Malcolm added these words to his Black Muslim narrative concerning his prison conversion. He recalled how the first thing he did to conform to the Nation of Islam's requirements was to abstain from eating pork: "Later I would learn, when I had read and studied Islam a good deal, that, unconsciously, my first pre-Islamic submission had been manifested. I had experienced, for the first time, the Muslim teaching, 'If you take one step toward Allah—Allah will take two steps toward you.'"[29] It may be that Malcolm's abstinence from pork at that point was a "pre-Islamic submission," but if it was so, it was not without precedent in his life. He remembered how his mother, in those most hungry and disastrous years of his childhood, had turned down a gift of pork from a kindly neighbor ("a whole pig, maybe even two of them") because she considered it unclean meat. Malcolm even remembered that the neighbors had called her "crazy" for doing so, but as a child he understood that her convictions were the reason "we had never eaten pork."[30]

Similarly, because Malcolm had never considered Jesus Christ to be different from prophets like Moses or Elijah this was also a kind of "pre-Islamic" advantage for him. Unlike Elijah Muhammad, whose roots were in Trinitarian Christianity, Malcolm never had the Christian faith. His later diatribes against the church, his lampooning of the Christian conception of Jesus, and his inclination to deify Elijah Muhammad with Christological terms from the Bible must all be understood in the context of his mother's benign rejection of Christian doctrine—not in the familiar contempt of Muhammad's apostate approach. With regard to his embrace of Islam, then, Malcolm already believed Jesus was a great prophet when he was confronted with cultic Islam while in prison. What actually hindered him from embracing traditional Islam was his belief, for the better part of two decades, that Elijah Muhammad's message was a sincere representation of traditional Islam.

Louise Little would likely not have approved of Malcolm's conversion to the Nation of Islam—that is, not to the extent to which he ultimately gave himself to belief in Elijah Muhammad. By the time Malcolm became a zealous proponent of the Nation of Islam, his mother had long been trapped in a techno-bureaucratic purgatory, unnecessarily institutionalized, and consigned to live among the mentally ill. Louise remained a virtual prisoner for a quarter of a century, until her adult sons Wilfred and Malcolm had her removed from institutionalization and sent her to live with their sister Yvonne. Louise lived until 1991—a healthy, sagacious woman whose later years negated the false witness of her institutional captivity. "She was not that aware of all of the things that [were] taking place with [Malcolm]," Wilfred recalled a year after his mother's death. "She knew that he was busy with the Movement and there was more to it than what she realized. She knew he was busy trying to build something." But perhaps Malcolm's mother discerned more than her children realized.

Once, Wilfred remembered, the family showed Louise a picture of her famous Black Muslim son and asked her about some of the things that were going on. "She said she felt that he was being manipulated," Wilfred remembered. Sometime later they showed her a picture of Elijah Muhammad, "and when she looked at the picture she said, 'You know, he's a person that manipulates people'—that was the way she referred to him. That's the way she saw it."[31]

6

"If a Man Die, Shall He Live Again?"

Malcolm X as a Fundamentalist Zealot

You see my tears, brothers and sisters. . . Tears haven't been in my eyes since I was a young boy. But I cannot help this when I feel the responsibility I have to help you comprehend for the first time what this white man's religion that we call Christianity has done to us.

—Malcolm X, *The Autobiography of Malcolm X*

How could one man do these things when a whole society couldn't do it? What he was teaching them, how he was holding them with his message, I don't know.

—Justice Jawn Sandifer, interview, March 28, 1992

If a man die, shall he live again? All the days of my appointed time will I wait, till my change come.

—Job 14:14, King James version of the Bible

"Do you believe in God?" the young inmate asked after accidentally-on-purpose bumping into another inmate in the prison courtyard. "God the father," he continued, "God the son, God the Holy Ghost, and all that crap?" The other inmate, a prisoner-philosopher named Bembry, wasn't offended by the young man because he recognized the sober intent of his question. In a short time the two prisoners, Malcolm Little and John Bembry, became friends—but it was a mentoring friendship, the kind of camaraderie and exchange that fed the intellect and imagination of young Malcolm, helping him to initiate a process of "mental resurrection" which he later attributed to Elijah Muhammad. As he recalled in his autobiography, Malcolm had already been observing Bembry—whom he calls "Bimbi" in his story—and was impressed with the inmate's great store of knowledge. Erudite and seasoned as a student of history, philosophy, and religion, Bembry enjoyed the respect of prisoners and correction officers alike. More interesting, however, is what particularly attracted Malcolm to Bembry: "What made me seek his friendship was when I heard him discuss religion." Even as a young hustler, it seems, religion was never as far from his mind as he would like to have had his readers believe. Not that the teenage Malcolm was seeking religion, but he was thinking about it, if only in rebellion. One Harlem associate even remembered him reading a good deal more than Malcolm admits in *The Autobiography*. Though most of what he was reading was admittedly shallow material, this friend distinctly remembered Malcolm also reading the Bible.[1]

Despite Malcolm's self-portrayal as a rebel and a prison atheist, it appears he carried within him an interest in religious thought throughout his youth. To be sure, as his career in criminal mischief and debauchery deepened, Malcolm's immoral behavior seems to have derailed his religious development. His fascination with lively, sensual urban culture proved to be a far greater force in his adolescence than were the moral teachings of his mother. Still, despite the depravity in which Malcolm became involved, one has a sense that—given his mother's religious orientation and instruction—he had never entirely done away with his personal altar. It is impossible to ascertain what it was about religion that Malcolm found fascinating, but it is safe to suggest that his interest in religion was not simply born from the desperation of his prison cell.

In his years as a teenager running on the streets of Boston, not all of Malcolm's haunts were nightclubs, bars, and pool rooms. In keeping with his mother's example, young Malcolm apparently found at least one church attractive, and for good reason. The Reverend Samuel Laviscount, pastor of St. Mark's Congregational Church

(United Church of Christ) in Roxbury, held regular community meetings which drew young people, including some "rough young fellows" like Malcolm Little. It is possible, in fact, that it was Malcolm's involvement that brought such otherwise street-oriented youth to a church—foreshadowing the kind of charismatic influence he would have in drawing people into the Nation of Islam many years later. Malcolm paid attention and participated in questions-and-answers in these forums, and decades afterward Laviscount still remembered teenage Malcolm expressing interest in the condition of blacks living in Scandinavia. The fact that Laviscount later remembered Malcolm is no surprise, since they had established a relationship—the pastor having considered young Malcolm quite nice despite his waywardness. For his part, Malcolm may have been drawn to Laviscount for a number of reasons. Born in Antigua, British West Indies, and schooled at Atlantic Union College (Lancaster, Mass.) and the School of Religion at Howard University, Laviscount manifested two characteristics that Malcolm perhaps found attractive—Caribbean culture and advanced education. Much like his later attraction to the well-read prisoner Bembry, Malcolm was invariably drawn to intellectuals who displayed intensity of thought and learning. Laviscount's West Indian background may have struck a chord of familiarity in Malcolm's life and, of course, there was his abeyant interest in religious matters, which made the learned pastor seem quite appealing.

Like Malcolm's mother, Laviscount came to the United States via Canada, and then went to college in New England, where he was graduated valedictorian of his class. His religious studies at Howard University's School of Religion in Washington, D.C., went equally well: he was graduated *summa cum laude* with a Bachelor of Divinity degree in 1917. His first two pastorates were in the South, after which he moved to Detroit, where he married and embarked on a long and notable pastoral career in the North. By the time young Malcolm darkened the doors of St. Mark's in Boston, Laviscount had been pastoring there for about a decade, after successfully developing a congregation of less than fifty to over a thousand people. An intellectual and race leader in his own right, Laviscount advanced religious programs that were attuned to the spiritual, social, and political concerns of the Roxbury community. During his thirty-three-year pastorate at St. Mark's, Laviscount served in many community and pastoral associations, including a seat on the board of directors for the Urban League. His impact on young people was hardly limited to Malcolm—who actually may have proven far more resistant to the Pastor's counsel than other young people, some of whom eventually became leaders in the community. Not that Malcolm did not appreciate Laviscount's advice, but the pull of the urban underworld was still too great. Whatever religious or spiritual advice Laviscount had offered to Malcolm did little good, and there is no way of knowing if he was aware of Malcolm's later incarceration before the young man contacted him. Obviously, throughout his hustler days, Malcolm did not consider an active religious and spiritual life desirable. It was in the shadows of incarceration that a ripening interest in religion occurred, and only after a period of reactionary atheism in which Malcolm delighted in his notorious career of cursing God and mocking faith—an act that caused him to become known around the prison yard as "Satan."[2] However, in the swing back toward religion that occurred in his first conversion, Malcolm personified the very kind of religious experience that his mother had sought to discourage in her children. Investing his faith in Elijah Muhammad, Malcolm became a fundamentalist of sorts, a religious zealot whose canon was not a text, but a man.

When the Reverend Laviscount heard from Malcolm again it was late 1950, and Malcolm had already converted to the Nation of Islam. At just under two years before his parole (August 1952), Malcolm had become quite advanced in his studies and writing, having already embarked on strategies to enhance and advance the cause of Elijah Muhammad within the Massachusetts prison system. "I've never been one for inaction," Malcolm recalled regarding his first letter-writing endeavors from prison. He says in his autobiography that he made significant efforts to reach his former associates in "the hustling world," though none ever responded, and he assumed his former friends either could not read or found his message too bizarre. But Malcolm apparently wrote to many other people, including the Reverend Laviscount.

In a format that Malcolm would invariably follow in writing letters as a representative of the Nation of Islam, he began with a "Muslim" heading, "In the Name of Allah," which was actually a reference to W. D. Fard ("our Almighty Savior"). Malcolm's conversion had included what he called a "pre-vision" of Fard, a primal experience that seemed to confirm the correspondence he was receiving at the time from Elijah Muhammad. Malcolm's sacred salutation to Fard as the savior who had "come down into hell unto His long-lost people" thinly veiled one of Muhammad's most controversial theological tenets— the negation of an afterlife, both paradise and hades.[3]

To the Black Muslims, both heaven and hell were biblical metaphors for the quality of life on earth, respectively, for whites and blacks. As Elijah Muhammad said in a 1964 interview: "There is nothing like consciousness after you're dead. *Here* is our heaven; *here* is our hell. 'Life after death' really means freedom from the white man." Muhammad considered the belief in eternal life a landmark deception that kept "poor black people" gravely deceived by Christianity. "There is no such thing as hell or heaven after death," Muhammad wrote several years earlier in one of his columns. "Death is the end of everything, righteous or wicked. When we die that is the last of anyone."[4] Throughout his career as a religious leader, Elijah Muhammad consistently preached this doctrine of posthumous nihilism, and he especially applied it to the Savior of Christianity. In one of his "Mr. Muhammad Speaks" columns, the Black Muslim leader made it clear that the resurrection of Christ at Easter was only a "fancy story of your Bible." "No one after death has ever gone any place but where they were carried," Muhammad wrote to a mostly Christian audience. "There is no heaven or hell other than on the earth for you and me, and Jesus was no exception. His body is still embalmed in Palestine and will remain there."[5]

Malcolm's introduction in his letter to the Reverend Laviscount, then, was ripe with allusion to biblical terminology regarding spiritual and physical resurrection—terminology Muhammad had turned upside down in his racial reading of the Bible. "[Allah] has brought the truth to the Black Man of North America," Malcolm announced to Laviscount, "and is raising us up from out of our Shallow

Grave of Ignorance." To Muhammad, of course, resurrection was only a renewed mindset—a consciousness informed exclusively by his black-white worldview. Unlike Jesus, who used "resurrection" to speak of spiritual renewal and of a literal, future event in the lives of believers, Elijah Muhammad nixed all hope of an afterlife—instead stressing the present social, political, and economic conditions of a racially defined world. Far from being faithful to the Qur'an, which also teaches a future resurrection, Muhammad was as much an infidel in this matter as any Western secularist.

As Malcolm later described in his autobiography, when Nation of Islam members passed away, the funeral services were conducted with poignant nihilism. According to Malcolm, when he presided over funerals as a Black Muslim minister, a piece of chocolate was given to each of the guests, who were then instructed to think of the deceased as melting like candy into sweet memory. In place of future hope, Malcolm offered the guests an existential resurrection of the mind in which black people were given the opportunity to find new life by following Elijah Muhammad's religious and economic programs. As Malcolm recalled, the followers of Elijah Muhammad liked to say that their funerals were conducted for the dead, while Christian funerals were actually held for the sake of the living. What they meant was that since there was ostensibly no life after death, Christian funerals really only catered to the emotional needs of the living, while Black Muslim funerals actually reflected a true recognition of mortality and the "mental death" that plagued those yet alive. Yet, like everything else he found in the Nation of Islam, Malcolm improved upon Muhammad's teachings, inevitably lending its approach a studied, reasoned argument that was far more sophisticated than Muhammad's less cunning denials of biblical doctrine. Indeed, Malcolm undoubtedly excelled in his ability to use the Bible, scouring its pages for verses that could be framed in his arguments against Christianity. His readings in other religious traditions, and probably his study of literature that was critical of Christian doctrine (such as Watchtower Society material), also informed his approach. However, if anyone ever honed Black Muslim biblical application to a fine art, it was Malcolm X.

In preaching those funeral services, Malcolm skillfully decontextualized certain biblical passages to which he refers in *The Autobiography*. For instance, he found precedent for Muhammad's nihilism by quoting the ancient discourse of Job (7:7–10 and 14:7–14), where the agonized biblical character declares the finality of death (e.g., "he that goeth down to the grave shall come up no more"). Malcolm also would recount the story of David's adulterous affair with Bathsheba and the death of the infant born from that illicit union (2 Samuel 12:23). "Can I bring him back again?" one can almost hear Malcolm repeating the words of King David. "I shall go to him, but he shall not return to me." Recalling these funeral sermons, Malcolm wrote: "To the audience before me, I explained why no tears were to be shed, and why we had no flowers, or singing, or organ-playing." The dead should have been honored while they were alive, preached Malcolm. Now that they were unaware of the world of the living, nothing needed to be done. Instead, Malcolm instructed that monies were to be given to the family of the deceased. The strength of his approach is obvious, recognizing as he did the clarity with which the biblical writers viewed the finality of death and the ultimate tragedy of mortality. However, the fact that Job and David elsewhere prophesied concerning future resurrection seems to have conveniently eluded Malcolm's treatment of the biblical topic.

Another vignette, recounted by a former Christian who joined the Nation of Islam, reflects how persuasively Malcolm was able to negate the biblical doctrine of eternal life before his audiences. During a sermon at Mosque No. 7 (after 1960 temples were called mosques) in New York City, Malcolm was teaching about Jesus and, according to one guest, was also denying life after death. When the guest became disturbed at hearing biblical teaching being contradicted, he challenged Malcolm. "[A]t the close of the meeting I asked a question: 'Do you mean to tell me that there is no life after death? If you are right, what am I good for?'" Malcolm responded by turning to the chalkboard and writing "Life after Death." With this phrase displayed, Malcolm turned around and asked how one could have life after death. "He made it so real to me and I found that it was impossible for me to have life after death," the man concluded. "*I decided perhaps I should have life before death rather than after."* Yet Malcolm had never fully answered the man's question, instead using the apparent contradiction of "life after death" to put him to silence. In fact, the man was asking a very *Christian question* pertaining to the brevity and temporality of life and the ultimate despair of the human condition, aside from the hope of the resurrection and eternal life. If Malcolm were consistent in his readings of the Bible and the Qur'an, he would have at least addressed the man's question more philosophically. Still, with such a persuasive approach it is no surprise that Malcolm was successful in debunking the doctrine of the resurrection. He later wrote that he had probably gained "a couple of hundred" converts to the Nation of Islam just from speaking at Black Muslim funerals.[6]

Malcolm was twenty-five years old when he penned his first prison letter to the Reverend Laviscount, who was sixty-one at the time. The manner of his greeting—the kind generally reserved for peers—was telling. "Dear Brother Samuel," he wrote assuredly, and with the intention of lecturing the pastor, "[w]hen I was a child I behaved like a child, but since becoming a man I have endeavored to put away childish things." This phrase, which Laviscount would certainly have recognized as a reiteration of the words of St. Paul, demonstrated the certainty of the young man's faith in the message of Muhammad. Malcolm continued: "When I was a wild youth, you often gave me some timely advice; now that I have matured I desire to return the favor."

Malcolm may have seemed imperious to Laviscount, whose years of study and experience in the ministry far extended those of the young convert; others had certainly been put off by Malcolm's approach. Earlier in his imprisonment, Malcolm had sought the tutelage of the Watchtower Bible and Tract Society, and a representative consequently initiated a series of visits with him during his stay at the Norfolk Prison Colony. At Norfolk, Malcolm was engaged in an intense and self-motivated period of study prompted by his desire to advance the Nation of Islam. According to J. Prescott Adams, the Watchtower representative, Malcolm was particularly interested in Jesus; however, the Jehovah's Witness was apparently perplexed by Malcolm's inclination to compare Jesus with Prophet Muhammad of

Islam. Malcolm had sought out the Watchtower Society for study materials, but his thoughts on religion were quite out of reach to Adams, who had undoubtedly hoped to bring the young inmate into the fold. Instead Adams was privately flustered by his self-assurance, later concluding that Malcolm was nurturing a "great ego."[7] Unfortunately, without access to the full correspondence between Malcolm and the Reverend Laviscount, it is impossible to know if the clergyman drew similar conclusions about his young friend, though it is quite certain that Malcolm would have rejected any counsel that ran contrary to the teachings of Elijah Muhammad.

While Malcolm was clearly self-assured, his assertiveness was not driven by arrogance but was more an expression of his absolute faith in Elijah Muhammad and the debt of gratitude that he felt for his conversion. As frequently as Malcolm's story has been told, it is often overlooked that his characteristic zeal, tireless labor, and enthusiastic defense of Elijah Muhammad were really a religious expression. While many historians tend to see Malcolm's subsequent work in expanding the Nation of Islam as a profoundly political activity, they err in not recognizing that Malcolm's methods, apologia, and motivation were akin to the evangelistic programs and activities of religious organizations, especially fundamentalist Christian groups. This is not to imply that Malcolm had no political motivation or interest, but it was not until he began to mature that he increasingly saw the Nation of Islam in this manner. Given the predominance of religion in the black community, it is doubtful that a separatist, nationalist-oriented organization like the Nation of Islam could ever have been built to the extent that Malcolm succeeded without it being overtly religious, evangelistic, and fundamentalist in orientation. Yet Malcolm was not merely appropriating religion in order to do so, as might be suggested in revisionist interpretations. "An earthshaking REFORMATION is taking place among the so-called Negroes in America," Malcolm later wrote in the preface of Elijah Muhammad's first self-published booklet, *The Supreme Wisdom* (1957). "Almighty God ALLAH has appeared in our midst and raised from among us a REFORMER in the person of the Honorable ELIJAH MUHAMMAD, the MESSENGER with a Message for us."[8] The dynamic behind the building of the Nation of

Islam, then, was the work of religious zealotry, and the keynote of Malcolm's early years in the movement was reformation, not revolution.

"This sojourn in prison has proved to be a blessing in disguise," Malcolm wrote to Laviscount, "for it provided me with the Solitude that produced many nights of Meditation." There are so many things that one never considers, Malcolm concluded, until "embraced by Solitude, one meets the FACTS face to face." While the "facts" probably entailed meditations on his intensive course of reading, Malcolm undoubtedly found a great deal of time to reflect on his own life, too. "I have to admit a sad, shameful fact," Malcolm later wrote in his autobiography. "I had so loved being around the white man that in prison I really disliked how Negro convicts stuck together so much." However, Malcolm concluded, after Muhammad's teachings had "reversed my attitude toward my black brothers, in my guilt and shame I began to catch every chance I could to recruit for Mr. Muhammad."[9]

While Malcolm undoubtedly came to regret the moral debauchery of his hustling days, the sins of his youth, like his initial attitude about race relations in prison, were not shameful in and of themselves. His sins, as he came to believe as a Black Muslim, represented a mind clouded by ignorance of self, resulting in a life of compromise and surrender to the evil influence of white people. Malcolm expressed this quite eloquently in his letter to the Reverend Laviscount:

> The devil[']s strongest weapon is his ability to conventionalize our Thought . . . and rather than exert our own Conscience, we willfully remain the humble servants of every one else's ideas except our own . . . not even having our own opinions of ourselves or our very own people. . . . [W]e have made ourselves the helpless slaves of the wicked [O]ccidental world.[10]

It seems that Malcolm's prison meditations, encouraged by insightful hours of reading and correspondence with Elijah Muhammad, actually enhanced his shame by the racial associations that now seemed to undergird his former life of sin. In a letter several months before the one to the Reverend Laviscount, Malcolm wrote to his brother Philbert: "Brother, you don't really know the devil until you've lived with him. He is one thing that I'm an expert on! I have lived and participated with him in *every* phase of his life!"[11] Malcolm was undoubtedly thorough in his understanding—perhaps more than any other African American leader of his era, the young man who would become famous for heaping contempt upon "white devils" was intimately acquainted with the ways of white folks. From the church and the classroom to the nightclub and the brothel, Malcolm's troubled sojourn had allowed him to see the full spectrum of white racist attitude and behavior. "I can talk much trash about the devil, convincingly," Malcolm also wrote to his brother Philbert. In another letter, written to Philbert's new wife, Malcolm likewise declared: "The many contacts I have had with the devil made it easy for me to recognize him as the devil. I find that the only reason many Originals [*African Americans*] are hesitant to accept the Truth is that their association with the devil has been superficial and they don't know him well enough to *see* his true character."[12]

Malcolm's conversion to "Islam" was in many ways similar to fundamentalist Christian conversion. First, it had required him to kneel in prayer, a decisive act on Malcolm's part. "But bending my knees to pray—that *act*—well, that took me a week," Malcolm wrote in his autobiography. Malcolm, who characterized himself prior to conversion as "the personification of evil," found the act of prayer particularly difficult, and later attributed that difficulty to inward rebellion against God. Second, Malcolm's conversion was premised on the acceptance of the literal truth of Muhammad's teachings (which included his interpretations of the Bible), and belief in Allah *via* Elijah Muhammad. Third, the conversion resulted in a radical renewal of life practices and moral behavior, epitomized by Malcolm's pious self-discipline and independent learning in the prison library. Finally, Malcolm embarked on a soul-saving crusade in which he zealously endeavored to "witness" to every person within his sphere of influence.

The act of prayer having been accomplished, Malcolm's confession of faith went beyond mental assent to Muhammad's doctrines, as he wrote in his autobiography: "My comprehending, my believing the teachings of Mr. Muhammad had only required my mind's saying to me, 'That's right!' or 'I never thought of that.'" But prayer, which he called the "hardest test I ever faced in my life," was the inner bridge over which Malcolm crossed into a new world of belief and submission. While he would thereafter become a man of prayer, that "test" gave to him a sense of transformation he would never duplicate—not even in his later conversion to Sunni Islam. The contrast between his life of sin and his life of submission was dramatic to Malcolm, who would actually find himself startled when he remembered his "earlier self as another person." Even his first couple of years in prison (1946–48) had been difficult, as he recalled in a letter to his brother. He had faced "dark moments" that overwhelmed him. "Of course I don't have dark moments anymore because Allah now keeps me in His Light."[13]

As a Black Muslim, Malcolm adopted the kind of fundamentalist faith that Muhammad himself had carried with him from the Christian church and modified according to his own desires. One of the most notable aspects of this faith is the belief in personal encounters with satanic forces. For the fundamentalist Christian, demonic forces are actual agents of Satan who are antagonistic toward believers; in Malcolm's fundamentalist reading of "Islam," white people were those demons, very personal foes in a very personal arena of spiritual conflict:

> Every moment of the day I walk and talk with Allah. His Presence is my protection. . . . The devil has the power to do to us only what we let him; if we are weak in faith he is strong. By continuous prayers Allah shows us the pits of Satan, and when we submit to Allah He guides us around all stumbling-blocks. If I *submit* to Allah I am a *Muslim*, thus I shall never fear ole Satan.[14]

Despite the fact that Malcolm's commitment to prayer (which he called the "Voice on the Royal Telephone") was very personal and individual, it was nevertheless premised on Elijah Muhammad's claims. Yet it seems that as long as Malcolm was incarcerated his zeal for Muhammad was framed by limitation. Thus, despite the fundamentalist nature of Malcolm's commitment to Muhammad while in prison, the religion of his incarceration was necessarily far more individual and privately philosophical than would be the blazing ministry of his first years as a Black Muslim spokesman. After his release in 1952, therefore, Malcolm became intensely enthralled with Muhammad, and the more he consequently invested in building the Nation of Islam, the more he seems to have transformed himself into a true zealot.

For Minister Malcolm X, then, personal discipline and moral integrity were not simply rooted in religious piety but were actually a kind of a racial holiness necessitated by the shame of his history of collusion with the devil and the urgency which he felt for rescuing his black brothers and sisters from that same evil force. This conviction was not translated into a tender, pastorly style of leadership, but rather a strict, demanding, and extremely legalistic ministry where every setback within the movement was probably considered by Malcolm to be a major coup by the devil. "He had the basis of religion . . . the restrictive laws," one of his critics remembered years later. "He would uphold them and he would put you out if you violated them. . . . He was a strict disciplinarian." Another observer pointed out that Malcolm X "condemned moral vices as much as skin and hair bleaching." In one presentation made prior to Muhammad's trip abroad, Malcolm challenged followers and guests with a call to rigorous involvement that likely reflected his own inexhaustible drive: "If a man is lazy let him go to the Christian church. But if you are ambitious and hardworking, come to the Temple of Islam."[15]

If Malcolm appeared to be an exacting Puritan captain with respect to the followers, he was no less demanding of himself. "A true Believer is never hesitent [sic] to make a sacrifice to see that this teaching is spread among the dead," Malcolm wrote to his brother in late 1954. By this time, Malcolm had become a seasoned evangelist with several temples established in the northeast, and had been duly awarded the pastorate of Muhammad's Temple No. 7 in Harlem. "[F]or the True Believer knows that Allah lets NO Work go *unrewarded*. To think that it might prove too costly to us if we make what ever sacrifice needed to wake the dead," he concluded, "bears witness that we yet don't fully Believe that Allah is the Best-of-Rewarders."[16] For Malcolm, "needed" sacrifices largely entailed material gain. Even though one scholarly observer considered his style of life as middle class, Malcolm's suit-and-tie appearance and his preference for Oldsmobile 98s belied a genuine vow of poverty. A kind of modern urban ascetic, Malcolm actually accumulated very little, except perhaps for books and jazz albums. "I own nothing, except a record player," he said in an interview. "I have no material possessions. The house where I am living is owned by the Temple. The clothes I wear are made (sewn) by the Muslim women." Malcolm said that when he entered the pastoral ministry, he made a vow that he was "never going to own anything." He told the same interviewer, "because frequently a very sincere leader becomes trapped by material possessions and consequently he becomes alienated from the aspirations of his followers."[17]

Malcolm's dedicated life of sacrifice had even preempted marriage and family life, and even after he was married in 1958 (at the urgence of Muhammad), the needed sacrifice of his service to the Nation of Islam inevitably touched his wife Betty and their growing family. Years later, when Malcolm would find himself betrayed and disowned by the movement, the issue of the parsonage in Queens, New York, would become an occasion of legal and literal warfare. By then, of course, Malcolm realized too late that his "needed" sacrifice on behalf of the Nation of Islam had only fattened the pockets of Muhammad and his family, leaving Betty and the children without a home. Indeed, it was the firebombing of the parsonage by the Black Muslims in February 1965 that preceded his assassination by one week.

In the first years, especially within prison, Malcolm had done a significant amount of recruiting and teaching. Even his most cynical biographer notes that Malcolm's work at Norfolk was "no small achievement," since he had recruited more than a dozen of the eighty blacks incarcerated there.[18] Malcolm's drive to fish for converts was characteristically strong, leaving no stone unturned in his quest for recruitment in the black community. Initially, Malcolm's methods were basic, such as working the fringes of other speakers' audiences in the streets, holding public rallies, waiting to speak to Christians exiting from their churches on Sunday, and distributing printed materials. As Malcolm developed new temples in various cities, of course, he had additional bases from which to reach out to the black population. Along with his growing familiarity with the black community in differing cities across the country, Malcolm developed a keen and sometimes opportunistic use of the black press, especially the major black publications of the day. In some cases it seems he fed exciting articles about Muhammad and himself to papers like the *New York Amsterdam News* and the *Pittsburgh Courier*, lending the impression that the Black Muslims were far more sophisticated and successful than they were in actuality. With national notoriety, Malcolm mastered the art of negative publicity, capitalizing on appearances on antagonistic talk show forums and other unsympathetic radio and television broadcasts, to give the Nation of Islam air play that would otherwise have been unattainable by Elijah Muhammad.

Early in his public ministry, however, Malcolm zealously advanced Elijah Muhammad while the private, philosophical aspects of his prison reflections on God and redemption seem to have receded. There was perhaps a pragmatic side to this development, since Malcolm recognized that other Black Muslim evangelists were probably less capable at explaining and defending the theology of the Nation of Islam. "Never try and teach them too much on the personal [identity] of ALLAH," Malcolm urged his brother Philbert in 1954, "but let your every word and effort be pointing toward the Messenger, letting all your followers know that ELIJAH THE PROPHET is in the land. Lead them toward Him, and HE will lead them toward ALLAH. You bear witness to the one [whom] YOU know, and HE bears witness to the one whom HE KNOWS." However, it is also the case that Malcolm truly came to believe that Muhammad had a unique and authoritative insight into the nature of the divine by revelation. Rather than speak of Fard, whom he believed he had seen in a prison pre-vision, Malcolm emphasized Muhammad. To Malcolm, Elijah Muhammad was "the only Muslim in North America qualified to represent ALLAH (that is, His IDENTITY)," while his ministers would only "mess it up" and "drive the people away." "So let them know that ELIJAH is in the land," Malcolm concluded, "lead them to him, and you will see the people come to you in droves. That is what is making the

East Coast remain AFLAME. ELIJAH THE PROPHET Is the KEY." Of course, Malcolm's sincere faith and upper-case letters notwithstanding, it was not Muhammad who had set the East Coast aflame, but his own zeal.

The epitome of Malcolm's zealot gospel is found in his reiteration of the Nation of Islam's resurrection theme. In a frenetic piece published in the magazine of an opportunistic Sunni Muslim who had befriended the Nation of Islam, Malcolm rallied under the banner of "mental resurrection." Employing his characteristic upper-case letters for emphasis, Malcolm expounded on the black man's condition in "the GRAVE of IGNORANCE," being spiritually dead "like Dry Bones in the Valley," and enamored with a blond-haired, blue-eyed God. Elijah the prophet having come, Malcolm continued, the hearts of black people were being turned eastward and now many were being "RAISED FROM THE WHITE MAN'S GRAVE." Elijah Muhammad is Allah's "Last and Greatest Messenger to us here in North America," Malcolm preached, and the good things of life now available to black people "must be enjoyed *while we are living*." The "Noble and Honorable MESSENGER OF GOD," he continued, has now brought "the Message of Life for 17 Million American so-called [N]egroes." Interestingly, Malcolm then notes that he had been visited by federal agents who had "questioned me so thoroughly concerning" Elijah Muhammad that "I spent sleepless nights wondering what it is about his teaching that has the agents of such a powerful country so concerned and upset." Indeed, Malcolm wrote, the more he contemplated this, "the more I came to believe in this man, and know that he is a DIVINE-GOD-SENT-MAN." The "Messenger-Prophet," Malcolm concluded, Elijah Muhammad was the one foretold in both the Hebrew Torah and the Christian Gospel.[19]

In this light, Malcolm's conversion to the Nation of Islam clearly consisted of three phases. The first was the intensely private, philosophical, and independent years of his prison "ministry." A time of study, contemplation, and restrained outreach, young Malcolm perhaps stretched the boundaries of his religious life and emerged from incarceration with a significant armament of intellect, experience, and vision. The second phase was the period of fundamentalist zealotry, roughly from 1952 through 1960, during which Malcolm virtually built the Nation of Islam into a coast-to-coast organization, attracting thousands of members and even more sympathizers. In this phase Malcolm not only expanded the Nation of Islam from a virtual back-street cult to a prominent new religion, but he himself elevated Elijah Muhammad on a platform of his own religious enthusiasm. Malcolm's eldest brother, Wilfred, noted this change in his brother, making a distinction between Malcolm's early spirituality and his later religiosity. To Wilfred, Malcolm ultimately devised the means of his own spiritual undoing. "It was a gradual thing . . . and it happened mostly after he got busy teaching—at the same time he converted himself. While he was converting the other people he converted himself."[20] Indeed, it was in this phase that Malcolm's own blind faith in Muhammad led him farther and farther away from the principles and practices of his religious upbringing.

In the final phase, the waning years of his involvement in the Nation of Islam, approximately 1960 through 1963, Malcolm would manifest an evolving reconnection with his native spirituality and religious thought—ultimately necessitating a break with Muhammad. However, while in the second phase, Malcolm was ensnared by the very antithesis of his childhood religious training—personal faith *in another* as spiritual mediator. In short, Malcolm's faith and confidence in God were transferred to the domain of Elijah Muhammad, the underside of his conversion being the surrender of his personal altar to a man.

If any one factor prompted Malcolm X to rediscover his own native spirituality it was not theology or doctrine, but struggle. For Malcolm, the ongoing struggle of black people for justice was the arena where faith was ultimately to be demonstrated. In the zealous second phase of his Nation of Islam years, Malcolm sounded off against "white devils" and poured contempt upon the Christian church. In this period, he upheld the Nation of Islam as an action-oriented organization, and just as he applied his own piety and self-discipline to Muhammad, he also ascribed to him his growing sense of involvement in the black struggle in the United States and abroad. Mocking the "pie in the sky after you die" religion of Western Christianity, Malcolm actually believed that Muhammad was different, that the Messenger of Allah would not only speak the truth about the white man but take action in the crisis hour. The crisis hour came, as Malcolm later realized, not all at once, but one painful, agonizing minute at a time. In the late 1950s and early 1960s, not only was the Southern civil rights arena heating up but police attacks on the Black Muslims in the North and West highlighted the discontent of urban blacks as well. While the white liberal media would never admit that the northern theater of the black struggle was as much an imbroglio as the South, Malcolm was painfully aware that the great urban centers of the United States were reaching a point of convulsion. Unlike Elijah Muhammad, however, Malcolm's faith came to bear on these circumstances, and he began to realize that the Nation of Islam was really not much different from the fundamentalist and traditionalist black churches that Muhammad loved to lampoon. Malcolm's "conception of a *wholistic* religion—that is, one that did not separate the imperatives of the spirit from the needs of the flesh—and his growing pursuit of its *programmatic expression*, set him apart."[21] Indeed, it not only distinguished him from Black Muslims and Christians in specific terms, but it categorically set him apart from the Western conception of religion that had shaped both, as well as the ultraconservative religion of the highest echelon of the Muslim world.

In terms of struggle, the grassroots orientation that characterized his last phase in the Nation of Islam began to outgrow and, eventually, overshadow the fundamentalist zealotry that had empowered his pioneering labors. The borders of the Nation of Islam having been expanded into new frontiers, "the wilderness of North America" now had to be filled with Black Muslim settlers worthy of the banner of Islam. Since Muhammad had never imagined his Nation would attain such size, it is likely his vision for its growth was far smaller than Malcolm's conceptualization. The Nation of Islam, to Malcolm, was "the *best* organization the black man's ever had," and its citizens were to be wholistically "resurrected" black Americans. It was for this purpose that W. D. Fard had come into this "hell," Malcolm believed, and the reason he had also called Elijah Muhammad as his messenger. It was a message for the lowly, and to the lowly Malcolm was determined to carry it.

If any aspect of Malcolm's pioneering work among the "grassroots" has been overlooked, then, it is his prison ministry. The importance of his prison ministry is twofold, for it not only represents the new dynamic of Islam (cultic and, eventually, traditional forms) as a vital religious presence in the prison system, but also the requisite corollary to Malcolm's activism against the racism of urban policemen. One inmate, Mahmud Ramza (whose Black Muslim name was Walter 5X), recalls that it was Malcolm who first won the legal privilege to administer religious rites to him while he was incarcerated in New York State's Green Haven Correction Facility in the late 1950s. Through Malcolm's tutelage, Ramza became a significant promoter of "Islam" in the prison system and later an active member of the Nation of Islam.[22] Malcolm's impact on prisoners went far beyond Ramza's case, according to Justice Jawn Sandifer, who served as chairman of the Legal Redress Committee for the New York State Conference of the National Association for the Advancement of Colored People (NAACP). In the 1950s and early 1960s, Sandifer and another NAACP lawyer, Edward Jacko, had their law office in Harlem on 125th Street and came to know Malcolm, serving as counsel for the Nation of Islam in a number of legal suits. Sandifer, who became a New York State Justice in 1964, remembers Malcolm "recruiting people who had previously had some encounter with the law," including drug addicts and hardened criminals, and that he was particularly interested in prisoners. At first, Malcolm was prevented from ministering in the New York State prison system because he was an ex-offender and because his credentials as a "Muslim" minister were not recognized. In that era, Sandifer says, only Protestantism, Roman Catholicism, and Judaism were recognized and represented in the system. "We had to find a way of getting Malcolm recognized as a minister," Sandifer recalls. Despite the fact that the two NAACP attorneys were authorized to move throughout the state prison system, they could not bring Malcolm inside with them. After a number of trips were made to the state capital of Albany in order for Malcolm and the lawyers to appeal to officials, Sandifer began to realize that the bottom line was that they were afraid of Malcolm X because they didn't know what his real intentions were.... [B]ased upon their background checks on Malcolm and who he was, they were afraid of what Malcolm might potentially do if he were able to convert large numbers of these people inside the prison walls.[23]

Sandifer says that Malcolm eventually won the right to do pastoral visitations only because his positive influence on ex-offenders was undeniably successful. "Malcolm worked magic," Sandifer recalls. "I can't give you the answer as to what it was, how one man could take people with criminal backgrounds—practically every one of them were people that came out of those prisons." Though Malcolm was quick to credit Elijah Muhammad with the remarkable rehabilitation of so many ex-offenders, Sandifer recognized the real influence. "How could a man like Malcolm come into the prisons, communicate with them, and after they were out, bring them down to [Temple No. 7 in Harlem]? Malcolm gave them dignity, he made them productive ... the same men that came out of these prisons."[24]

Given Malcolm's determination to use *The Autobiography* to glorify Elijah Muhammad, it is no surprise that his narrative overlooks his strenuous determination to reach incarcerated men. While Muhammad had interest in prisoners, Malcolm single-handedly cut a path into the prison system on behalf of "Islam," a path that has since become well traveled by Black Muslims and traditional Muslims alike. Malcolm was never allowed to speak to large numbers of prisoners, but he worked out an arrangement whereby he received referrals from Sandifer and Jacko, allowing him to travel throughout the state prison system, even visiting inmates at maximum-security facilities like Attica. According to Sandifer, Malcolm particularly focused on prisoners who made no religious self-identification at the time of their entrance interviews. He may have chosen this approach to avoid being perceived as a threat to Christian chaplains, but it may also reflect his hope of reaching men who were wide open to the message of "Islam."

Malcolm's early and often overlooked work in prison ministry and justice issues demonstrates his determination to work with integrationist-oriented groups like the NAACP long before his brief and notable last year of independent activism. Furthermore, his prison ministry shows that Malcolm's interest in justice continued to grow as an *expression of his religious activism*, not in tension with it. Sandifer says that while he, Jacko, and Malcolm worked extensively on the prison project, their partnership evolved into an aggressive confrontation with police brutality. Prior to Malcolm X's presence in New York City, white racist policemen ran roughshod over black communities like Harlem, often brutalizing citizens in broad daylight. While the two attorneys and the Black Muslim minister privately debated the political philosophies of integrationism and separatism, they were practical allies in a struggle against the uniformed white racists who made no distinction as to black people's religion or politics in their attacks.

Spike Lee's *Malcolm X* does a significant job in re-creating the drama of the famous Johnson X case in 1957, which culminated in a Harlem showdown between Malcolm and the New York City Police Department. Largely due to the humble narrative of *The Autobiography* upon which Lee's film is based, however, it does not convey the strategic aspect of Malcolm's determination to launch a campaign against police brutality in New York City. Just as the organization and strategy behind Rosa Parks's famous bus ride has often been overlooked in popular civil rights narratives, Malcolm's commanding influence on the Harlem population in the Johnson X case has been seen only as a testimony of his spontaneous political savvy and the awakening of his sleeping-giant leadership in Harlem. While these aspects are true, they overlook the fact that Malcolm and the two NAACP lawyers, Sandifer and Jacko, were looking for an occasion to face off with racist policemen, whom Malcolm verbally castigated for their "gestapo" tactics. "Malcolm was in a capsule compared to what was going on [in the South]," Sandifer says, but despite being overshadowed by the civil rights movement, the three worked out a strategy in handling police brutality cases following the successful suit lodged on behalf of Johnson X.[25] According to Sandifer, victims were permitted to file charges of police brutality within ninety days of the incident, so the two lawyers would not file until their clients were acquitted of the usual accompanying criminal charges. While the Johnson X case was the most notable victory on the part of the black community against the police department, according to Sandifer, the police were willing to settle a good many other cases before judgments were rendered in order to avoid being exposed. In fact, the police department was forced to modify their training systems as a result of these cases and, while gestapo tactics did not cease, the Malcolm X era brought an end to flagrant public displays of brutality by white racist officers.[26]

That Malcolm's prison outreach and quest for justice were so unusual in the urban North is as much a tribute to his religious commitment to the downtrodden as it is a sad commentary on the introversion of many black Christian churches. On the other hand, as Malcolm's sense of duty to Allah and his community were heightening, Elijah Muhammad's personal mission was degenerating to the low point of accumulating wealth and sexual pleasures. Many Christians, white and black, had forsaken justice for the life to come, and Muhammad had forsaken his Nation for a life of pleasure. Like the revelation about race that he already saw but could not believe until reaching Mecca in the spring of 1964, it is likely that Malcolm X could not see that he was beginning to outgrow Elijah Muhammad's fundamentalist cult orientation. As long as he believed "the Messenger" was interested in wholistic redemption, however, Malcolm X would endure as a Black Muslim. Thus, one of his close associates remembers receiving a postcard from Malcolm, who had gone South on a crusade for the Nation of Islam. The postcard had the printed message, "Gone Fishing," and featured two men in a boat enjoying a leisurely time with rod and reel. Malcolm, who was a master at getting his message across even on postcards, added a line by hand so that the card read: "Gone Fishing *For the Souls of Men.*"[27] In time, however, Malcolm would realize that Muhammad's nets were torn and that he would have to launch out into the deep to fish for himself.

7

Jesus ReduX

Malcolm and the Religious Jingoism of the Nation of Islam

The white man never had a God and never will.
—Elijah Muhammad, *The Truth*, vol. 1

Why does Mr. Muhammad treat our Bible as if it were just a sacred obituary of men long dead? Mr. Muhammad's interpretation cheats us of the larger, deeper meaning of the passage in our Bible.   —A *Pittsburgh Courier* reader, January 17, 1959

When we tell you that Allah is a supreme black man, you laugh, because you can't conceive of God as black. But when the white preacher tells you that Jesus had blue eyes and stayed in the ground for three days and got up and went to heaven, you believe it. Now, which is more ridiculous?
—Malcolm X, in Peter Goldman,
The Death and Life of Malcolm X

In the early 1960s, journalist William Worthy visited some businessmen in Boston who had converted to the Nation of Islam. Worthy had known them before they encountered Malcolm X and heard Muhammad's gospel of "mental resurrection." Playfully, Worthy told them he still had the pin-up calendar featuring a nude Marilyn Monroe, which they had given out to customers back in 1955. "Yes," they responded, "but that was while we thought white, lacked light and were still Christians."[1] The response to Worthy was only a clever reiteration of the standard teaching of the Nation of Islam, which for all intents and purposes had reduced Christianity to a dirty word. As was the case with the Bible itself, however, despite its assault on Christianity, the Nation of Islam sought to salvage Jesus from the wreckage of its own attacks, propping him up as a justification for the movement and its teachings.

Thus, one of Malcolm X's theological and rhetorical responsibilities as the standard-bearer of the Fard-Muhammad legacy was to heap calumny upon the Christian church, its teachings, its clergy, and its laypeople. Since Malcolm had no background of devotion to Christian orthodoxy and since he undoubtedly had realistic reasons for resenting the Christian community's de facto commitment to racial segregation, playing the role of enemy of the cross came quite easily to him. Like the other doctrines in his Nation of Islam sermons, Malcolm undoubtedly reiterated Muhammad's teachings about Christianity. Muhammad, whose bizarre, apocryphal New Testament narratives could become droll to the point of absurdity, had built his ministry in part by contradicting the church's teachings on Jesus.

In his newspaper column, Muhammad railed against the Christian message of the black church, characterizing black ministers as "yelling and spitting out foam all over the pulpit," and dismissing as "nonsense" their messages about "hell-fire after death, and the dying of Jesus on the cross." Muhammad expressed relief that black people were abandoning the doctrines of the black Christian minister as they advanced educationally. If Muhammad had been honest, of course, he would have admitted that the educated blacks who had abandoned the church were hardly rushing to join the Nation of Islam. In another column, Muhammad declared that Christianity had "falsely accused Jesus as being its founder," and was consequently "plagued with spiritual darkness and confusion," and that Christianity erroneously taught its adherents to anticipate the return of a spiritual savior. "Jesus did not leave us to look for a spirit—unnatural, not human— but to look for a Man Who is the Son of Man, and this great Man is not to be expected to come from another planet." Instead, the "natural" savior that Muhammad believed to have been foretold by Jesus was W. D. Fard, the "Master" and "Great Mahdi." In the Savior's Day convention in 1957, for instance, Muhammad thus proclaimed that Christianity had taught black people "to pray to a God who isn't God," and to love their enemies but to hate their own. The cross, the symbol of Christianity, could do no one any good, "whether you wear it around your neck or hang it in your bedrooms." Of course, behind Muhammad's irreverent gainsaying there remained the charge that always grounded his cultic diatribes in the undeniable fact of white Christian racism. "What has the Christian World done for you and me? Why should we want to remain in it? They have shown that they don't treat you as a brother." Like the cross, Muhammad concluded, Christianity simply did not "suit" black people.[2]

The denial of the Christian doctrines regarding Jesus Christ were obviously necessary in order for Muhammad to advance Fard, and Malcolm certainly followed obediently in this manner. However, Muhammad differed in that his *public* treatment of Christianity, and Jesus in particular, was premised on a self-righteous tendency to gainsay the biblical narrative and replace it with his own fabrications. Malcolm, too, became quite clever at gainsaying Christian doctrines and traditions but it seems he reserved most of these kinds of remarks for Black Muslim audiences. In contrast, Malcolm's public discourse was invariably premised on a kind of self-abasement in which he consistently attacked Christianity by portraying himself as an ex-Christian whose former life of debauchery and sin reflected on Christianity itself. This is not to suggest that Malcolm did not lampoon Christianity and the church. Indeed, in the final phase of his Black Muslim career he showed willingness to outdo even Muhammad in attacking Christianity—undoubtedly an attempt to hang on to his position in the movement. In general, however, Malcolm's public discourse on Christianity was by far more carefully crafted toward persuasion, while Muhammad's was essentially polemical.

The most blatant example of Muhammad's attack is found in his home-spun apocrypha on the life of Christ, which was printed by the *Pittsburgh Courier* in the "Mr. Muhammad Speaks" column, complete with a disclaimer by the paper's editor. In one installment supposedly providing the true account of the death of Christ, the plot is surreal and Muhammad deliberately sketches the characters in the scenario of a modern inner city. According to Muhammad, a reward of $1,500 initiates the arrest of Jesus, and two "officers" apprehend him—consequently getting into an argument as to who would collect the reward. Jesus then settles the argument by pointing out that one of them had actually touched him "about three-tenths of a second before" the other. The prevailing officer then suggests to Jesus that he kill him on the spot rather than hand him over to be tortured. Jesus complies, and the officer leads him to an old storefront, standing him in front of a boarded-up window. Driving his sword through Jesus and into the board behind him, the force of the officer's thrust causes Jesus' hands to jut outward "like a cross." In this way, Muhammad continues, Jesus dies transfixed, his arms outstretched. Afterward, Joseph of Arimethea secures the body of Jesus and has it mysteriously embalmed by Egyptian chemists and placed in a glass tube. Buried in this airtight container, the body of Jesus is laid beneath Jerusalem in a secret vault in order to befuddle his enemies. Of course, Muhammad says, Christians can view the body of Jesus if they pay $6,000 and obtain a papal certificate. The tomb is guarded by Muslims, who escort Christian visitors during the viewing, although Christians who view the body are strip-searched and handcuffed for the occasion. Muhammad happily concludes that Muslims, "the brothers of Jesus," can view the body any time at no charge.[3]

Even granting Muhammad a degree of fun at the expense of Christianity, whether or not he was smiling when he wrote this vapid narrative did not change the fact that readers, both followers and Christians, took him quite seriously. Clearly, it was Muhammad's intention to spite the church by putting Jesus into the grave and then dancing on it. There was, however, a logic to Muhammad's dance, which was to discredit the essential doctrines of Christianity; his story of Jesus is intended as an explanation for the origin of such supposed myths as the cross and at the same time inherently denies the resurrection. The claim that Muslims were in control of the body of Jesus not only gave Muhammad's followers a sense of superiority over Christians, but figuratively expressed Muhammad's claim to have control over the body of Christian scripture. "We (the Muslims) took Jerusalem and the tomb of Jesus in 1187 A.D.," Muhammad boasted, "and it is still in our possession and will remain in our possession."

> Certainly there is a Jesus predicted for you but not the one of two thousand years ago, but the one that Jesus prophesied would come after him, who will redeem us from the hands of our enemies. He came in 1930 under the name of Mr. Wallace Fard Muhammad (to whom be praise[s] forever). He suffered here for three and one-half years to pay for our redemption.[4]

That Muhammad intended to replace Jesus Christ with W. D. Fard is obvious; what tends to be overlooked is the corollary treatment of the historical and biblical Jesus.

Despite their insistence that he was dead, Muhammad had to re-call Jesus from the grave, if for no other reason than to revise him—cutting him away from the biblical context and reintroducing him to black people in a manner that complemented "Islam." Not surpris-ingly, however, Muhammad chose not to conform to the Qur'an in his presentations. While Islam certainly contradicts the biblical view of Jesus as deity, it denies that Jesus suffered martyrdom. Muslims, then, would be no more pleased with Elijah Muhammad's story of Jesus than they would be with the narratives of the four gospels of the New Testament. For his part, Muhammad aggressively presented Jesus as a flawed hero-victim, whose tragic, failed ministry required someone greater to succeed him. "Jesus' history refers more to a fu-ture Jesus than the past," Muhammad wrote. In fact, the Jesus of his-tory "admitted he could not guide [his followers] into all truth" and prophesied that Allah would send Fard, who would be successful as a teacher and guide. Now, Muhammad declared, Jesus could do neither good nor harm to blacks, since he was dead. "It is outright ignorance to believe that he can," Muhammad concluded.[5]

While the leading black Christian ministers apparently chose to ig-nore Muhammad's column, some rank-and-file clergy and laity re-sponded. "I cannot see how anyone who reads the Bible can agree with this writer," one minister wrote. "His claims are vague and empty, without proof or foundation. . . . I think it's about time some-one came out and answered this man's wild ravings and false interpretations of the Bible." Like other critics of the Nation of Islam, however, the minister tended to emphasize the "hate" behind Muhammad's message. Contrary to Muhammad's teaching, what disqualifies whites, the minister concluded, was not their ability to "influence" blacks to become Christians, but rather their inability to practice Christianity with respect to their fellow man. Another response came from a woman who identified herself as a "Bible student and instructor" and complained that "[e]ach week, Mr. Muhammad grows more wild, fanatical, ridiculous and vicious." This reader pointed out the gross contradictions in Muhammad's story of Jesus when compared with the Bible—an observation she had apparently made the year before, when she also wrote complaining that Muhammad "not only contradicts the Bible" but was making "an obvious, subtle effort to further divide racial groups" in contrast to the conciliatory work of groups like the NAACP.[6]

In general, Christian reactions to "Mr. Muhammad Speaks" were varied in their criticism. One clergyman lamented that blacks already had too many "self-sent messiahs, root-merchants and conjurers," and that Elijah Muhammad "walks out too far saying that Islam is the only salvation for the Negro." Another clergyman complained that Muhammad's column would have an "adverse effect" on society and was an affront to "intelligent Negroes." Operating under "the guise of religion," he continued, Muhammad's organization was only "a perverted form of Negro nationalism," and "Mr. Muhammad Speaks" was an "emotional, rabble-rousing, race-hating" column. Two other ministers wrote, one stating that he could not understand "how a mortal man can preach an ideology of hate as this man," and that he rejected the notion of separatism, apparently believing that Muhammad intended his followers to literally leave the United States. The other simply concluded that Muhammad "isn't even a good philosopher" and that his followers "need enlightenment."

Other laypeople wrote criticizing Muhammad of misleading readers who "had not taken time to find the true meaning of God's word for themselves," and challenging that "[t]rying to do away with God's Holy Bible and Christianity is like spitting in God's face so to speak. It will never be done." Of course, Muhammad's column drew some peculiar readers out of the woodwork as well. One man, who announced that he was also prophetic, took advantage of Muhammad's pronouncements to predict the day "when there will be no pale-faced, blue-eyed people on the face of this earth," a day when "billions and billions of colored peoples" will finally live in "peace and harmony."[7] Of course, many of Muhammad's followers wrote short, approving letters in support of the Messenger—probably at the urgency of Malcolm X and other Black Muslim ministers.

"We saw him incompletely," writes Malcolm's most eloquent biographer.

> We were accustomed to the public Malcolm, worldly and well read. . . . We did not see him in the mosque, calling the black dead to the shelter of the Sun, Moon and Stars of Islam, flinging down the Christian Bible and stomping on it, announcing as revealed truth that white people have vestigial tails and that the blacks are the chosen of God. We saw Malcolm as a politician, not as a priest.[8]

But priest he was—a point that one FBI informant in Temple No. 7 noted when Malcolm, during one of his fiery sermons, raised a Bible in the air, dared God to verify its miraculous claims, and then threw it on the floor. The audience yelled their approval while Malcolm shouted that the Bible was no different from any other book. Malcolm may have physically battered the Bible for special effect, but he did not so easily disregard its message. Faithful to Muhammad's teachings, Malcolm taught that the Bible was full of lies in its present version, and that an untainted version was concealed in the Library of Congress in Washington, D.C. Fortunately for the Nation of Islam, Malcolm told his Temple No. 7 audience in 1958, Elijah Muhammad had translated this Bible from its original Arabic into English in order to bring the truth to black people. Without Muhammad's true knowledge of the original Bible, Malcolm taught, black people would be lost, since the common Bible was translated to suit white people and white religion. Christianity was thus an "unnatural," "concocted" religion based on the Bible's lies—lies that were cleverly designed to keep black people ignorant.[9]

In general, another way in which Malcolm assaulted Christianity was by targeting aspects of Christian worship that were either directly or indirectly associated with the Bible in the minds of common church folk. Thus, in his sermons and in *The Autobiography*, when he lampooned the idea that an infant who dies becomes an "angel baby,"[10] he was not only negating the idea of a spiritual afterlife, he was also mocking an African American Christian folk tradition. Malcolm scored other traditional afterlife images in a 1959 radio interview on Harlem's WLIB, skillfully contrasting them with the practical claims of Elijah Muhammad: "Christianity offers Negroes its economic program of milk and honey (food), white robes, golden slippers (clothing), and mansions (shelter) up in the sky after they die . . . whereas Mr. Elijah Muhammad teaches us that in Islam we can get all of life's necessities right here on earth in this life."[11] Of course, the significance of ridiculing these traditions, such as heavenly white robes and golden slippers, is not that they are biblical. Malcolm was precise in recognizing that "angel babies" and "golden slippers" are sentimentalities that have nothing to do with Christian doctrine. However, in debunking religious myths, Malcolm and the Black Muslims dismissed significant biblical doctrines along with them. It is one thing to strip away the Eurocentric icon of a blue-eyed, blond-haired Christ as the poster child of white supremacy; it is quite another to dismiss doctrinal Christianity with no distinctions, branding it as a faith that robs African Americans of social, economic, and political justice.

In the most literal sense, therefore, the cross was an object of derision to the Black Muslims. At a meeting in Boston's Nation of Islam temple, Malcolm poked at the popular hymn, "The Old Rugged Cross," which celebrates the Christian concept of the atonement. Malcolm told the "Muslims" that they didn't need a sign of suffering and shame, only freedom, justice, and equality. Likewise, Malcolm mocked black Christians for wearing the traditional cross symbol as jewelry; he told them doing so only showed they were confused and deceived. "The religion of Christianity will make you double-cross yourself," Malcolm concluded before a Cleveland, Ohio, audience. "You are a nut to believe in such things."[12]

Inside the temple, Malcolm frequently took up the topic of Jesus, attacking Christian beliefs directly and indirectly pertaining to him. In a meeting at Temple No. 7 in 1960, for instance, Malcolm belittled the doctrine that Jesus could die for people's sins. Believing such a thing, Malcolm said, was like one getting on the train to California thinking that someone else had paid the fare—only to find the conductor demanding payment anyway. Yet, like Muhammad, Malcolm was able to underscore these flagrant doctrinal attacks with bitter truth: "They say he suffered for us, we are still suffering. They still hang us in trees." Malcolm told his audiences that Jesus' death had availed nothing for them, and assured them that Jesus had not resurrected and was therefore of no benefit to them: "How can a dead Jesus help anyone? He couldn't help himself." Since Jesus had not resurrected from the grave, according to Malcolm, his ascension into heaven was equally unbelievable. In what must have been a humorous moment, Malcolm toyed with the notion that Jesus went back to heaven riding on a cloud (itself a distortion of the biblical text). Since clouds move so slow, Malcolm teased, Jesus probably was still on that cloud trying to get up to heaven. Rather than hope in Jesus, Malcolm told his parishioners in 1959, they had someone greater than Jesus, "someone to open the eyes of the blind, the ears of the deaf, heal the sick, raise the dead—Elijah is doing all of this." Indeed, Malcolm told the same congregation that what the Bible said about Jesus' suffering and death was really only a symbol of black people themselves, who have been crucified by the white man and raised from mental death.[13]

Despite his faithfulness to Muhammad's treatment of Christian doctrine in the temple, Malcolm's public voice, which increasingly gained scope in the late 1950s and early 1960s, was given to assaulting Christianity for its fundamental expression of white supremacy, not its doctrinal content. To be sure, Malcolm's attacks were laced with doctrinal remarks, but for the most part his public discourse was grounded in the history of black oppression. In this context Malcolm constantly sought ways in which he could build up Elijah Muhammad and, in so doing, he developed the theme of reformation as his strongest weapon against Christianity.

The theme of reformation was a two-edged sword which, depending on the nature of the discourse, could be used defensively or offensively. Defensively, Malcolm's appeal on behalf of the Nation of Islam was to point out the extensive success Muhammad had in changing the lives of his followers. Who would find fault with a movement that had turned convicts, drunkards, drug addicts, and other moral dropouts into upstanding citizens? Offensively, reformation suggested that Muhammad's followers had been saved from the dead-mindedness of white Christendom. Like William Worthy's friends in Boston, Black Muslims were taught that their former lives, no matter how wretched, were essentially "Christian." Indeed, it was a matter of routine that Malcolm X, whether speaking inside the temple or in public, attributed all the vice and evil of his former life to Christianity.

In the 1957 Savior's Day convention, which was held at the Tabernacle Baptist Church on Indiana Avenue in Chicago, Elijah Muhammad's keynote address was especially filled with the religious jingoism of the movement. Muhammad catalogued the failure of Christianity to "get recognition and respect" for blacks, accused it of producing "more division and hate than all the other religions combined," claimed it had robbed and destroyed the peace and unity of black people, and kept them "worshipping and praying to something that didn't even exist." Like all of the Nation of Islam's polemics against Christianity, it was a biased interpretation informed as much by personal religious dissent as it was historical fact. Indeed, in every aspect cited by Muhammad, Christianity had also generated great forces for black advancement—especially producing the single most important institution in African American history, the church, which served as a bastion against white racism and became the bassinet for some of the most influential leaders in black America, including Muhammad himself.

While Muhammad and Malcolm sang the praises of color-friendly Islam and mocked Christianity as a "slave-making lie," the irony regarding religion and black enslavement is that in rendering the institution benign, Islam consequently reinforced its presence in the Muslim world. In contrast, when the Christian world finally began to vomit up the poison of chattel slavery, Christianity in the British and

North American contexts engendered some of the most militant and tireless abolitionists. None of this was palatable to Muhammad, however, since recognizing the good fruit of Christianity entailed recognizing its good root—which would then obligate him to make rational, balanced distinctions in matters of religion and race. Such adjustments, of course, would require a level of integrity that was mitigated by the very nature of the Nation of Islam.

In the same convention, Malcolm X spoke to the assembled Nation of Islam, but chose to employ his finely honed ex-Christian approach: "There was a time when I didn't know the Truth. I was then in total darkness. I was deaf, dumb and blind. I did many things that were bad. I was a dope-addict. I was a liar. I was a thief. I hated my own kind. I was a drunkard. But then I couldn't help being what I was. I WAS A CHRISTIAN!"[14] Both speeches having been published in *The Moslem World & The U.S.A.*, Malcolm's words especially drew sharp reaction from Elizabeth Kinnear, a representative of the National Council of Churches of Christ in the United States of America. "Surely it is unfair," Kinnear wrote, "to indicate that a man was a dope-addict, a liar, a thief, etc. because he was a Christian. There is nothing in Christianity which condones evil-doing and all that we write and say should conform to the highest in religion, and that of others as well as our own."[15] Kinnear's reasonable objection, however, could not be heard above the howling sarcasm of the Black Muslims, especially in a proselytizing publication like *The Moslem World & The U.S.A.*, whose editor was clearly attempting to attract Muhammad into the Muslim fold. Any insult to Christianity was music to the ears of Muslims such as the editor of *Moslem World*, who dreamed of turning African Americans away from the church en masse.[16]

Malcolm X continued to blame Christianity—a religion he had never embraced—for his former life of debauchery, and in the waning of his influence in the Nation of Islam in the early 1960s, his attacks on Christianity became especially graphic. *The Autobiography*, which Malcolm undertook in the hopes of improving his standing in the movement, is rife with Malcolm's remarks about his former criminal life as a "Christian." He apparently engaged in this personal style of religion-bashing in speeches, such as one where he declared: "No one drank more alcohol or smoked more reefers than I did when I was a Christian." In another interview, a journalist was amazed at the extent to which Malcolm spoke "of Christianity with hatred," quoting him in one particular screed: "I went to prison as a Christian, and while I was a Christian, I did what most Christians in this country do, which means I engaged in many vices. That's the Christian way. Christians are drunk. Christians are dope addicts. Christians rob banks. . . . But when I became a Muslim, I put that life behind me."[17] This is not to suggest that the "Christian way" as demonstrated by clergymen and laypeople was without problem. Malcolm's description of black Christians as corrupt and hypocritical may have had propagandistic purposes but it was not without some basis. Whether or not Malcolm knew Jesus, he certainly knew church folks, and he was well aware of the unfortunate contrast between church appearances and life behaviors that afflict many congregations. As a young man he recognized that many evangelists "peddled Jesus," and he likewise knew that some ministers and laypeople were hardly living *christianly*. "Even before I went to prison," Malcolm reflected in a 1963 interview, "I could see the hypocrisy of Christianity."

The fact that human inconsistency and hypocrisy plagued the church only served to reinforce the Black Muslim polemic against Christianity. (Of course, moral inconsistency also plagued the tribe of Shabazz, but it was not convenient for Malcolm to speak about the disciplinary actions he had taken as a minister.) One can imagine, for example, the absolute delight with which one church scandal was greeted by the Black Muslims, when a pair of dramatic photographs appeared in Harlem's *New York Amsterdam News* in the summer of 1958, exposing the affair of a prominent clergyman and the beautiful wife of another clergyman in a midtown New York hotel. The guilty minister, an official in the National Baptist Convention, was caught naked with another minister's semiclad wife. The photos, taken by the woman's husband (whose "raiding party" apparently gained entrance by a ploy), captured the horror and shame of the adulterous couple, the embarrassed flight of the naked minister into another room, and the scowl of the unfaithful wife. An extraordinary scandal like this not only sold copy, but undoubtedly reinforced the Black Muslim belief that the Christian church was in whole a corrupt institution where, as Malcolm said later, "Negro men" were always "patting" and "pawing" black women. "I had faith in the Nation," Malcolm wrote in *The Autobiography*, "we weren't some group of Christian Negroes, jumping and shouting and full of sins."[18]

But Malcolm's faith was not as much in the Nation of Islam as it was in Elijah Muhammad, and he tended to attribute to the Black Muslims his own austere morality—a morality he believed was only a reflection of the man he adoringly christened "the Little Lamb." In *The Autobiography*, Malcolm wrote: "The 'lamb of a man' analogy I drew for myself from the prophecy in the book of Revelations [*sic*] of a symbolic lamb with a two-edged sword in its mouth. Mr. Muhammad's two-edged sword was his teachings, which cut back and forth to free the black man's mind from the white man."[19] Malcolm continued by saying that his admiration for Muhammad had grown to adoration, an adoration that approached reverent fear. The appropriation of the "lamb" imagery of Revelation was perhaps the ultimate affront that Malcolm could have paid to Christianity, since it is clearly the supreme reference to Jesus Christ in the New Testament. Interestingly, however, Muhammad had never seized that title nor claimed such imagery of his own accord. Throughout his entire career as a religious leader, Muhammad was content with being proclaimed God's last and greatest messenger, the new Elijah raised from among his people to declare the millennial age of Allah.

Ironically, it was Malcolm X who elevated Elijah Muhammad to the level of Christ, usurping the symbolic christology of the Bible on behalf of the slight, mild-mannered little Georgian. In one sense, of course, Malcolm's appropriation was hardly malevolent; he had never believed in the divinity of Jesus, so stealing his crown on behalf of Muhammad was hardly theological grand larceny. Still, Malcolm knew, undoubtedly, the value of the "little lamb" reference to Christians, and he knew what impact it would have on the thousands of former Christians who were following his lead. Indeed, as Wilfred Little recalled, Malcolm was quite deliberate in taking divine Christian titles and applying them to the man that he himself adored. Little says that Malcolm went so far as to study how other historical leaders had been propagandized into virtual divinity, and he sought to emulate them.

> He made the decision, he was going to elevate Elijah Muhammad, and cause the people to see him as a divine person. And he went through the Bible and found all the different ways that they use words in there to describe the men of God who were considered as divine people. And then he began to use those with the name [*of*] Elijah Muhammad.[20]

In *The Autobiography*, Malcolm inadvertently shows how his own elevation and adoration of Muhammad had become infectious throughout the movement, and how his interpretation of the Messenger gave to Black Muslim meetings a sense of the cultic, even idolatrous. Malcolm says that his work in introducing Muhammad in Black Muslim rallies was "specifically to condition the audience to hear Mr. Muhammad," and his own reflections of those preliminary remarks suggest that he exceeded mere laudatory introduction, perhaps even going beyond psychological manipulation. From his own description, Malcolm's personal idolatry fueled a fire of adoration that may even have brought the assembly into contact with metaphysical forces—such phenomena being far more accessible to the African diaspora, given the lack of prejudice against the spiritual realm that characterizes non-"Enlightenment" cultures. In these rallies, Malcolm X became high priest to the Nation of Islam, recounting the sacred history of the tribe of Shabazz, cursing the white man and his Christian God, and invoking the black divinity and his messenger. Within the Nation of Islam, Malcolm had even been compared to Aaron, the high priest who served with Moses, and it was this role that he relished the most. Those who later accused him of wanting Muhammad's position could not possibly have understood why such ambition was so foreign to Malcolm; he had anointed Muhammad with his own sweat, blood, and tears, almost single-handedly transforming him into a semi-divinity. Malcolm X was a worshipper and a servant by nature, and like David's famous general Joab, he desired the conquest, not the crown.

"Tears would be in more eyes than mine," Malcolm recalled of those adoring moments as he introduced Muhammad to the assembled Nation. Reflecting on how Muhammad had rescued him, Malcolm wrote further, his emotions never peaked as they did when the Messenger ascended to the platform, surrounded and embraced by his admiring ministers. Malcolm wrote that he could literally *feel power* in Muhammad's presence, and this only heightened the intensity of his introductory remarks, which climaxed in "vacuum-quiet"—a momentary postponement of gratification that exploded with Muhammad's first greeting: "As-Salaam Alaikum." "WA-ALAIKUM-SALAAM!" the enraptured audience roared back in anticipation of a message that would probably go on for another two hours. Despite his frail appearance and the concerns of his followers, the weak-voiced "little lamb" drove home his message while many in the audience blurted out their worshipful support: "All praise is due Allah!" "*Teach*, Messenger!" "Little Lamb!" Muhammad once declared his Nation of Islam a world in itself, but if it was a world, it was one created largely by Malcolm X.[21]

In his sermons, Malcolm characteristically employed Christ in uplifting Muhammad and the movement. Speaking at Harvard University in 1961, Malcolm compared Elijah Muhammad to Jesus, stating that both had been "missioned" by God to preach to their own lost sheep. "Jesus also found himself opposed by the scholars and scientists of his day," Malcolm told the Ivy League audience. The scribes, priests, and Pharisees that Jesus opposed "are symbolically described in the Bible," Malcolm said, in reference to Muhammad's modern-day opponents, "the learned, educated intellectuals of his own kind." And just as Jesus and the Prophet Muhammad had ushered in their respective dispensations, Elijah Muhammad had brought about another change, albeit one that was final and complete. Ultimately, Malcolm declared, just as the scribes and Pharisees had bowed to Jesus, all of Muhammad's opponents would acquiesce to the truth of his message.

In another speech, delivered at Atlanta University in 1961, Malcolm continued to invoke Jesus in speaking of Muhammad. "How well [Allah] has enabled us to see that this little meek and humble man is he of whom the Bible says: 'How knoweth this man letters (such great wisdom) having never learned (being unlearned).'" The description, which Malcolm excised from the seventh chapter of John's gospel, pertained to the comments of the Pharisees about Jesus, who despite no formal training was able to baffle his scholarly critics. "No man in history has ever fit such a prophetic picture more perfectly than this little 'unlearned' man who is teaching us today with such great authority," Malcolm concluded.[22] In keeping with Black Muslim hermeneutics, of course, Malcolm forced a simple narrative into serving as a prophetic picture of Elijah Muhammad, invoking the story of Jesus only to prove the unique place of the Messenger in history. Malcolm's invocation of Jesus was not only the way he proved that Muhammad's ministry was a fulfillment of prophecy, but it also explained how it was that the Messenger obviously lacked formal training and was not a very good orator. Embarrassed by his own superiority, and by the fact that many of his audiences preferred hearing him over Muhammad, Malcolm told his listeners that their reaction only verified the influence of the devil, who conditioned black people to focus on the manner of a speech as opposed to the content of a speech. He sealed his defense by referring to the stuttering Moses and his spokesman Aaron. The biggest trick that whites had played on blacks, Malcolm concluded, was teaching them to prefer "eloquence."

By invoking Jesus and Moses as prophetic templates, Malcolm could rationalize the obvious inferiority of his superior. The more expansive the Nation of Islam grew, of course, the more Allah's Messenger needed Malcolm's help to condition his audiences, persuading them that Muhammad's two-hour harangues were brilliant revelation. Even when Muhammad was safely hidden away in Chicago, or in his winter home in Phoenix, Arizona, Malcolm remained vigilant in his duties as Muhammad's apologist. Malcolm naturally embraced irony in his presentations on the Nation of Islam, forever explaining away the problems of the movement—like a messenger who could not speak or a nation that had no land of its own. In one presentation before the Boston followers, Malcolm told his audience they had left beautiful churches to come to the Temple of Islam, and even though the latter might appear more like a shack in comparison with their former churches, it was better to be in a shack with wise people than to be in a palace with fools. Fools, Malcolm continued, believe in life after death, golden slippers, and pie in the sky. Fools believe in a God that does not serve them, and in a future resurrection of the literal dead. To understand Jesus they would have to realize that Jesus was a black man sent to the Jewish devils. In those days, he added, whites were savages and Christianity had a future. But nowadays, Malcolm X told his audience, Christianity—like its dead Jesus—only had a past. Instead of turning to the Christian God, they should turn to Allah, the God who would help them. He concluded triumphantly that it was Islam that had a great future.[23]

8

This Bitter Earth

Black Muslims in a Christian World

This bitter earth, well, what fruit it bears
What good is love that no one shares?
— "This Bitter Earth," as sung by Dinah Washington (1959)

We so-called Negroes were supposed to be a part of the Christian church. Yet we lived in a bitter world of dejection, caused by our being cast aside and being rejected by the white Christian church of our cruel slavemasters.
— Malcolm X, in *Los Angeles Herald-Dispatch*, November 14, 1957

By 1957, Elijah Muhammad and Malcolm X had really begun to rock the boat of black religion in the United States. Though whites tend to act like no social phenomenon is of any significance until they are aware of it (and thus define it), the African American community was well aware of the Nation of Islam about two years before Mike Wallace's famous exposé, "The Hate That Hate Produced," brought the movement to nationwide attention. Of course, the black press had already brought the Black Muslims to nationwide attention in the African American community, and the black church in particular became all too aware of the epithets and challenges being hurled at them by Malcolm X in particular. "He just devastated the Christian church," recalled the editor of the *New York Amsterdam News*. Speaking in Los Angeles before a Nation of Islam audience, Malcolm was quoted by the *Pittsburgh Courier* as saying the "Negro preacher" is "the greatest pretender of them all"; and while he acknowledged that individual preachers were not being condemned, Malcolm maintained many were nevertheless "leaders of a great conspiracy which blocks the development of their people." By telling black Christians that heaven "is in the sky," Malcolm said, the preachers were able to enjoy "heaven right here on earth." In the Los Angeles area alone, Malcolm concluded, black churches controlled millions of dollars in assets, yet these assets were being placed in the hands of white bankers who practice discrimination and injustice in their businesses.

Several months later, the *Courier* picked up another polemic against black clergymen by Malcolm, noting that he had been a guest on the Newark, New Jersey, radio station WHBI's "Voice of Radio Free Africa." During this broadcast Malcolm emphasized the need to refute "all the religious lies taught in the churches," and indicted "ignorant Negro preachers" for accusing Muhammad of inciting hatred. Having become "willing tools" of whites because of their greed, Malcolm said, these black ministers were parroting the "religious lies" of a "pacifying religion" which was skillfully designed "to keep us in 'our place.'" In contrast to the "naked truth" being preached by Muhammad, Malcolm concluded, the "Negro preachers are quickest to prove themselves to be the biggest fools."[1]

Like the message of the Nation of Islam itself, the contempt expressed toward black preachers was a blend of genuine concern and cultic dissent. As to the former, Muhammad and his ministers were all too aware of the injustices being perpetrated upon black Christians in the South, and in the late 1950s there were likewise incidents of black ministers being assaulted, beaten, and brutalized by white racists. For instance, two separate incidents were reported in one issue of the *Courier* where black ministers were attacked by Klansmen. The first took place in Tuscaloosa, Alabama, when the Reverend O'Hara M. Prewitt was abducted at gunpoint, blindfolded, and taken to a remote setting where he was stripped naked and strung up with a noose, his feet barely touching the ground. He was then flogged until unconscious, after which he was made to dress, was forced into the trunk of a car, and released on the roadside in the early morning hours. Another minister, Charles Billups, was accosted by a mob of whites in

Birmingham, Alabama, then blindfolded, bound, and tied to a tree. Praying for his captors aloud, Billups was verbally abused and derided, especially when he kept saying he was a "minister of God." The crime, presided over by a man identified as "The Prosecutor," became a two-hour session of torture, Billups being chain-whipped and his open wounds jabbed with splinters. Reports said that the minister was beaten so brutally that the bruises actually looked like the chain was imbedded in his skin. In both cases, the ministers were apparently targeted by organized racists because they were suspected of involvement in integrationist efforts.[2]

The Nation of Islam was understandably outraged by these incidents, and at the same time disgusted that blacks would suffer on behalf of the integrationist cause. Writing in the "Mr. Muhammad Speaks" column, the leader of the Nation of Islam called for a unity of all "black mankind" under the "unifying religion" of Islam. "It is needless for you to put your trust in Christianity," Muhammad wrote, since Christianity had neither helped blacks unite nor defended them from their enemies.

> It even does not help the black preachers when the enemy attacks them, though they may be praying in the name of Jesus. You will come to know the kind of Christianity that you are believing in is none other than the white race's tool used to trap the black people into a state of helplessness to the white race. God nor Jesus seems to care for it.[3]

Responding directly to the *Courier* story on the Billups incident, Muhammad said the minister had been beaten "by a mob of devils," and lamented that "poor black people are gravely deceived in their faith and belief in Christianity." Interestingly, Muhammad then invoked the Christian teaching of heaven and hell, though one would have expected him to discuss "turning the other cheek" and praying for one's enemies, which clearly characterized the Billups case. "Death is the end of everything, righteous or wicked," Muhammad concluded. "When we die that is the last of anyone."[4] It might seem like this was a peculiar reaction to the Billups case, but Muhammad obviously felt that the only reason black Christians permitted themselves to be so abused was because they did not sufficiently value the present life as a result of Christian teachings. On the other hand, belief in an afterlife had not stopped other Christian peoples from advancement, and Muhammad's insistence upon posthumous nihilism seems to be rooted as much in religious bias as zeal for black liberation.

Muhammad's lack of objectivity in evaluating Christianity and the Christian church was already a sore spot for many black Christian readers. While many pastors were perhaps too intimidated to go one-on-one in confronting the Nation of Islam, the editor of the *New York Amsterdam News* acknowledged that "many Christian leaders" had taken "stern exception" to Muhammad's writings in the Harlem paper. After the *Amsterdam News* had run a column by Muhammad entitled "Islamic World" (sometimes it was published as "Islam World"), Christian leaders began to complain to the editor, deploring Muhammad's "attacks on the Christian religion." In an attempt to provide balance, the editor decided to invite a Christian minister to contribute a countercolumn on behalf of Christianity. The short-run column, "Christian World," ran throughout December 1957 in the *Amsterdam News*, featuring the writing of the Reverend George C. Violenes, then pastor of the Christian Community Church in Harlem.

Unfortunately, while Violenes's column was scholarly, historical, and evenhanded, it read more like a minisurvey than a response to Muhammad's religious polemics. Violenes began by retracing the history of the Hebrews and the Muslims in the first two issues rather than taking on the biblical-theological topics that actually merited attention. Meanwhile, on the very same page, Muhammad's column appeared—the Black Muslim leader claiming prophethood while pounding away on the same black-and-white keys. When Violenes finally did meet Muhammad on theological ground, his writing waxed homiletical, touching upon the theme of Christ's nativity in keeping with the Christmas season that year. Far too dispassionately, Violenes issued a gentle rebuff to Muhammad for his disparaging doctrine of the Christian God, calling it a "false accusation." Violenes wound up his argument by suggesting that since Muhammad was not a follower of Christ, he needed to repent of his sins and be baptized.

> Today Mr. Muhammad is a self-styled follower of Islam, who has been trying to confuse the Negro and put a cleavage between the white and Negro races.

If Mr. Muhammad would only pray, God through His only begotten Son will forgive him of his infidel mind, and give him new spiritual birth. Then and only then will Mr. Muhammad see clearly that this is not the time to condemn the white race and smear the loyal American Negro who has contributed so much to the democratic way of life.[5]

It was an admittedly direct, orthodox Christian response, but what the *Amsterdam News*—and what the black press in general—needed was a clergyman who would do more than preach at Muhammad from a paper pulpit. What was lacking (and what seems to be lacking with reference to Louis Farrakhan's contemporary Nation of Islam) was a black Christian leader who would hold Muhammad accountable for his extravagant, distorted theological assertions, his homespun biblically styled tales, and his awkward adventure in unitarianism. Violenes, like many other Christian pastors since then, responded to the Nation of Islam's rhetoric more in the name of "good race relations" than on behalf of the Christian faith. The lack of a rigorous, exegetically oriented counterattack left the impression that Elijah Muhammad, for all of his controversy, was espousing a legitimate religious alternative. To this day, because the response to the Nation of Islam by churchmen tends to be focused on race relations, many fail to differentiate the Black Muslim doctrines from traditional Islam. Others, like the Reverend Benjamin Chavis whose conversion to "Islam" in 1997 was premised on the notion that he could serve Christ and Farrakhan, reflect the same failure on the part of many black Christian leaders to identify the problematic religious nature of the Nation of Islam phenomenon.

The Reverend Chavis's recent conversion to Farrakhan's Nation of Islam is not without precedent. In fact, during the days of Muhammad's Nation of Islam, the Black Muslim phenomenon attracted more than one Christian clergyman, and in one high-profile case, it drew an entire congregation into Muhammad's fold. According to reports in the *New Crusader*, a black publication in Muhammad's hometown of Chicago, the mass conversion took place when the Nation of Islam held a rally in Phoenix, Arizona. The Phoenix Madison Square Garden rally took place in January 1962, and was also opened to whites and Native Americans. The audience heard Muhammad speak for two hours in an attempt on his part to refute the heavy criticism he had faced since moving his winter quarters to Arizona for health reasons. According to Malcolm X, Muhammad had faced a "united front of hostility and opposition" from an interdenominational ministerial alliance in Phoenix. Malcolm told reporters that despite his illness, the Messenger wanted to face the Phoenix audience in order to "offset the malicious propaganda" of local black clergy. At the climax of the rally, the Reverend J. P. McGowan, pastor of the Mount Zion Baptist Church in Phoenix, "stood up and declared allegiance to the Muslim leader," bringing the entire Zion congregation along with him. When asked about this conversion, "Muslim officials" back in Chicago told one journalist that "it has been a long practiced procedure for Christian ministers[,] when converted to Islam but desirous of remaining in their Christian denomination, to accept the Muslim edict to teach the religion of Islam instead of the precepts of Christianity." These Nation of Islam officials did not explain how this compromise could be attained, though they seem to have assumed that converted Christian pastors, being relatively independent, would posture as Christian ministers in order to maintain their denominational affiliation and privileges even though their doctrine and philosophy would come in line with the teachings of Elijah Muhammad. If this was the case, it presumed that the ministers' denominations either did not care, theologically speaking, or simply never found out about the conversions. The "Muslim" officials went on to say that the issue of winning black Christians who wanted to remain affiliated with the church was still a question under consideration. "[I]f a way could be found for those who want to do so to continue identifying themselves with Christianity," one of the representatives concluded, it would likely mean gaining thousands of "so-called Christians" in the movement.

Of course, that question was never really broached, let alone answered in any strategic sense. Christians who chose to join the Nation of Islam did so with no concern for maintaining a Christian identity, and those who did wish to maintain affiliation with the church inevitably found themselves straddling an uncomfortable fence of religious contradiction that could not be resolved with any theological integrity. In fact, the Reverend McGowan and his three hundred X-Christians learned from the onset what the price of trading religions would be, since Muhammad climaxed his Phoenix message with a statement of faith. In that statement, Muhammad proclaimed "mental resurrection" over against the hope of physical resurrection; the prophethood of Jesus over against the divine sonship of Jesus; and the messianic nature of "Master W. Fard Muhammad," who revealed himself "as Allah" and who will "bring about a universal government of peace."[6] Of course, given the preponderant racism these black Christians were probably enduring in Arizona, it is understandable why McGowan and his congregation might be drawn toward the racial honesty and blunt resolve of the Black Muslims to separate themselves from whites. As black people, even Christians might find themselves wishing to join the Nation of Islam; but as Christian blacks, they could never answer the question of how they might fit into the Black Muslim world. A bitter impasse, the unanswered question worked as much to keep Black Muslims from their Christian brethren as it did to keep black Christians from the Nation of Islam.

While journalists who discovered the Nation of Islam readily classified the movement in terms such as "puritanical" and "paramilitary," they inevitably saw Muhammad's Nation through a civil rights lens. In *The Autobiography*, however, Malcolm also makes a disparaging allusion to black ministers who criticized the Nation of Islam, calling it "anti-Christianity." These critics, whom Malcolm spoofed as the "Right Reverend Bishop T. Chickenwing," however, were easily repulsed when Malcolm declared: "Christianity is the white man's religion. The Holy Bible in the white man's hands and his interpretations of it have been the greatest single ideological weapon for enslaving millions of non-white human beings." Malcolm told his critics that the white man salved his conscience by calling people heathens and pagans, which provided a justification to send in his armies, and "then his missionaries behind the guns to mop up."

Like his view of Christianity, Malcolm's view of Christian missions was generalized to suit his arguments. While white religion was

broadly used as a tool of oppression in European conquest, missionaries were not originally operative as "mop up" crews, especially in
Africa. In fact, many missionaries preceded the colonial endeavor,
having been compelled by religious awakening and inspired by the
success of abolitionism in the British Empire. There were often significant differences between early-nineteenth-century missionary
churches and the religion of later European settlers. For instance,
some early missionaries in South Africa were caught between the
racist Boers and the Zulu people, and paid for it with their lives. In
early West African missions, the thin, unrelenting line of Christians
was comprised of blacks and whites, and in many cases they served as
the "tribune of the oppressed," watching closely the expanding colonial interests of European governments and interceding on behalf of
African peoples.[7] This is not to suggest that Malcolm's criticisms are
invalid. For the most part his assessment of western Christendom was
correct, yet his view was typically black-and-white, with no shadings
or exceptions permitted.

Malcolm's public approach to Christianity primarily reflects the necessities of the Nation of Islam—particularly at a time when it was important to grasp a moral upper hand over the black church and its
leadership. Whether or not Muhammad ever seriously intended to
overtake the church, it seems that Malcolm X really believed that religious primacy in the black community was in reach. In this sense, then,
the Bishop Chickenwings not only represented a serious hindrance to
the advancement of the black community but also to the Messenger
himself. Prior to the broad-scale notoriety that came to the Nation of
Islam in 1959, however, this sentiment is best observed in Malcolm's
zealous writing on behalf of the Nation of Islam—particularly in a little column he wrote called "God's Angry Men," which ran in the *New
York Amsterdam News*, the *Westchester Observer* (New York), and the
Los Angeles Herald-Dispatch in 1957–58. In essence, "God's Angry Men"
is a finely crafted view of the Christian world—far more compelling
and challenging than Muhammad's writings, and clearly premised on
an understanding of United States history that Malcolm X drew from
his prison studies, as well as his intensive exploration of the Bible and
his penetrating view of society and its institutions.

Malcolm premised his introductory remarks in "God's Angry Men" by announcing that Muhammad's "Islam" had become a rocky barrier to Christianity, an obstacle that "all the black and white preachers combined seem incapable of removing." Now, Malcolm declared, thousands of black people were "turning daily away from the segregated Christian Church." In so doing, blacks were leaving behind "our own ignorant religious leaders." The keynote message of these leaders was "designed to make us feel inferior to the white Christian slavemaster." Borrowing from Muhammad's interpretation of the Parable of the Rich Man and Lazarus, Malcolm pictured African Americans as sitting "amid the rubbish of the Western World, at the feet (or gate) of the rich white Christians, begging for something (civil rights) to fall from their table." Instead, blacks received hard, dirty labor, slum housing, high rents, the poorest quality food, and the highest prices.

In keeping with Muhammad's perspective, Malcolm draws complete continuity between the days of slavery and the civil rights era. Whites are slavemasters, blacks are slaves, and Christianity is the religion of manipulation and control. Thus, Christianity is a "new religion," made up to fool blacks into seeking their freedom after they die. Ironically, however, while Christianity was given to blacks, they found themselves cast aside and dejected, even mocked and ridiculed by white Christians for attempting to imitate Christian worship: "We called ourselves 'Negro Christians' yet we remained an ignorant, foolish people despised and rejected by the white Christians whom we so greatly admired. What fools we were!" Out of this rejection, Malcolm writes, came the "Negro Church," which was kept "a separate church, distinct and apart" from the white Christian church. A "futile attempt by us (ex-slaves) to IMITATE the white church of our Christian slavemasters," the black church promoted the "lying Christian doctrine" of black inferiority. Just as Christianity proved to be a bitter world in which to live, neither could it unite black people, since it reduced them to "mental slaves and willing tools of the wicked white race," and then divided them by the manipulation of "petty Negro preachers" seeking wealth and power. This divisiveness, Malcolm concluded, was the source of factions and denominations within the black church.

Pitifully, Negro Christians idolized white Christians, living for the day when they could enter a "'white heaven,' where their plurality (TRINITY) of white gods" would allow them to freely integrate.[8]

Stating that a "DEAD" person is one who is deaf, dumb, blind, and lost, Malcolm said African Americans had been "made a DEAD PEOPLE here in the West, buried beneath a heap of 'rubbish' (false religion and false education) for the past 400 years." This condition resulted from the "lying doctrine" of black Christian preachers, who betrayed their "very own kind" in doing the will of the white slavemaster. These preachers were educated in "special schools" established by the slavemaster, called seminaries, in which "choice slaves" were trained to "come back among us and preach his false religion to us." Their lying doctrines, then, are not the teachings of "the righteous Prophet Jesus," Malcolm said, but were invented by the "wicked white race." The influence of Christianity was to make blacks "look upon everything white as being right, which automatically compelled us to believe that dark had to be wrong . . . and all dark people were cursed."

Another aspect of their oppression, Malcolm wrote, was the inability to accept "LIVING LEADERS." Their minds having become superstitious, blacks do not recognize greatness in a man until he is dead: "Tribute is still being paid to a DEAD Moses. Worship is being wasted on a DEAD Jesus. Millions honor a dead Muhammad. And, many respect and revere a DEAD Mr. Garvey." Indeed, these followers are "so busy whooping and hollering over THE DEAD" that they are missing Elijah Muhammad, "the greatest LIVING EMANCIPATOR and TRUTH BEARER that the world has ever known." Unlike many black preachers, who are well dressed and drive in Cadillacs at the expense of their starving parishioners, Malcolm said, "Mr. Elijah Muhammad is not one of those pseud[o]-religionists. He is not a religious faker. He is not practicing 'MAGIC' such as the Negro Preachers have practiced and duped our poor people with for years." A "MODERN MOSES," Elijah Muhammad was filling "those of us who follow him with an unquenchable thirst for education, knowledge and wisdom," and curing "us of drunkenness, dope addiction, reefer smoking and other evils we engaged in as "Negro Christians."[9]

There is a strong sense that Malcolm perceived Muhammad's appearance on the scene of black religion in the United States as a kind of neo-Protestant movement, whose prophetic voice was sounding a new era that the established church would find irreversible. Not only was Muhammad like Moses, a prominent biblical character in black Christian preaching, according to Malcolm, but he also referred to Muhammad as "A REFORMER," and announced that "an earth-shaking REFORMATION is taking place among the so-called Negroes right here in the LAND OF BONDAGE." In this case he could not have been connecting Elijah's name with the biblical Elijah, who was, in fact, a reformer of Mosaic faith among the Jews. Rather, in Malcolm's terms, "the long-hidden truth" now revealed through Muhammad was producing

> a REGENERATION (an awakening) among us of such astonishing degree that the world now must bear witness that this Great Awakening now going on among the so-called Negroes, due to that which is being taught by MESSENGER ELIJAH MUHAMMAD, is indeed the ONLY RESURRECTION that the Bible was ever speaking of or pointing toward.[10]

"Reformation" and "Great Awakening" were terms that Malcolm likely acquired in his prison studies about Christianity, and his use of them suggest the Protestant orientation of the Nation of Islam.

One journalist perceived this when he described the Nation of Islam's opposition to Christianity as being particularly anti-Roman Catholic. Indeed, Elijah Muhammad was sharply anti-Roman Catholic, and in his "Mr. Muhammad Speaks" column he attributed to Roman Catholicism the intention of setting "organized Christianity above the true religion of Allah (Islam)" and turning the people from "the spiritual center of Allah's Mecca, Arabia." Muhammad said that Rome's history showed many false gods and was "backed by the wealth and might of the white race." In another article, Muhammad made a very Protestant criticism, alluding to Christians worshiping "idol gods in their churches," with "statues of wood, metal and imaginary pictures of God, angels, prophets and disciples that they bow [to] and revere . . . as if they could speak." Likewise, in his sermons, such as one recalled by an admirer, Malcolm X questioned how it was that the Holy Land had been moved from Jerusalem to Rome. He also questioned how blacks could be considered "Roman" Catholics. He went so far as to find an obscure passage in the book of Job, where Satan was said to have walked "to and fro, up and down on the earth"; Malcolm told his audience this was a reference to the signing of the cross by Roman Catholics. Throughout his time in the Nation of Islam, Malcolm's assessment of Roman Catholicism did not grow less acerbic. In fact, in an interview with Alex Haley published in *Playboy* in 1963, Malcolm was the most blunt, saying that "Catholicism conditions your mind for dictators. Can you think of a single Protestant country that has ever produced a dictator?" Indeed, Malcolm concluded, the "two heresies" of fascism and communism had come out of Roman Catholic Italy. Another journalist who interviewed Malcolm the same year made the observation that "[t]here is no love lost between Muslims and Catholics." Malcolm told the journalist that with the rise of President Kennedy, Roman Catholics were ascending because Protestants had lost the will to fight. However, even though the scales were tipping toward Catholicism, Malcolm said, blacks would still be used and "end up with nothing as usual." On a personal level, Malcolm said, he made no distinction between white clergymen and white racketeers when it came to the exploitation of black people. "You can throw the Pope in, too," he added.[11]

As far as "God's Angry Men" was concerned, Malcolm heard from one white preacher, whose letter he said "really sounded too pitiful" to merit a reply; however, in the next installment, Malcolm revealed that he had mistaken a black minister's letter as having come from a white clergyman. "He fooled me completely! His letter sounded like no one but a 'white man' could have written it. It was a good defense for the white race." Malcolm concluded that the black minister could only have sounded so "white-minded" because he was "BRAIN-WASHED," and despite his black skin he had become "white on the inside . . . white in his way of thinking . . . white in his loves and desires . . . white in his offenses . . . and a defender of his white Christian 'brothers' who have enslaved us." Malcolm then chided black preachers who dared attack the Nation of Islam, comparing them to "yapping puppies" and trained hounddogs who defend their master's property but not themselves. These doglike preachers, Malcolm concluded, ought to bite their white masters "instead of wasting time breaking their little teeth on the ROCK OF ISLAM."

"God's Angry Men" established the journalistic presence of the Nation of Islam in the black community and opened the door for the "Mr. Muhammad Speaks" column. Malcolm wrote in his autobiography that eventually Muhammad agreed to take over "that valuable *Amsterdam News* space"—bumping "God's Angry Men" into the pages of other black publications. Malcolm may have invited Muhammad to start a column, but he was probably responding astutely to the veiled jealousy he sensed from the elder and his family over his success in the *Amsterdam News*—a foreshadow of the later takeover of the *Muhammad Speaks* newspaper by Muhammad's family in Chicago. Nevertheless, "God's Angry Men" stands as a testimony to Malcolm's absolute faith and confidence in Elijah Muhammad, and his belief that the Messenger was not only a successor to all the great biblical prophets but also the real heir of Marcus Garvey's legacy. In Malcolm's eyes, the bitter world of white Christianity was not the world of Jesus, "the righteous prophet and servant of ALLAH," nor was it a world worthy of those, like Malcolm X, who considered themselves ardent followers of "the Honorable Marcus Garvey." Only in following Elijah Muhammad could one ascertain the religion which Jesus taught, Malcolm concluded, and those who truly loved Garvey likewise could not help but "recognize, accept, and follow Messenger Elijah Muhammad today." Allah came down to "this hell," Malcolm wrote, and left his Messenger standing fearlessly "in the midst of hell" to gather the black Nation and "destroy this wicked white race and the Slave Empire with plagues." The Christian world was the white man's heaven, Malcolm concluded, and the white man's heaven was most certainly the black man's hell.[12]

9

"We're Living at the End of the World"

The Second Coming of Earl Little

His voice never wavered. He gave birth to words, ideas and thoughts and made our minds receptive to his ideas about churches in which we had ministers.

—Hakim Jamal, *From the Dead Level*

No! I didn't learn anything about the Bible from my father.

—Malcolm X, on "Community Corner,"
WADO Radio, New York, July 1962

It is God who will come, not Jesus. It is God who will come. If Jesus was going to do it he would have done it a long time ago. . . .God is going to bring the white man down to his knees and make him let you go.

—Malcolm X, in New York City Police Department
Bureau of Special Services files, April 16, 1961

A scholarly observer of the black community wrote an essay in the early 1960s based on his observation of the religious parallels between the Nation of Islam and Christianity. He noted that early Christians appealed to the downtrodden and, just like the Black Muslims, the Jesus movement offered the lowly a sense of dignity and self-respect. Both groups looked to a future of bliss for their followers and for certain judgment to fall upon the wicked. Both worshiped an incarnate deity, and both "appear to be intolerant of other faiths," he concluded.[1] It was a clever analysis, especially at a time when most people saw the Nation of Islam as a mean-spirited, race-oriented organization in competition with the civil rights movement. Still, his observations were also premised on the generalizations and biases of secular scholarship.

Early Christianity may have been appealing to certain people who found themselves disenfranchised or socially disadvantaged, but from the beginning the religion of Jesus stood conspicuously between the rich and the poor, never actually joining either. Invariably focused on the interior life, Jesus and the apostles warned about the dangers of loving wealth and condemned the arrogance and selfishness that often plagues the privileged, though they never advanced the doctrine that poverty was a superior or righteous state. Subsequently, when Christians have shown excessive devotion either to amassing wealth or ridding themselves of it, they have become inevitably preoccupied with only those aspects of the Christian faith that justify their agendas. The relationship of Christianity with the wealthy and the poor has always been fluid and personal—which is why postbiblical developments like organized Christian "communism" and other forms of devout self-deprivation are as awkward as the pray-and-grow-rich movement so prevalent among fundamentalists in the late twentieth century. Malcolm X once warned an audience about the potent dangers of "dollarism" in the United States. "This country can seduce God,"[2] Malcolm said in what seems an irreverent hyperbole—until one considers the state of the Christian church in the United States, especially the prevalence of televangelist ministries.

The Black Muslims, too, had an appeal to the dispossessed in the African American community, but the Nation of Islam was not a poor people's movement. Elijah Muhammad, like Fard, did not challenge poverty per se, nor was he interested in disparaging capitalism, especially regarding his own interests. Muhammad could boast that dysfunctional men were being recycled into productive citizens of the black nation, but the reputation the Nation of Islam acquired as a movement of economic uplift was gild more than guts. Elijah Muhammad had always aspired to bourgeois status and, like the Puritans of New England, he dreamed of setting up a city on a hill to ex-emplify that status. Indeed, Muhammad was more like the Puritans than many realize; what has been said of them can also be said of him: that he came to do good, and did *very, very well.*

Christians and Black Muslims do envision a coming eschatologi-cal deliverance, which includes judgment falling on the infidel. But at least in theory (which is often how religions must be discussed if they are to be appreciated), Christians believe the community of the re-deemed to be an international, multiethnic body based on faith, while the Nation of Islam was always *doctrinally* defined by race. That the scholar saw Christianity as being intolerant, of course, expressed the prominent Western notion that redemption must imitate democracy lest God be proven a tyrant. However, neither Moses, Jesus, nor Muhammad of Islam were Western secularists: the idea that a precise medium of redemption might be considered narrowminded and that godliness entails tolerating everyone's gods would have struck them as quite bizarre. Indeed, if Moses, Jesus, or Muhammad were guided by this modern assumption about religious tolerance, it is likely that neither Judaism, Christianity, nor Islam would ever have been born.

As far as Malcolm X was concerned, of course, no parallels between the religion of Muhammad and Christianity could outweigh the dif-ference between them. For Malcolm, this difference was especially clear in the very symbolism of the "white man's religion." The cross, he told one Nation of Islam audience, was really a sign of the devil. "We all know that the white man's religion is the one that uses the sign of the cross, and he tells us that this is a good sign, a sign of God, a sign of love. But is it?" According to one listener, Malcolm then suggested they think of the cross in a different way. The cross, he said, is usually seen in a graveyard, a place of death. The cross meant death to Jesus, Mal-colm declared, yet black Christians foolishly continue to wear it around their necks. "What if Jesus had been given the electric chair," he asked, "would you all wear little electric chairs around your necks?" Unlike Islam, Malcolm continued, Christianity always meant war and bloodshed for black people throughout the world. The white man's theme song, he said, was typified in the hymn, "Onward Christian Sol-diers," and his byword was "Praise the Lord and Pass the Ammunition."

Of course, just as Malcolm X held Christianity blameworthy for all the violence and injustice suffered by black people worldwide, so he upheld it as being responsible for the tragedy of his own youth. In a "Harlem Freedom Rally" sponsored by the Nation of Islam in New York City in 1960, Malcolm told the audience that he had gone to jail as a young man, but "quickly added that he was a Christian when he went to jail, and all of his associates in jail were Christians." One of the worst evils perpetrated on blacks by Christianity, Malcolm taught, was the doctrine of pacifism in the face of oppression. In a radio debate with civil rights leader Bayard Rustin in 1960, Malcolm pointed out that while blacks are taught to be nonviolent, oppressed Europeans are given arms by the United States to fight. Indeed, these armed Europeans are then labeled by propagandists as "freedom fighters," while blacks who advocate the use of force are labeled as "violent." For this reason, Islam was in "direct opposition to Christianity," Malcolm concluded. In a sermon at the Los Angeles mosque, Malcolm raised the issue quite forcefully. "You teach yourselves nothing, you teach your children nothing," he said, pounding his fist on the lectern, "except to love Jesus and to love those who hate you and hurt you!"[3]

In contrast to Christianity, Malcolm X portrayed the religion of "Islam" as the solution to the plight of black people in the United States. As such, it contained the one ingredient that rendered a religion either right or wrong: the freedom of the black man. However, as he told Bayard Rustin, Muhammad's religious approach was also distinct from nationalism, even though the Black Muslims and black nationalists had many similar goals. The alternative presented by the Nation of Islam was a distinct "religious approach," which stressed a "moral reformation" that would give people dignity and self-respect. "God Himself has to have a hand in it," Malcolm said, "especially because the problem of the so-called Negro is so unique." Many black nationalists have since employed Malcolm's words, reshaping them into a secular message. Malcolm X did not perceive the message of the Nation of Islam as an ideology, but rather as a gospel premised entirely on the familiar religious paradigm of the Exodus:

> We believe every condition that the Negro is in today was preordained,
> predestined, and prophesied. And we believe that we're living in the
> fulfillment of that prophecy today. We believe that our being here in
> America is in terms of biblical prophecy. We believe that the slavemas-
> ter's oppression of us is in line with biblical prophecy.[4]

To Malcolm, the Nation of Islam was the new, if not the true, Israel in
that all biblical references pertaining to the election, oppression, and
deliverance of the ancient Israelites by God were actually prophecies
about African Americans.

In April 1961, Malcolm spoke at the Embassy Auditorium in Los
Angeles in an event sponsored by the Nation of Islam. His message
was rife with biblical references, allusions, and arguments premised
entirely on the paradigm of the black Israel. At the core of the message was a merciless critique of the black Christian minister and his
failure to properly teach and intercede on behalf of his oppressed
people. The "Negro preacher," Malcolm declared, "is telling you about
some kind of action that is supposed to take place after you are dead,
but somewhere else, at some other time and at some other place." Instead of challenging the suffering and wickedness of the present system, he continued, the black minister kept black Christians looking
into the past, at the suffering of the Hebrews in ancient Egypt and the
wickedness of Sodom and Gomorrah. As to the charge that the Black
Muslims were preaching a religion of separatism, Malcolm pointed
out that blacks are already separated by whites in every sphere of life,
but that religion was one area where they could exercise self-determi-
nation: "Your religion depends on you."

> You go to China and find a Chinaman that believes in Jesus and ask
> him to paint a picture of Jesus and he will paint a picture of Jesus that
> looks like a Chinaman. You go to Alaska and find an Eskimo that be-
> lieves in Jesus and ask him to paint a picture of Jesus and he will paint
> a picture of Jesus looking like an Eskimo. You come back here to
> America and find a white man that believes in Jesus and he will paint
> a picture of Jesus looking like a white man.

But when one approaches a black man who believes, Malcolm concluded, "he will paint a picture of Jesus looking like a white man."[5]

The inability of the black Christian to envision Christ as black was only a symptom of the general malaise that had been introduced to the African American community through the preaching of black ministers. Their preaching, Malcolm said, had made black people averse to the idea of black rule. Malcolm argued that "black supremacy" was a good thing: "Man, if you don't want black supremacy, you don't want to see a black man rule something, some time, then you don't belong on this planet." Thus, black ministers would have to be removed: just as oppressors were being removed in revolutions throughout the world, Malcolm said, the time was coming when black Christian leaders, along with the rest of the Uncle Toms, would have to be uprooted and discarded like weeds. "The time is coming when we will weed the world just like you weed a garden. . . . They will strangle you in your community and never have anything to offer other than strangulation."

As to the ethics of pacifism proclaimed by Christian preachers, Malcolm lamented that blacks were never allowed to have the Qur'an, because it is the "Bible of the dark world." Instead, blacks are given a Christian Bible, which the white man put in every room of the black man's house, from the attic to the bathroom. "They put you in the electric chair with their Bible," he added. However, even if the black man read the Bible closely, Malcolm said, he would see that it says "an eye for an eye, a tooth for a tooth." As for the admonishment of Jesus to pray for one's enemies, Malcolm said Christians did not understand what he meant. "He meant pray for them, pray that God comes and gets them."

> We pray for our enemy, we pray that the airplane of the man who made a slave out of us will crash with him in it. You pray for the death and destruction of your enemy. There is no man who can find fault with a prayer like that. Jesus prayed for God to come and destroy his enemies, every man in the Bible prayed that God would come and destroy their enemies.

Unfortunately, he concluded, the "Negro preacher has you like a fool on your knees, saying that God will forgive your enemies." Malcolm's analysis was partially correct. The Hebrew prophets might call fire down upon the heathen and the Psalmist might long to smash the heads of his enemies' children but not, as many suppose, because the Old Testament God was different from the New Testament God. The theme of divine intervention and vengeance is abundant in the Hebrew text because those biblical writers perceived themselves in a covenant with God that included their physical and national well-being over against other nations and peoples. As long as national Israel was in covenant with God, its prophets, priests, and kings could rightly pray for the deaths of their enemies. Since Malcolm understood the election of the Nation of Islam in terms very similar to the covenant with national Israel, he was at least theologically consistent in asking for the white man's planes to fall from the sky, and for white America to be plagued with cancer and polio.[6]

However, Malcolm X never came to terms with Christian theology, not only because he rejected orthodox tenets like the virgin birth and the divinity of Jesus but because the prerequisites of the spiritual nationalism of Christianity could not be superimposed upon the Nation of Islam. Christianity sees itself in continuity with the covenant Hebrew nation, not with Judaism, but that continuity is spiritual instead of national or genealogical. Jesus and the apostles improvised a doctrine of nationhood that included Gentiles, and which therefore necessitated the abandonment of political, ethnic, or racial identity as a condition of inclusion. Consequently, Jesus had no use for physical force, nor did he wish his followers to be so involved, because the conquests of Christianity were supposed to be indifferent to political, national, and ethnic boundaries. Jesus was not interested in establishing a kingdom "of this world," which relieved him and his followers of the burden of defending it by force of arms. On the other hand, in theory Elijah Muhammad was quite interested in establishing a nation with boundaries that were political and racial, and consequently the paradigm of the Hebrew nation worked far better for him than did the church.

Even after he was put out of the Nation of Islam, Malcolm consistently expressed tension with the supposedly pacifist philosophy of Jesus. However, as a Black Muslim with a mandate to correct the lies of the "poisoned book," Malcolm's treatment of the words of Jesus was sometimes more wishful than exegetical. For instance, his insistence that Jesus taught his followers to pray for the deaths of their enemies was a prime example of Muhammad's manner of biblical interpretation: finding the right interpretation, Muhammad said, was like fitting a hat. Just as the size of the head determined the size of the hat, the mental attitude of the person determined the meaning of the biblical text.[7] Long before "by any means necessary" became a political motto for Malcolm's independent organization, it was a actually a rule of thumb for Black Muslim Bible interpretation.

Malcolm's speech at the Embassy Auditorium was actually occasioned by his serving as a substitute for Muhammad, who had been scheduled for a series of meetings with blacks in the press, business, and religious communities of the Los Angeles area—the summit having been orchestrated by Sanford Alexander, publisher of the *Herald-Dispatch*. In 1957, Malcolm had established Temple No. 27 in Los Angeles, and although he credits Muhammad in *The Autobiography* with sending him there, one FBI informant claimed that the Los Angeles temple was preferred by Malcolm, not Muhammad. According to this report, Temple No. 27 was considered "Malcolm's Temple," and Muhammad did not "think much of it" because he himself favored other locations in California over Los Angeles. Consequently, Malcolm exercised a great deal more authority in Los Angeles, having also chosen the temple officials. Another report stated that Malcolm's congregation in New York City financed his Los Angeles endeavor, though Muhammad contributed to the balance of his expenses. In *The Autobiography*, Malcolm modestly records that having established the work in Los Angeles, he "went visiting" at the *Herald-Dispatch* and "worked in their office." Malcolm's "visit" obviously resulted in his making a significant impression on publisher Alexander, a Caribbean admirer of Marcus Garvey who quickly became quite supportive of Malcolm's endeavors for the Nation of Islam. Their mutual commitment to black nationalism and the Garvey legacy may help to explain how Malcolm was able to obtain an office at the *Dispatch*, share the paper's secretarial support, and obtain publication space for "God's Angry Men."

Muhammad's summit with Los Angeles leaders was ill-fated, however, the Messenger falling prey to a severe cold, cough, and bronchitis. Having given only an initial press conference in Los Angeles, Muhammad departed the next day, requiring Malcolm to stand in his place. In his speech before the mostly male audience that filled the Embassy to its 1,800-seat capacity, Malcolm complained that more businessmen had turned out than clergy, even though Muhammad had come with an agenda of unity that would allow them to fight against "a common enemy." The lack of support from the clergy, then, set the tone for Malcolm's speech, which began with the observation that it is better to talk to a black minister in front of his congregation "rather than in a corner somewhere," because most of these ministers would "talk with the Honorable Elijah Muhammad behind the door and agree with every thing he says." Yet despite the private harmony between Muhammad and these Christian ministers, Malcolm said, "they will come into the church and try to tell you that Mr. Muhammad is wrong. We are tired of this."[8]

Though Malcolm complained about the inconsistency of these black ministers, their behavior is understandable in retrospect. After all, the Nation of Islam was an extremely controversial movement which, despite the congeniality of Muhammad and Malcolm X toward individual ministers, consistently vilified the black church and its clergy as much as it did the white man. While some ministers might have been attracted to Muhammad's blunt assessment of white society, they would hardly want to be identified with his movement for obvious reasons. Muhammad had labeled the black clergy "the white man's right hand," showing himself particularly peeved when a Methodist pastor in Indianapolis reneged on an offer to allow the Nation of Islam to use his church facilities for a meeting in 1959. The pastor, Muhammad said, showed more "natural fear of the devil than Allah" and consequently negated the salvation of himself and his followers.[9]

In a high-profile case, Muhammad was far more critical of the eminent clergyman, Lightfoot Solomon Michaux, for similar reasons. Born in Virginia, the talented pastor and evangelist founded the Gospel Spreading Church of God, an organization of seven congregations over which he presided as Elder. Having organized his min-

istry in late 1919, Michaux was one of the first black radio and television evangelists, and was known throughout the world for his "Happy
Am I" broadcasts. One of the distinctives of Michaux's teachings was
that because "Christian" is a term that originated as a pagan epithet,
the followers of Jesus should call themselves "saints" instead, particularly because it was the term used by the apostles. For his own reason,
then, Michaux agreed with the Black Muslims when they used the
term "so-called Christian." Interestingly, Michaux was also a friend of
Presidents Franklin Roosevelt and Dwight Eisenhower and other
high-ranking officials in the nation's capital—which may suggest why
he also preferred to make his public relationship with Muhammad
appear polemical.

In 1961, Michaux and Muhammad began to correspond about the
possibility of holding a public debate, the discussion having been
broached because of Michaux's undesired link with the Black Muslims in the person of his brother, Lewis Michaux. Lewis had worked
in his brother's ministry up through the 1940s, but their relationship
became strained. When Lewis, who lived in Harlem, became an admiring friend of Malcolm X, the tension between the Michaux brothers increased even more. In Harlem, Lewis Michaux was affection-
ately dubbed "Professor Michaux" by writers, scholars, and other
bookworms who frequented his bookstore on 125th Street. The bookstore, which was originally owned by Elder Michaux's religious organization, became a prominent meeting place for black nationalists in
Harlem. According to his biographer, however, Elder Michaux was
quite disturbed by Lewis's touting of Malcolm X, and "partly out of
anger and frustration with his brother" he "set out to expose and discredit the Muslim movement."[10] The complex situation of brotherly
tension and religious rivalry served Muhammad's agenda, since he
was undoubtedly looking for an occasion to gain more attention in
the African American community with his antagonizing rhetoric
about Christianity.

The program, "Christianity vs. Islam," was billed as a sort of clash
of the titans and advertised in the Washington, D.C., area by
Michaux's church, including a full-page spread in the organization's
Happy News publication. The advertisement portrayed Michaux as a

"champion in a war against the devil," a man of "strong Christian convictions," and a veteran of Christian broadcasting, while Muhammad was noted as a "man of experience and capability" with a "vigorous following." Since both men were dedicated, the event was "expected to be forceful and deliberate in presenting the views that make their cause outstanding." Michaux's stated purpose for involvement was to demonstrate that Christianity was being called into question because "those who preach it and practice it have been so false themselves," though Christianity would ultimately triumph.

The debate took place on Sunday, September 10, 1961, in Griffith Stadium in Washington, D.C. At it turned out, the baseball stadium was packed, undoubtedly much of the audience consisting of the followers of both leaders. As programs go, neither man could have asked for more: Michaux's popularity had begun to wane in later years and he was undoubtedly pleased by the renewed attention it afforded him. The two leaders were dressed appropriately for the drama of the hour. Representing "Islam," Muhammad wore his trademark star-and-crescent pillbox hat, and a dark suit with white shirt and bow tie; on the side of Christ, Elder Michaux was attired in a white suit and shirt ensemble, with dark cravat. Muhammad, who appeared with an entourage of the spartan Fruit of Islam bodyguards, made an especially impressive appearance on the speaker's stand. Bedecked in the stars-and-stripes of the U.S. flag, the covered platform was thoroughly flanked by Muhammad's guard, all of whom were dressed in dark suits and bow ties—and an additional line of men also stretched around the entire baseball diamond, presenting a formidable display of security for the Messenger. (Michaux's *Happy News* later reported that the attitude of Muhammad's security force had created great disgust among the Christians in the audience, their bitter expressions reflecting disregard for all except Muhammad.) In turn, Michaux was provided personal protection by an officer from the Metropolitan Police Department and, unknown to Muhammad, "the Police had concealed within the Griffith Stadium in strategic positions, a security force of their own, thoroughly prepared for anything the Muslims wished to initiate." Of course, Malcolm X was also present on the stand, having led a motorcade of as many as fifty buses from the New

York mosque, which the Black Muslims probably shared with Michaux's New York followers. After the debate, the leaders posed for photographs with their bespectacled wives—Michaux's spouse attired in a conservatively styled dress, with corsage and dress gloves, and Clara Muhammad's apparel an all-white "Muslim" gown, the suit including head veil and dress gloves. The two couples momentarily posed together on the platform—the leaders appearing to be quite pleased while their wives seemed elegantly uncomfortable.

An event of sacred bells and whistles, "Christianity vs. Islam" was hardly significant in theological terms. Indeed, despite the attention it provided him, Elder Michaux probably regretted the affair afterwards. In its wake, he was "labeled a racial conservative by many witnesses and receded further into the national background." Worse, the event seems to have marked the hardening of tensions into real enmity between the brothers Michaux. Lewis remained devoted to Malcolm X; unable to rein him into the church, the Elder eventually broke with Lewis and even wrote him out of his will. Of course, Elder Michaux was a conservative who vehemently criticized black activists whether they were nationalists or civil rights types, blaming them for exacerbating the racial schism between blacks and whites. However, it seems that his harshness may have been more an expression of personal resentment, because he generally tended to diminish those over whom he could not exercise authority. Since he had no influence on either nationalists or civil rights activists, Elder Michaux denounced them, even though he privately shared sentiments of race pride that were perhaps more honestly reflected by his brother Lewis in Harlem.[11]

Furthermore, Michaux was afterward criticized by Muhammad himself, the Messenger charging him with the same hypocrisy that other Christian ministers had demonstrated toward the Nation of Islam. In one installment of his regular column, Muhammad published an article entitled "The Blindness of the Negro Preachers" shortly after the event at Griffith Stadium. In the article, he castigated Michaux (and Martin Luther King, Jr., though on a different point), revealing that prior to the "Christianity vs. Islam" event, Michaux had actually traveled to Chicago and met Muhammad in his home on

September 7, 1961. "In secret, this Elder Michaux had agreed at my home," Muhammad wrote, "that he believed in what I was teaching and that he believed the white man to be the devil." According to Muhammad, however, because there were "devils" in the Griffith Stadium audience, Michaux openly declared his "love" for white people, showing himself to be a "double-crossing, hypocriting [sic]" preacher who "cannot be trusted with good leadership."

Of course, Muhammad's words must be weighed carefully. On one hand, he was probably telling the truth. It is likely that in private conversation the two leaders found it easy to agree on the indecent and often criminal behavior of whites. Both Muhammad and Michaux were not only sagacious observers of white society, but as Southern men they each knew the depths of racial depravity to which whites would go in attacking black people. Behind closed doors, it seems, Michaux could shed the "good Negro" garments he had perhaps chosen to wear in the presence of men such as President Eisenhower and FBI director J. Edgar Hoover. Muhammad naturally saw Michaux's approach as hypocritical; he expected black ministers to be as straightforward about their feelings in public as he had been, and he felt betrayed when these supposed black allies retreated to Christian rhetoric in public statements. On the other hand, Muhammad was as much an opportunist and hypocrite as Elder Michaux, if more so. Muhammad was well aware that he was entering into a temporary working relationship with a fellow black leader whose theology and ideology required a different strategy with regard to race relations. To attempt an exposé on Michaux after the fact was dirty work.

According to an FBI telephone surveillance (TESUR) report, in August 1961 the two leaders had an agreeable conversation in anticipation of their joint effort in Washington, D.C. They discussed expenses, security, and other details, after which Muhammad promised: "This can be the most, ah, greatest meeting, of your whole career. You can have half of Washington there." While Michaux was probably pleased with the potential it afforded, he emphasized to Muhammad that "he would only stand up for the point of Christ," though Muhammad should feel free to say anything his doctrine allowed. Interestingly, both men concluded by agreeing that the meeting could "bring this nation to God"—though the only nation Muhammad was interested in was the black nation over which he presided. In contrast, by virtue of his Christian philosophy, Elder Michaux held his arms open to whites, and his hope for the "nation" obviously entailed a spiritual renewal for all people, including racial reconciliation. The Elder's ambition to exercise authority and enjoy renewed popularity aside for the moment, Michaux was a conservative by philosophy and his presence in the nation's capital inevitably brought him into contact with white leaders. Rather than viewing him as a hypocrite, Muhammad failed to credit Michaux with an astute level of diplomacy necessary for any black leader to survive, especially one living on the threshold of the "devil's" capital. Perhaps Muhammad also held feelings of contempt and jealousy toward Elder Michaux going back to his own inglorious days in Washington, D.C., prior to his imprisonment. In their phone conversation, Muhammad noted that he had not heard Michaux's voice "since the late 1930s"—probably a reference to his having listened to Michaux's "Happy Am I" radio broadcasts. Unlike Michaux, Muhammad's career in Washington ended in defeat; without Malcolm X to build the Temple People movement into the Nation of Islam, Muhammad's work in Washington, like his overall organization, would have remained far less impressive than Michaux's thriving, multi-city ministry.[12]

In retrospect, if anything remarkable came out of the Michaux-Muhammad affair, it was a little-known sermon that Malcolm X gave at Michaux's New York church in anticipation of the Washington debate. The appearance of Malcolm X in Michaux's church demonstrates the extent of the planning of the two groups in endeavoring to create an orientation of cooperation and unity—an orientation that is more reflective of Malcolm X's maturing vision than of Muhammad's bitter, opportunistic approach toward black Christian ministers. According to a surveillance report prepared by New York City's Bureau of Special Services, a fellowship meeting was conducted on June 19, 1961, at Elder Michaux's church at 220 West 145th Street in Harlem. Apparently, Lewis Michaux had served as the go-between, the plans for the service being made on site at the "Professor's" bookstore, which he apparently renamed the "National *African* Memorial

Bookstore" and dubbed "the House of Common Sense and Home of Proper Propaganda." To no surprise, the Michaux bookstore became the favorite site for lone street-corner orators and huge street rallies, many of which featured the fiery Malcolm X.[13]

The premise of the service, which included Black Muslims in the audience as well as Michaux's congregants, was to cultivate a mutual understanding between the groups. Michaux preached prior to Malcolm, using the Qur'an as a sign of good faith, while Malcolm X preached from the King James version of the Bible—something he normally did, anyway. In some respects, of course, Malcolm's message in Michaux's church was typical of all his Nation of Islam sermons. Most notably, Malcolm reiterated the centrality of Elijah Muhammad, alluded to the Exodus theme in discussing the enslavement and oppression of blacks, and proposed that the only solution for blacks was separation from whites under the banner of Allah. On the other hand, Malcolm's sermon in Michaux's church was significantly different from his Nation of Islam sermons, not only because his oratory and style were far more Christian than "Muslim" but because the message itself showed evidence of Malcolm's reemerging religious roots. In a broader sense, this sermon likewise stood distinctively between the Nation of Islam and his later independent work in 1964–65: its essence was far more religious than the politically oriented addresses that characterized his closing months in the Nation of Islam (resulting, as he admitted, from his disillusionment with Muhammad) and his independent work. On the other hand, the Malcolm X preaching behind Elder Michaux's pulpit was not so much a fundamentalist zealot as he was a prophet emerging on his own terms; though he still sounded like Muhammad's representative, he also sounded like the preacher son of Earl and Louise Little. Indeed, in a very real sense, the sermon was the second coming of Earl Little.

Malcolm premised his talk by differentiating Elder Michaux from the mass of black preachers and characterized his host as "a very charming man" unlike "the ordinary preacher," who usually does not "hit it off" with the followers of Muhammad. This compliment brought applause from the mixed audience and, after commending Lewis Michaux's high regard for black studies, concluded that since he "has a brother like Elder Michaux, you know that both of them have got to be good men." Malcolm next established the religious identity of the Nation of Islam by pointing out that they believed in the God of the biblical patriarchs and prophets, whose name in the original language was Allah.

Malcolm explained to his audience that the biblical characters spoke Arabic. Emphasizing that "Jesus didn't speak English" and thus did not use the term "God," Malcolm said that in biblical time even the English-speaking people were not yet speaking English. "They were up in the caves and hills of Europe on their all-fours and they didn't know how to talk!" (*applause*). Still, apart from this standard presentation of early Europeans as beastlike people, Malcolm's insistence that Jesus and the other biblical characters spoke Arabic was equally self-serving. In fact, had Malcolm been consistent with what he had undoubtedly studied in his famous prison readings, he would have acknowledged that the biblical characters spoke ancient Hebrew and Aramaic, not Arabic. But teaching that the biblical characters spoke Arabic reinforced the integrity of "Islam" in the ears of the unlearned, and Malcolm knew it. "When Jesus met his followers in those days," he continued, "he said 'Salaam Alaikum' and they replied 'alaikum Salaam'—which means, 'Peace be unto you' and in return 'And unto you be peace.'" Even when Jesus was hanging on the cross, according to Malcolm, he cried out "*Allah Allah* lama sabacthani." Of course, Malcolm was wrong; he was forcing Arabic onto biblical texts that were based on the Aramaic that was spoken in the time and culture of Jesus. To be sure, Arabic is far more similar to Aramaic than English, but Malcolm nevertheless distorted history in order to persuade his listeners that Islam was the religion of the Bible.

Malcolm's continued commitment to the message of Muhammad was also evident in his harsh treatment of the black Christian minister. Carefully putting aside Michaux as an exception to the rule, Malcolm blamed the lack of unity among African Americans on "*ignorant* preachers" who "served more gods than One," which Malcolm said was the source of the division. "One God, not two gods, three gods, four gods or five gods, but one God. And as Elder Michaux will tell you, when you serve one God then you have unity." It was a remarkable piece of theological diplomacy, especially since Michaux himself embraced Trinitarian doctrine. By attributing to Michaux a belief in the unity of God, Malcolm was simultaneously telling Michaux's Christians that the doctrine of the Trinity was incorrect and divisive. Malcolm also compared black preachers to the priests of Baal, whom the prophet Elijah defeated in a contest on Mount Carmel, and then repeated the Nation of Islam's favorite claim that Muhammad was the prophesied Elijah who was to come. As Elijah the Prophet, then, Muhammad was facing off with the false prophets of the land. "And the Baal prophets to us means everyone of the so-called Negro preachers here in America who have been teaching our people to believe in mystery gods and strange gods." The black preacher was thus sharing the religion of the slavemaster: "Go to their church—they're going into the same church that the slavemaster does."

Malcolm proceeded to discuss the Muslim world, emphasizing that Islam was the original religion "where the white man kidnaped us from, and brought us from in chains four hundred years ago." Citing Billy Graham's recent trip to Africa, Malcolm repeated the report given by the famous Christian evangelist concerning the dominance of Islam in Africa. The religion of Islam was growing, Malcolm said, "because the black man in Africa today is waking up," throwing off the chains of colonialism and "turning away from the religion of Christianity back toward the religion of their forefathers, the religion of Islam"—the same religion being taught by Elijah Muhammad to "the masses of black people right here in America."

"Elder Michaux, you have to excuse my Bible if it's a little worn out—it's worn out because I *use* it," Malcolm said in an aside to his host. "If it was new you'd know I've been sitting on it a long time" (*audience laughter*). Turning to the book of Genesis, Malcolm began to expound on prophesies of enslavement and deliverance, tracing them to fulfillment in the modern United States. "So the Bible is a good book," Malcolm concluded.

> It's the Word of God. But you have to understand it. The book says when it's about to close: "Blessed are those that read and understand."

It don't say reading it will make you blessed. You've got to understand it to be blessed. If reading the Bible [*pounding his fist on the podium*] would make you blessed, there wouldn't be a Negro in America suffering. But nobody reads Bibles more than the Negro and no one catches more hell than the so-called Negro here in America.

Recognizing the Christian reverence for the Bible, Malcolm did not refer to it as the "poisoned book." Despite his Black Muslim appeal to the need to properly understand the Bible, it was uncharacteristic of the Nation of Islam to speak of the Bible in such overtly Christian terms as "the Word of God." At this point it becomes clear that Malcolm was not making an appeal primarily to Elijah Muhammad's authority, though the sermon is replete with references to him. Malcolm characteristically quoted the Bible a great deal in his Nation of Islam sermons, but his guiding principle was always Elijah Muhammad. To the Black Muslims, the Bible, like the Qur'an, was revelation, but always mediated through the Messenger. In this sermon, however, Malcolm became a Christian preacher whose text was "thus saith the Lord." Likewise, his sermon was not merely a potent, spirited lecture typical of his sermons in the mosque, it was preaching—preaching the way Earl Little preached. Not merely a representative of the Nation of Islam, in Elder Michaux's pulpit Malcolm Little found himself standing in the shoes of Elder Earl Little, the "visiting preacher" — and found himself filling those shoes with his father's spirit, his father's voice, and his father's righteous indignation:

> . . .black people who are strangers in this land right now. Strangers so much so you're called a second-class citizen. Strangers so much so that you are not granted civil rights. Strangers so much so you have to ride on the back of the bus up North as well as down South. Is that right or wrong? (*From the audience: "Right!"*)
>
> But the *Bible says*, and *God says in this book*, "but also that nation whom they shall serve will I judge. And afterward they shall come out with great substance."

Malcolm was working his way back home now—still carrying Elijah Muhammad with him, to be sure, but nevertheless moving closer to home, a home he once had and a life he once lived. Preaching like his father, he was also watching Earl preaching, watching from his seat on the church pew—a little boy watching his daddy with amazement, all "goggle-eyed" and confused at the movements and shouts, at the cadence, and the ebb and flow of his father's spirit moving onto the church like a great black wave. Malcolm X had grown up thinking, perhaps priding himself on his own indifference to the ways of the church, to his father's jumping and shouting, and to the people's response, "their souls and bodies devoted to singing and praying." He had worked hard to cultivate that other aspect of his father's oratory, the side he loved and admired—the "intelligent" presentation of Marcus Garvey's representative. But this night, in Michaux's pulpit, both sides came alive.

"As Elder Michaux said, we're living at the end of the world," Malcolm continued. Quoting from Ecclesiastes, Malcolm declared: "'Generations come and generations go, but the earth abides forever.' God is not going to destroy the earth." Then the black wave mounted up from inside him, flowing out onto Muhammad's "Muslims" and Michaux's "saints":

> God is going to destroy people! There's more than one world on this earth: There's an eastern world and there's a western world. There's a dark world and a white world. There's an old world and a new world. There's a righteous world and wicked world. Now which world is God going to destroy? He says in this book, "*Behold—*"

Suddenly, in midsentence, he paused. It was as if he had come to his Black Muslim senses again, like he suddenly realized he had been preaching out of character. He was pounding his fist steadily while speaking, but even this he slowed and then stopped; then an apology: "Excuse me for going a little fast." Malcolm quickly explained that his excitement was a result of being taught the truth by Muhammad while seeing "our people misunderstanding." But his excitement went far deeper, farther back, back to a pew in a little Baptist church on the edge of his childhood memories. In the twinkling of an eye, in the pounding of a black fist on the pulpit, Earl Little had returned, and for a brief moment Malcolm Little was goggle-eyed and amazed all over again. Malcolm X the great orator had startled himself into silence.

There seems to have been spiritual tension at this point, but Malcolm pushed forward, refocusing his attention on Muhammad— Elijah as prophet, Elijah as the prophesied one, Elijah as the liberator of blacks and the "warner" of whites. It was almost as if Malcolm had checked himself, gathered up his thoughts and emotions, and put on the Black Muslim identity he had inadvertently set aside for the journey. Now he began to expound on the moral uprightness of Muhammad's followers—"as young as they are," Malcolm said, "none of them drink, smoke, take drugs, gamble"; he listed these righteous abstinences as if he were reading from a page inscribed within his own soul. "They don't lie, they don't cheat, they don't steal, they don't use profanity, and they try their best to be as polite as it is possible to be." Above all, neither did Muhammad's followers commit fornication or adultery. More references to Muhammad followed, yet one gets the impression that beneath the level of Malcolm's sermon another story was being told, a confession made on a plane of conscience and spirit quite out of reach to his audience.

Malcolm continued by expounding upon the work and wisdom of Muhammad, inevitably finding his way to the theme of separation. Separation is not like segregation, Malcolm told his listeners. Unlike segregation, separation is done "voluntarily of your own free will." Using the example of a father and son, Malcolm noted how a boy remains submissive to his father as long as the father provides all his needs. "But when I become twenty-one, I don't want to be inferior, I want to be equal. I want to be a man." Separation, Malcolm said, emerges from the tension between a father and a son who has grown to adulthood. This, Malcolm concluded, is the way Elijah Muhammad says things are with blacks in the United States; it was finally time to stop begging the white man so that he would stop treating the black man like a boy. Muhammad was therefore asking the white man for some land in the United States, Malcolm concluded, "and let us go for ourselves. And if we do that we'll have peace, if we don't do that we won't have peace."[14]

Malcolm's use of the father-son analogy for separation was probably also a spiritual commentary on his own life. Without Earl Little, Malcolm had turned to Elijah Muhammad. Without his natural father Malcolm had turned to the "little lamb" of Georgia, who gave him the necessities of flesh and spirit and, even more, gave him a legacy that he could build. "There was a genuine affection," recalled C. Eric Lincoln, "between these two, not unlike the affection between a father and son who has done well for the family name." Indeed, Lincoln remembered, the first time he saw Elijah Muhammad smile was when Malcolm X entered the room.[15] Malcolm was still clinging to Muhammad, but perhaps he had begun to sense that some day he would also have to leave home.

Interestingly, Malcolm had begun the sermon with an example he attributed to Elijah Muhammad. According to Malcolm, "We can learn a lesson from the bee and the fly. The bee travels from flower to flower," Malcolm said. "It doesn't land just anywhere, and it doesn't land just everywhere." The bee lands on a flower, staying there only long enough to get the best of what that flower offered, and then moved onto the next flower. It is this movement that allows the bee to produce honey, Malcolm said. In contrast, the fly lands in one place and is satisfied, Malcolm explained, "and a fly never has been known to make any honey." The audience laughed at Malcolm's clever illustration, but they obviously understood his point. "But when you sit in one place all of your life, you be like the fly. . . . The fly's mind is closed but the bee's mind is open." Malcolm meant to encourage the interchange between the Nation of Islam and their Christian hosts, but it is likely that the lesson of the bee and the fly did not come from Muhammad, whose approach to religion was exclusive and self-exalting. For all intents and purposes Muhammad *was* the fly, producing nothing vibrant or sweet, and clinging to the same religious claims and boasts. On the other hand, Malcolm was the bee, his nature being to search from life's garden of religious and political variety just like his mother had taught him.

About two weeks later, Malcolm appeared on an evening talk show program in New York called "Community Corner," hosted by Bernice Bass. Considering that the program was airing on a Christian-oriented radio station and that Bass was herself a devout Baptist, it was inevitable that the topic of religion would arise. In fact, it arose immediately. Malcolm characterized Muhammad as a teacher of high morals and reformation among those whose morals were deteriorating. Bass immediately challenged Malcolm as to whether he was suggesting that black non-Muslims were necesssarily people of low morals—a good point, since the Nation of Islam consistently portrayed black Christians as their moral inferiors. Malcolm sought to elude the challenge, suggesting that while most blacks agreed with Muhammad's teachings, they did not feel they could exercise the same restraint demonstrated by the Nation of Islam. Bass would not relent, however, and she reminded Malcolm that many African Americans, including herself, had been brought up in strict Christian homes with equally high moral standards. Malcolm was cornered, and the only way to escape was to play to the conservative values of the listeners. Malcolm lamented that society had become godless, that by not making drunkenness and drug addiction a crime, society had actually made these behaviors legal. Furthermore, Malcolm said, the Supreme Court "did something concerning obscene literature that made it right to be obscene, which means it makes it alright to contribute to the delinquency of people, to incite lust within people and things of that sort." It was a rare moment indeed when Malcolm X was not in the driver's seat during an interview; in debates, his opponents would do well if they were simply able to hold their own. But Bernice Bass clearly had Malcolm reacting to her determined pursuit, and he was reacting badly—his information vague, his point undefended. Bass moved onto another topic, but she had won—at least she had repulsed one reckless Black Muslim charge, succeeding in her defense of the church where many Christian ministers had not even tried.

Perhaps the reason that Bass did so well, of course, was that the general air of the interview was anything but polemical. Indeed, if one word describes this fascinating interview it is charm. There is no doubt that Bass, though strident in her defense of the faith, was quite charmed by Malcolm; at one point going into an advertisement," she even called his name as if to flirt—after which one can almost hear them both smiling. Malcolm, too, was charmed by Bass, and all of his remarks, no matter how caustic, were thus wrapped in a gentleness that one rarely hears in a Malcolm X interview.

"[T]he whole trend of *your* western culture is turning away from spiritual values and moral values toward values of their own, and their own values are not very high at all," Malcolm declared further. Bass responded with the example of drug addiction among people of the East, to which Malcolm immediately invoked the infusion of opium into China by Europeans. Bass countered that drug addiction existed in the East prior to European colonialism, but Malcolm insisted this was not so. Such a notion, Malcolm said, was produced by Europeans in order to misrepresent other cultures.

Bass then raised the question of black preachers, and Malcolm responded with the standard references to Elijah and the prophets of Baal, and Moses and Pharaoh's magicians. When Bass challenged that Muhammad was not the only legitimate religious leader, Malcolm insisted that all Christian ministers are false, no matter who they are. Bass adjusted her strategy, complementing Malcolm on his usage of the Bible and suggesting he had learned about the scriptures from his father, whom he often said was a Baptist minister. "No! I didn't learn anything about the Bible from my father," Malcolm responded bluntly. "Oh?" Bass replied. "How did you learn it?"

> I learned it after becoming a follower of the Honorable Elijah Muhammad. I didn't learn anything from my father other than how to suffer peacefully and love my enemy, and forgive those who misuse me. But it was after becoming a follower of the Honorable Elijah Muhammad. He teaches us to read everything, to read Christian literature, Buddhist literature, Jewish literature, we read everything—we're supposed to keep an opened mind and weigh everything.[16]

It was an incredible declaration, even taken at face value. Never had Earl Little looked so bad, never had Elijah Muhammad looked so good. One would have thought that Malcolm's father was the passive Martin Luther King, Jr., instead of the devoted Garveyite activist who shot his pistol at two white arsonists fleeing into the night. Likewise, one would have thought that Elijah Muhammad was Bembry the prison philosopher or, better, yet, Louise Little, encouraging her children to read widely on religion, "keep an opened mind and weigh everything." Like the lesson of the fly and the bee in his sermon at

Michaux's church, Malcolm was clearly attributing things to Muhammad that came from deep within himself, just as he was imposing things upon his father that came from outside the Little family.

For Malcolm, it was ironic that the Nation of Islam always announced that Elijah the prophet had finally come in fulfillment of the ancient prophecy, "to turn the hearts of the children to their fathers." As long as Malcolm X embraced Elijah Muhammad as his father, he was dutybound to deny the man who had brought him into the world, to minimize the powerful orator and dedicated activist who charged his earliest memories, and skew the legacy of his "Christian" struggle on behalf of black people. "We are living at the end of the world," Malcolm had announced at Michaux's church in Harlem, exalting in what he believed was the imminent demise of Western Christian dominance. Yet another world was also waxing old like a garment, and soon its skies would be rolled up like a scroll. In the wake of Earl Little's second coming, Malcolm X did not realize that his own world was soon to go up in flames.

10

A Double Portion of Fire
Malcolm X in the Wilderness of North America

Jesus was born nine thousand miles from here, and you can call on him as much as you want to and the white man will still put his rope around your neck.

—Malcolm X, speaking in a Harlem rally,
in *Daily Defender*, June 20, 1963

Now it came about when they had crossed over, that Elijah said to Elisha, "Ask what I shall do for you before I am taken from you." And Elisha said, "Please, let a double portion of your spirit be upon me."

—II Kings 2:9

The voices questioning me became to me as breathing, living devils. And I tried to pour on pure fire in return.

—Malcolm X, *The Autobiography of Malcolm X*

Malcolm X never aspired to become an orator before a white audience. He wrote in his autobiography that, while still in prison, he used to lie on his cell bunk and picture himself "talking to large crowds," but he did not say if those imaginary audiences were integrated or even all white. From the time of his earliest work for the Nation of Islam while incarcerated, Malcolm reached exclusively to blacks, and all of his later efforts in building the movement were concentrated on the black community. By virtue of the organization's philosophy alone it would have mattered little to him if whites had never heard him at all. "The trouble was that history overtook Malcolm and the airtight little Nation of Islam," and once it had, Malcolm X had to develop a ministry with no precedent in the entire history of the Nation of Islam phenomenon, especially Muhammad's movement. Gradually, one interview at a time, one college speaking engagement at a time—one "devil" at a time—Malcolm X became what *white* people considered a public figure.

At that point, of course, civil rights leaders—perhaps out of jealousy—often charged the media with creating Malcolm X's public career. However, the most discerning and eloquent voice from the media rejects such a notion, recognizing that "Malcolm created himself." Still, white journalists "did find him irresistible," he adds, "and, through us and our media, he reached that other country called Black America."[1] But this is both sincerity and presumption: whites in the media, like whites in his growing audience on the college speaking circuit, were indeed charmed and enthralled by the public Malcolm X. However, it was Malcolm who introduced himself and the Nation of Islam to black America, not the self-defined white media. The African Americans that Malcolm X could not reach in his extensive road trips, speaking engagements, and "fishing" expeditions from Boston to Los Angeles and from Detroit to Atlanta, he reached through the black press and, if nothing else, the "grapevine." This is not whimsy: *whites have always underestimated the ability of black people to analyze and communicate their analyses throughout the community*. Neither is it to suggest that the mainstream media did not reach African Americans with word of the Black Muslims; but by the time they did, the Nation of Islam was already known. It is more correct to suggest that blacks merely *reacted* to the white man's reports concerning the Nation of Islam in ways they had not done previously. Those reactions, whether genuine or effected, were far less about Black Muslims and far more about black people in their perpetual role as the emotional babysitter of the *Afriphobic* white community in the United States.

In public, of course, black leaders reacted to "mainstream" media news about the Nation of Islam in predictable ways. When the first stories about Muhammad's movement hit the pages of *Time* and *Newsweek* in the summer of 1959, Martin Luther King, Jr., took his cue from white liberals and prophesied woe, calling the Nation of Islam one of the "hate groups arising in our midst which would preach a doctrine of black supremacy"—quickly adding that black supremacy was *as bad* as white supremacy. Of course, King—who was himself snubbed by Southern black ministers who feared association with his integrationist efforts—was no fool. Although he genuinely differed with the Black Muslim philosophy, King undoubtedly knew that "black supremacy" existed only in the black world of rhetoric, while in the United States only one form of supremacy reigned, either in ruthless terror or manipulative paternalism. If he did not realize this, he quickly learned from the stern rebuke he received from Elijah Muhammad, who lashed out against King in his "Muhammad Speaks" column. Muhammad reprimanded the minister for saying that black supremacy was as bad as white supremacy, charging that King was attempting to please "the white devils" and consequently proving himself "either neutral or a hypocrite on both sides—the black and white nations." King was not only motivated by "fear of the devils," Muhammad said, but his words showed that he had never experienced the horrors of white supremacy.

> He has never lived under his own people's rule. He never has seen the black man lynching and burning the black man. He never had the experience of having to go on freedom rides, sit-in strikes under black rule, to force them to serve him. Mr. King and his followers are showing the world that they love white supremacy, and hope it will rule them forever.

Muhammad concluded bitterly that King's words were the "worst teaching I have ever heard of in this modern day," and expressed his wish that the "scared, rotten, white-poisoned preachers should be driven to the rear of the people until they learn that we, the Black Nation ... will rule successfully ourselves—without the help of those devils."[2]

While other leaders had made similar condemnations of the Nation of Islam premised on the idea of black supremacy, Derrick Bell, executive secretary of the Pittsburgh branch of the NAACP, issued a statement over radio station KDKA, saying that "the Negro community is not shocked" at white revelations concerning the Nation of Islam, and were actually accustomed to groups arising in the community that espoused nationalist sentiments. Bell also stated that the NAACP had been "advised by several sincere individuals" (read *white liberals*) to "denounce the Muslims in no uncertain terms" by means of full-page ads in "local" (read *black*) newspapers, and to condemn even the *Pittsburgh Courier* for printing Muhammad's column. Rather than assuaging white fear, however, Bell took the mature position that the solution was not to censor the Nation of Islam but to put an end to "the human suffering and spiritual bankruptcy" that fueled Black Muslim hatred of the white man. (This eventually became the standard approach of civil rights leaders regarding the Black Muslims and, later, the independent Malcolm X. Civil rights leaders quickly learned to use Malcolm X as an example of "extremism," in a kind of scare-ology tactic that would make the integrationist movement seem far more appealing.) Pointing out that Black Muslim threats were so far quite empty, especially in comparison to the violence of white supremacists, Bell concluded with a final dose of reality: "As to [*the Black Muslim*] hatred of whites, this may come as a shock, but many, many Negroes did not need Elijah Muhammad and his Muslim doctrine for that. Correctly or not, thousands of Negroes have long since attributed their lowly position in the American social and economic scale to whites."[3] Of course, the pros and cons of black supremacy were never a concern to black leaders until the mainstream media made it a life-or-death issue to the black community.

In April 1962, after the terrible assault of Chief Parker's cowboy-police on the Nation of Islam mosque[4] in Los Angeles, Malcolm understandably wept, then raged. He had founded the Los Angeles mosque and, amid the seven unarmed victims of police gunfire, the man who died was a longtime friend. Subsequently, when an airplane full of Southern whites crashed in Europe, Malcolm vented in exultation that God had delivered some justice in lieu of the white man's system of law and order.[5] The immediate result was that black leaders were obligated to react to mainstream reports—not about the travesty of injustice in Los Angeles, but Malcolm's jubilation over the plane crash. "We want it clearly understood," declared an alliance of ninety Los Angeles area ministers, "that we are in no way related to the Muslim movement. We repudiate its total doctrine of black supremacy and the attempt to place one American against another. We suspect that the Muslim movement wears the garb of religion but in reality is just another nationalistic movement."[6]

The ministers were reacting because Malcolm had loomed over Los Angeles in the aftermath of the attack, harshly criticizing Chief Parker and Mayor Yorty, and reminding black Angelinos that the siege on the mosque was really just another case of the brutality of the Los Angeles police against black people. Another reactionary charge came from Ralphe Bunche, United Nations Under-Secretary, who called Malcolm a man with "a depraved mind" for his vengeful remarks about the plane crash. However, it is doubtful that either Bunche or the Los Angeles clergy would have responded had they not felt obligated to protect white sensitivities. A year later, in the summer of 1963, when Malcolm appeared on Barry Farber's radio program in New York City, Farber tried to browbeat Malcolm for his plane crash remark. Malcolm responded by questioning why Farber had not shown as much anger over the police assault on the Black Muslims in Los Angeles—at which point Farber blew his cool. Malcolm was right and Farber unwittingly proved it by his defensiveness.[7] As Malcolm's lone voice demonstrated, the mainstream media were much more disturbed by his bitter expressions about the plane crash than they were about cold steel being pumped into the heart of an unarmed black man. As far as black leadership was concerned, however, they would probably never have protested the Nation of Islam as a hate group unless whites had required it.

Interestingly, a remark made by the evangelist Billy Graham in New York City appeared in the *Pittsburgh Courier* in early 1959, expressing the growing concern of white leadership about New York's racial tensions, and perhaps hinting at the influence of the Black Muslims. "New Yorkers can scarcely afford to point a finger at the South for its handling of social problems," Graham declared. Graham, a Southerner, referred to the Big Apple's racial tensions and other social and economic ills as being on par with segregation in the

South. To be sure, Graham stood on feet of iron and clay when it came to racism, though at this stage he appeared to be progressive by desegregating his crusades and speaking out against prejudice in his messages. While admonishing New Yorkers, Graham perhaps defensively asserted a more responsible leadership was also emerging in the South.

Of course, New York's city fathers were well aware of their race relations problem—a problem that the media increasingly associated with the presence of Malcolm X and the Black Muslims throughout 1960. When New York City's Commission on Intergroup Relations (COIR) released its Annual Report for 1960, it listed the rise of "nationalist movements" as a "major development." The growing dissent expressed by "black nationalists," COIR said, included "Muslims . . . in the City's Negro areas." COIR clearly wished to allay the fears of Mayor Wagner and his administration by stating that even though "many Negroes are dissatisfied," most had rejected the "strident appeals" of the nationalists and the Nation of Islam. "But," COIR added, "the movements bear watching." COIR also reported that blacks were increasingly developing a "sense of identity" vis-à-vis the "civil rights struggles at home and the rising tide of African independence and leadership." The report concluded this section with two recommendations: that black nationalist groups be "investigated" and "interpreted" for "public and private leadership," and that New York City develop an educational and informational program "to place in proper perspective the City's substantial efforts to secure the rights of all residents." Whether or not Mayor Wagner's administration was able to advance educational programs demonstrating New York's commitment to equal rights, it is clear that the City renewed its determination to investigate and interpret the nationalists and Black Muslims for New York's private leadership. Malcolm X, of course, was already a major target of New York City Police Department surveillance, and as Malcolm's impact on city race relations continued to increase, it seems private leadership became even more concerned about his activities.[8]

If Malcolm's oratory and analysis were the vehicle by which he traveled to national prominence, then religion served as the wheels of that vehicle. Until the final phase of his time in the Nation of Islam, Malcolm's presentations were often religious—something that stopped only when he began to wrestle with the reality of Muhammad's religious and moral hypocrisy. It must have been a painful irony for Malcolm, after spending the bulk of his career castigating black ministers, to find that Muhammad was no better—and perhaps far worse than most of the black Christian preachers he liked to ridicule. "Please don't call me Reverend!" Malcolm X had told an interviewer in 1957. "Those who sought such a title and now wear it, have made it become one of scorn and ridicule—by not living up to what it implies." Malcolm told the same reporter that the black church was continually being torn by petty arguments, jealousy, and the quest for power by small leaders. Gradually, with the waning of the 1950s, however, he began to discover that the Nation of Islam was not immune from jealousy, including the Messenger and his family. After all he had done to highlight the problems of the church, Malcolm began to see that the Black Muslim movement was no different, although he did not acknowledge the similarities between self-serving Christian fundamentalism and the panacea of the Black Muslims until he had totally disassociated himself from the Nation of Islam. Later Malcolm would even differentiate between sincere people within the Nation of Islam and the movement's corrupt leadership. However, he never granted the same grace to the Christian church in any public statement.

As exemplified in his sermon at Elder Michaux's church, even though Malcolm often railed against Christian ministers and called Christian churches "iceboxes" where people's brains were "frozen" to the point of passivity, he was not personally hostile toward the clergy, nor was he averse to speaking in churches upon invitation. Perhaps the most high profile case in this regard is Malcolm's rapport with Adam Clayton Powell, Jr., the notable politician-pastor of Harlem's Abyssinian Baptist Church. As a guest speaker in what the *Pittsburgh Courier* called "an unprecedented display of religious unity," Malcolm addressed a joint audience of Christians and Nation of Islam members as part of Abyssinian's "Unity of Harlem's Black Citizens" program in June 1957. Though Powell had fallen ill in the afternoon and was not in attendance to hear him, Malcolm X praised Abyssinian's famous pastor as a "man who has today dedicated his life to the betterment of the black man's plight here in America." However, Malcolm's words of unity were hardly ecumenical, for only in alliance under Muhammad's "Islam," Malcolm said, would the black man find "dignity, pride and love of his own kind." Acknowledging the political influence represented in Abyssinian's large congregation, Malcolm nevertheless concluded by insisting once more on the unity of "Islam."

There was nothing unusual about Malcolm's strident, single-minded appeal to Muhammad, except that his remarks about "Islam" at the Abyssinian Baptist church sounded less like Muhammad's religion and more like the traditional religion of Islam. "Allah is the supreme being, creator of heaven and earth," Malcolm declared, "God of Moses, Jesus, Abraham, Muhammad and all other prophets."[9] There was no mention of W. D. Fard as Savior and God incarnate, which suggests that despite his faith in Muhammad, Malcolm may have begun to find the full gospel of the Nation of Islam awkward to preach outside of the Black Muslim context. Of course, this explanation might not appear to hold up given the fact that there are examples, even as late as 1963, when Malcolm proclaimed Fard in public remarks. However, those later comments about Fard likely reflect deliberate attempts by Malcolm X to prove his fidelity at a critical point in his relationship with the Nation of Islam. It is also likely that Malcolm's knowledge of traditional Islam, which dated back to his study of world religions in prison, haunted him at times: perhaps he felt more inclined to speak of the Islam of the Qur'an as opposed to the "Islam" of Elijah Muhammad, especially when he was addressing predominantly Christian and Jewish audiences.

In a speech given at Yale University in 1960, Malcolm opened by declaring himself a representative of Elijah Muhammad, whose appearance and teachings were "the fulfillment of divine prophecy." In discussing the religious credibility of Muhammad, Malcolm insisted that the Messenger was not teaching mere "racial, economic, and political philosophy" but "the real religion of Islam": "My friends, Islam is the religion taught by all of the prophets: Noah, Lot, Abraham,

Moses and even Jesus. Islam is the true name of the religion God gave
to the prophets in the past to cure their people of whatever moral or
spiritual ailments that were afflicting them in that day."[10] In 1961, de-
livering the first of three speeches he would give at Harvard University (but the only one he would deliver as a Black Muslim), Malcolm
X prefaced his address with a similar religious introduction:

> ... [Y]ou must first realize that we are a religious group, and you must
> also know something about our religion, the religion of Islam. The
> creator of the universe, whom many of you call God or Jehovah, is
> known to the Muslims by the name Allah. The Muslims believe there
> is but one God, and that all the prophets came from this one God. We
> believe also that all prophets taught the same religion, and that they
> themselves called that religion Islam, an Arabic word that means com-
> plete submission and obedience to the will of Allah.[11]

Malcolm concluded this very orthodox preface by claiming that the
Nation of Islam was an integral part of the Muslim world of over 750
million believers, "predominately in Africa and Asia, the non-white
world." Despite subsequent remarks about the unique way in which
African Americans had converted, Malcolm gave no hint to his Harvard audience that Muhammad's "Islam" was premised on an incarnate deity named W. D. Fard—though in both the Yale and Harvard
speeches he did make an attempt to address the Muslim critics of
Muhammad's "Islam."

Of course, at this time Malcolm was also building relationships
with traditional Muslims from the East, and he was becoming increasingly aware of the need to place a legitimate Muslim facade on
the religious claims of Muhammad. Along with this, the Nation of
Islam was increasingly subjected to the attacks of black Muslim opponents and their white allies who were attempting to embarrass and
discredit Muhammad. At Harvard, not surprisingly, Malcolm specially emphasized that Muhammad had been received, recognized,
and respected by religious leaders during his trip to the Muslim world
in early 1960. "Yet the American Caucasians, hoping to block his success among our people, continue to oppose him and to say that he is
not a true Muslim."[12] Beyond these claims to legitimacy in the Mus-

lim world, however, what is significant about these remarks is how they appear to deny Muhammad's doctrine of Fard/Allah. For if, as Malcolm told the Harvard audience, Allah was the same as "Jehovah," then Muhammad's teaching about the "Mystery God" of the Christians and Jews was negated. Malcolm's need to link the Nation of Islam to the Muslim world by orthodox declarations was not only the first sign of his developing second conversion (which would culminate with his ouster from the Nation of Islam and the pilgrimage in 1964), but a tacit acknowledgment that Muhammad's theology was heretical. Muhammad never claimed his divinity was the same as the God of the Christians, and by appealing to "God" and "Jehovah" as the creator of the universe, Malcolm was clearly switching from a Black Muslim doctrine (i.e., a primeval black male divinity with a pantheon of lesser black gods sharing in his creative work) to an Abramic doctrine (i.e., the one transcendent, spiritual God).[13]

Malcolm clearly identified with the Muslim world, and wanted the Nation of Islam to be understood as an essential part of it. This was nothing new, however, since Malcolm's attraction to the Muslim world dated back to his conversion in prison and even characterized some of his appeals to prison authorities for religious rights. As the doorway to the Muslim world opened wider, of course, Malcolm's international inclinations became pronounced. Rather than dwell exclusively on biblical texts with a provincial reading of race as did Muhammad, Malcolm increasingly drew strength from the Muslim world for his fight against Christianity. In Malcolm's thinking, the gains of Islam worldwide were bound up with the success of the Nation of Islam. An interesting illustration in this regard is found in an informant's report on a message Malcolm delivered at the New York City mosque on May 13, 1960. In the message, Malcolm held up a copy of the *New York Times*, referring to an article that had appeared that day about Billy Graham's visit to Africa. "It says right here in this white man's paper that Islam is growing faster than Christianity in Africa," Malcolm declared. The article reported statements made by the Christian evangelist during an eight-week crusade through east, central, and west African nations. "I have met a number of people who think Africa may eventually be overwhelmed by Islam," Graham was reported as saying. He added that Christianity and "Christian forces in Africa" thus faced "a tremendous challenge and responsibility," especially in competition with Islam for the devotion of an estimated forty million Africans who had not converted to any "world ideologies."

Reading Graham's remarks through the eyes of Malcolm X makes the article far more fascinating, especially the evangelist's obvious intention to sound an alarm, summoning more missionaries, "particularly American Negro and African missionaries." Graham's concern over the fact that more Africans were "turning to Islam than to Christianity at the moment" was not only reflective of the essential head-counting nature of his endeavor, but was similar to the competitive orientation that Malcolm expressed on behalf of Islam. Indeed, despite the opposite sides upon which they stood, Malcolm and Graham were developing as counterparts—a point that was not missed by Malcolm when he became an independent activist in 1964. Graham's approach to conversions in Africa, like his crusades in general, reflected a numerically oriented model of religious outreach and also resonated ancient hostilities toward the Muslim world. In turn, Malcolm's intense interest in the expansion of Islam among black peoples worldwide went arm-in-arm with his hostility toward Western colonialism and white supremacy, especially as it was manifested in white Christianity.

Likewise, Malcolm probably did not miss the irony in the fact that Graham's endeavors were called "crusades." In Muslim memory, the historical crusades were an expression of Christendom's hostility, aggression, and conquest, during which "Christian armies" (an oxymoron in the perspective of Jesus) moved on the Holy Land to seize it in the name of Christ. Graham's warning to "Christian forces" was embedded in a call for missionaries, but in Malcolm's astute reading it probably also seemed the evangelist was urgently telegraphing a message of great concern to Western interests in Africa. This is not to suggest that Christians ought not to have been concerned about the spread of Islam, nor that tensions between African Muslims and Christians are not indigenous concerns. However, for more than religious reasons, Billy Graham's nightmare was obviously Malcolm's dream-come-true, the former expressing great concern because of his sympathies toward Christian forces on the continent, including the "Christian" government of apartheid South Africa (whose unjust system Graham never reproached throughout his years of ministry). In the same article, Graham also said that the portrayal of Christ as a European had likely influenced Africans to "choose another religion" instead of Christianity. However, the evangelist concluded, Christ was neither white nor black. In contrast, Malcolm clearly saw the white man as being identical to Christianity, as his summary remark demonstrates: "Billy Graham needs Negro missionaries for Africa, do you know what that means brothers and sisters? It means that the Africans are wise to the white man and they don't want any part of Christianity. Now you see it, just as Christianity lost the crusades, he has lost his foothold in Africa."[14]

Finally, Graham's racial retreat, inherent in the statement about Christ's color, was probably not missed by Malcolm. In *The Autobiography*, the last scene in his prison narrative recalls a confrontation between Malcolm and a Harvard Divinity School student who was conducting Bible classes at the Charlestown Prison. "What color was Jesus?" the prisoner Malcolm challenged. The blond instructor blushed, looking perplexed as he walked nervously around the room. "Jesus was brown," he responded. "I let him get away with that compromise," Malcolm recalled. In his speech, Malcolm did not challenge Graham's assertion that Christ was neither black nor white, but he probably discerned that the Christian evangelist's remarks were a tactical compromise, not a challenge to the white supremacy inherent in Western religion.

As Malcolm's work in the Nation of Islam increased in scope, he clearly began to exceed the ability and interests of his leader. While Muhammad shrank away from the Muslim world after his overseas tour in 1959–60, Malcolm's inclination toward it continued to increase as his contacts deepened and his appeals to Muslim solidarity intensified. Similarly, his appointment as national representative of the Nation of Islam virtually put him on a collision course with Muhammad's jealous family, the Messenger being caught in a dilemma of his own making. Muhammad himself had said that the more Malcolm became well known, the more it would advance him.[15] Yet as fame fleshed out in media coverage and pure celebrity, Muhammad became dissatisfied, his notoriety having become largely a reflection on Malcolm's brilliant black armor. Jealous of Malcolm's campus speaking engagements and numerous radio and television appearances, the old prophet perhaps regretted that his young servant had become a prophet in his own right—a prophet with a double portion of his spirit, and a double portion of his fire. Indeed, perhaps Muhammad was secretly galled by the scripture that said no student could be greater than his master.

In 1960, a journalist expressed a surprising degree of admiration for the Nation of Islam, though his remarks undoubtedly pertained to Malcolm's specific impact in New York City. "They are the only group that seems to be able to maintain some stability and decorum in these diplomatic dog-days," he wrote concerning Malcolm's eminent presence at the side of Fidel Castro during his recent stay at Harlem's Theresa Hotel. Furthermore, as debates raged between rival nationalist groups in Harlem, the journalist concluded, the Black Muslim had risen above his peers: "Malcolm X is a very persuasive gentleman who knows how to keep his head and make the most of a bad situation." Of course, ever since his conversion in prison, Malcolm had been making the most of a bad situation, but along with his growing prestige he cultivated his fire so as to do the most oratorical damage without engendering physical harm. Though the media inevitably took Malcolm's controversial statements out of context (that is, out of the context of black experience) and generalized them into a frightening portrait of a black racist, few journalists balanced their assessment of Malcolm with his personal gentility, good humor, and thoughtfulness. For all of his fire, Malcolm X was no rabble-rouser; it has always been police brutality and simple injustice that have prompted violent eruptions in the black community—and despite the fact that Malcolm's words were labeled "violent," no one ever died from being called a "blue-eyed, bad-smelling white man." Malcolm's sharp diatribes were often sheathed in humor, proving to his listeners that turning the table on the white man was far more effective than turning the other cheek to the white man. Still, even when Malcolm's words were spoken in anger, he exercised an amazing ability to steer his followers and audiences across a terrain of cathartic outrage to an intelligent destination.

Malcolm X taught his parishioners that despite the philosophy of the Nation of Islam, they would have to cooperate with whites in circumstances where necessity overrode preference. Speaking before his congregation in 1959, Malcolm pointed out that some of the followers had children enrolled in "Christian schools," which seems to have meant the public school system, though it may have been a reference to parochial schools. Malcolm told his parishioners that despite the teachings of the Nation of Islam, they ought to train their children to live peacefully with white students and teachers. Parents, he said, were especially to come to an understanding with teachers, lest thinking of them as devils would create problems for their children. White teachers, Malcolm concluded, should have their respect and their children's respect "one hundred percent."

Whites were too wounded by his harsh public statements to realize that even though Malcolm used words like fire, his fires were purposeful. From political dogma to the shape of noses and skin color, Malcolm burned away the assumptions of a society steeped in white supremacy, many times ruthlessly. However, his derogatory comments about whites were also part of a larger picture—a scenario that included police assaults, coupled with increased media attacks on the Nation of Islam, *and* the shadowy background of Black Muslim jealousy and resentment that required Malcolm to outdo even himself in an effort to prove his faithfulness. Indeed, the public image of Malcolm X preserved by the media is especially based on this difficult period of 1962–63, when his popularity in the press was rising at the same time as he was losing his sense of security within the Nation of Islam.

Still, Malcolm was never out of control. In a 1963 Harlem rally in which he castigated the hypocrisy of Democrats and called the United States the black man's "concentration camp," Malcolm declared: "You can't change the white man; he is a born devil." Undoubtedly aware that there were whites sprinkled in his audience,

Malcolm told the Harlemites that if a white happened to be standing next to them, they should make believe that "white devil" was not there. Perhaps it seemed he was going out of his way to incite a snub, but it is more likely that this was Malcolm X's way of making sure that the few whites scattered in the audience would not be harassed.

At the same time, not all of Malcolm's white audiences were polite, and his response to their hostility was another way in which he demonstrated he could "keep his head and make the most of a bad situation." A writer who was studying theology in the early 1960s, recalled hearing Malcolm speak to a mostly white audience at the University of Pennsylvania at an event sponsored by the NAACP. The crowd hissed, booed, and some even waved Confederate flags while Malcolm was trying to speak. Malcolm, whose dignity was his armor, "seemed oblivious of their scorn" even though the jeering got so loud that he had to pause from speaking. "Are you sure this is the University of Pennsylvania?" Malcolm asked in a momentary lapse of hissing and booing. "It sounds more like Pitt—snake pit." Having delivered the rebuff, Malcolm calmly resumed his speech, completing it with a "cordial disdain" for the antagonistic white audience. Afterward, the writer approached Malcolm and began to quiz him regarding the Nation of Islam's lack of theology. It was a good question and it was delivered in private conversation—enabling Malcolm to respond in a manner different than he might have responded if the question had arisen in debate. Malcolm smiled and said: "You can't put down a pavement until you've laid the foundation."[16]

This response was another tacit admission that the religious teachings of the Nation of Islam were problematic. Malcolm seems to have been implying that the necessary foundation was the gathering of black people under a religious banner other than the cross. With this accomplished, the pavement—a sound theology—could be laid. Malcolm likely thought of Sunni Islam as the pavement most adequate for blacks, a smooth, solid surface upon which they could walk toward liberation. Thus, despite his growing inner awareness that the Nation of Islam was in tension with the Muslim world, Malcolm continued to advance the belief that Muhammad's teachings were the most appropriate manifestation of "Islam" for African Americans.

In a pretaped radio program in New York City called "Pro and Con," Malcolm appeared along with the Reverend William James of Harlem's Metropolitan Community Methodist Church in March 1960. Unfortunately, the discussion with Malcolm was taped separately from the one with the Reverend James, so the burden of religious inquiry was left to the host, William Kunstler, at that time a professor of law at the New York University Law School. In a program entitled "Is Black Supremacy the Answer?," Malcolm represented the Nation of Islam. In the ensuing discussion, Kunstler quoted Roy Wilkins, head of the NAACP, as saying that the Nation of Islam was no better than the Klan. Malcolm responded that Wilkins was only "parroting what he has been told to say or paid to say by those who have control over him." In contrast, Malcolm said, Muhammad had recently returned from his overseas trip to the Muslim world and was "warmly received." The "Muslim faith" could not possibly be compared to the Klan, and Wilkins's remark showed his lack of familiarity—if Wilkins had actually made such a charge, Malcolm concluded.

Quoting from the first major article on the Nation of Islam in the *New York Times*, Kunstler then highlighted the Black Muslim movement as an extremist group, and Malcolm responded that it is no crime to be extreme in one's "love and in his devotion to his race." He then switched to a religious example:

> Catholics say that the Catholic church is the only church and the only way to get to heaven is through the Catholic church. Baptists say that no one can go to heaven unless they're baptized. And Jews themselves for thousands of years have taught that they alone are God's chosen people and that he would some day come and place them and them alone in the promised land.[17]

Given these examples, Malcolm concluded, no one ever accused Catholics, Baptists, or Jews of practicing supremacy or race hatred. Furthermore, Malcolm added, the "Christian Bible" is "loaded or laced" with the teaching that non-Christians would face fiery hell. "I find it difficult for Catholics and Christians to accuse us of teaching or advocating any kind of racial supremacy," he concluded, "because their own history and their own teachings are filled with it."

Malcolm understood that the Bible and the Qur'an both shared the paradigm of salvific separation—that is, that God accomplished redemption by drawing definite lines between the believer and the unbeliever. Indeed, in a number of cases, both canons express the tension of the believer in the world of the infidel—some texts urging strict separation, others expressing sympathy and kindliness. Knowingly, Malcolm tapped into this biblical vein during his Yale speech, when he pointed out that Moses did not teach integration with regard to the liberation of Israel from captivity. He also quoted the words of Jesus, calling his disciples to hate their own families and follow him instead. "Yet," Malcolm declared, "you say Muhammad teaches hate and that Jesus taught love." Digging deeper into the Gospels, Malcolm produced the example of Christ's directions to his disciples to restrict their ministry to Jewish people, not going to the Gentiles. "He definitely advised his followers to discriminate and make a distinction between the Gentiles and the 'lost sheep.'" To seal his point with fire, Malcolm retold the parable of Christ about the "wheat and the tares," in which God ultimately separates the tares from the harvest, throwing them into the flames. Similarly, Malcolm became expert at responding to Muslim critics by pointing out the verses in the Qur'an that commanded Muslims to have no association with Christians and Jews, and often used an English interpretation of a text that could be applied to Allah's wrath coming upon whites.[18] On "Pro and Con," then, Malcolm was doing the same thing by pointing out the theological separatism that undergirds both Judaism's sense of identity and Christianity's doctrine of redemption.

Unfortunately, Malcolm was also good at manipulating scriptures. His easy reference to these biblical and Qur'anic passages made for a quick rejoinder, but had his argument been examined more closely it would have been necessary to remind Malcolm X that biblical separation was based on faith, not race. While Moses had separated his people from their oppressors, the Hebrew nation was inclusive of outsiders who embraced the God of Israel. Similarly, while Jesus had sent his disciples to the Jewish nation first, this was only a priority that was to be followed by a world mission to all "ethnic" (a term employed by Jesus signifying the Gentile nations) peoples. The parable of the wheat and tares, like the parable about the sheep and the wolves, expressed Christ's idea of spiritual tension, not racial segregation, just as his idea of hating one's family entailed prioritizing obedience to God over unbelief, not literal hatred.

These spiritual meanings were inconvenient to Muhammad's message, and since the Messenger had forced a racial reading upon the entire text of the Bible, Malcolm X could read it no other way without being found unfaithful. On the other hand, Malcolm's personal instincts about the Bible were hardly unspiritual. As his dialogue and debate with Christians continued, in fact, he began to reach deeper into the Bible, not searching for proof texts and scriptural scapegoats on behalf of Muhammad, but for the prophetic well-spring whose streams were justice and righteousness in a wilderness of injustice and oppression. Not surprisingly, when Kunstler quoted a civil rights leader as saying the Nation of Islam was only "a temporary movement . . . raised by a crisis," Malcolm again reached for the Bible. When the leadership of Israel opposed the blossoming Christian movement, Malcolm recalled, a wise rabbi named Gamaliel arose to warn his brethren to leave them alone. "He advised the people, 'don't touch that group,'" Malcolm said, "'because if they're not with God, as they say, they'll come to naught, but if they are with God and God is behind them, be careful how you deal with them because you might find yourself in opposition [to] God.'"

Kunstler and Malcolm became friendly after their work on "Pro and Con," and the former liked to remember the sides of Malcolm X which the public never saw. A favorite recollection was when Malcolm, in a favor to Kunstler's wife, did an interview for an upstate New York reporter working for a small newspaper. The reporter, a white man named Gil Joel, was also paraplegic. Kunstler recalled that when the unusual journalist entered his office, Malcolm sat with him for several hours while Joel painstakingly punched out his notes on a typewriter with his big toe. Joel remembered Malcolm X as a "handsome, sober young man with bronze skin, neat attire and soft but firm speech." Malcolm, he wrote, "answered my questions with the cordial, measured authority of one accustomed to being interviewed"—an interesting remark, given the fact that this was probably the most unusual interview Malcolm X ever gave to a reporter.

Joel's series, which was actually dominated by an interview with Kunstler, provides no in-depth reading of Malcolm X. Overtly pro-civil rights, Joel's interview with Malcolm was published in the tumultuous year of 1963, which for the Nation of Islam began with a number of police assaults and ended with Malcolm being silenced by Muhammad. However, in the spring of 1963, Malcolm was still declaring that the Nation of Islam "is a religion alone." Allah, Malcolm told his interviewer, is the Supreme Being and the One God. "Since there is only One God, all the prophets talk the same religion. We believe that God will establish a righteous Kingdom on Earth after all the wicked kingdoms have fallen." Joel probably did not realize it, but Malcolm had presented a *Muslim* witness—quite in contrast to the teachings of the Nation of Islam. The God of the Black Muslims, Malcolm now declared, was the "One God" worshiped by all peoples. This "One God" was clearly not W. D. Fard, for His coming would entail the establishment of a "righteous Kingdom" after all wicked kingdoms had fallen, not just the white man's world.

Throughout 1963 Malcolm's voice continued to echo across the urban wilderness of North America, his fire rising higher, his words eagerly transcribed by reporters, students, authors, and scholars. Cameras flashed and film rolled, and Malcolm kept handing out photos of Muhammad, eagerly pointing interviewers toward the Messenger. As Malcolm recalled, being "hypersensitive" to the jealousy emanating from Chicago's Nation of Islam officials, he began to decline campus speaking engagements and important interviews. Still, New York was a world away from Muhammad, and even though Malcolm could not yet see it, the real world was not interested in the Messenger. Consequently, Malcolm moved back and forth between New York City and Chicago, stretching himself like a bridge of anguished flesh and blood between the world he had made for Muhammad and the one he was now making for himself.

One journalist inadvertently captured Malcolm's urgent grasp at the Messenger during Muhammad's interview for *Cavalier*, a less glamorous opportunity than Malcolm's famous interview in *Playboy* earlier in 1963. While the elder spoke, Malcolm sat next to him, taking copious notes of Muhammad's every word. In this little-known interview, Muhammad spoke of his life, philosophy, method of Bible interpretation, and even that plane crash which Malcolm had said was the work of God. It was "Allah's doing," Muhammad said in support of his national representative. While the Messenger sat, talking in what Alex Haley called "choppy and illiterate" sentences, Malcolm sat quietly, offering his scribal sacrifice in the name of love. Finally, the journalist asked Muhammad about his successor, and the old man declared: "You can't take my place any more than someone could take Moses' or Jesus' place. Only God can name my successor. . . . There's nobody after me but God himself."[19] There's no way of knowing, of course, but at that moment Muhammad may have been thinking about Malcolm while whispers of jealous ministers and relatives echoed in his memory. After all, neither Moses nor Jesus had been upstaged by their assistants. They were followed by men considerably less capable, men whose aspirations were entirely dependent upon them. Moses was followed by Aaron and Joshua, one his priest, the other his successor. Jesus was followed by Peter and Judas, one his right-hand man, the other his betrayer. Malcolm, of course, saw himself as a priest and a right-hand man. But in the months ahead, Malcolm X found himself cast as Joshua and Judas—both dangerous roles, both against his will.

11

Malcolm, Martin, and Billy

> They called me "the angriest Negro in America." I wouldn't
> deny that charge. I spoke exactly as I felt. "I believe in anger.
> The Bible says there is a time for anger."
>   —Malcolm X, *The Autobiography of Malcolm X*

> Do you think Allah has brought about all this intending for
> you to leave the ring as anything but the champion?
>   —Malcolm X to Muhammad Ali, 1964,
>   *The Autobiography of Malcolm X*

In the spring of 1963, Martin Luther King, Jr., was quoted in the *Pittsburgh Courier* in speaking about Malcolm X. "I've never met him, but I've heard him a number of times," King said. "Some of his critiques are sound. For example, I'm inclined to agree with him when he points out the laxities of Christianity." King said further that all the civil rights leaders "seem to have a similar diagnosis for the (racial) disease," but that he could not accept Malcolm X's cure. "It's totally unrealistic."[1] Of course, the Nation of Islam felt the same way toward King and his nonviolent crusade. In an interview in Washington, D.C. around the same time, Malcolm said:

> Christianity sets up such a concept of religion that what the Negro
> Christian has, is so spooky, so way out, so unscientific, so unreal that
> it makes it almost impossible for the Negro who is a Christian to use
> logic in analyzing his problems and getting anywhere near a sensible
> solution.

In contrast, Malcolm said, the religion of Islam provided black people the physical and spiritual strength necessary to overcome their problems.

In a more direct sense, Malcolm had been very critical of King, calling him at various times a "twentieth-century Uncle Tom," holding him up to ridicule as one of the "ignorant Negro preachers" for advancing his pacifist campaign, and accusing him of being a traitor who was used by whites to further their own aims. In another interview, Malcolm even called King a coward because he had apparently asked television talk show host David Susskind not to permit Malcolm to appear on his program with him. Recognizing Malcolm's harsh diatribes, one of King's biographers suggests that Malcolm was partially motivated out of jealousy, since *Newsweek* had rated the Nation of Islam least popular among the civil rights groups in 1963. Several years before, the biographer says, Malcolm had spoken of King with more respect, and had even invited him to a New York rally. This assessment, however, is plainly wrong and for more than one reason. First of all, the fact that King had been invited to participate in a rally in Harlem in 1960 suggests neither admiration nor contempt on Malcolm's part. The rally, billed as the "Harlem Freedom Rally," was one of several attempts by Malcolm while in the Nation of Islam to bring black leaders together in "a united effort." Besides King, a variety of black leaders were asked to attend, including a number of Harlem clergymen, New York City politicians, prominent lawyers, and celebrities like Jackie Robinson, Joe Louis, and Max Roach.[2] On the other hand, Malcolm staged a similar rally in the summer of 1963, inviting King, along with the rest of the most prominent civil rights leaders.[3] Malcolm was no less disposed to recognize King's leadership and meet with him in 1963 as he had been in 1960, while his criticisms of King were consistent over the years. Furthermore, to suggest that Malcolm became jealous over a *Newsweek* poll is jocose; unlike some of the civil rights leaders, perhaps, Malcolm X was not emotionally dependent on mainstream news polls. Furthermore, many in the black community who would never join or support the Nation of Islam on a formal basis were in agreement with much of what Malcolm X was saying, and he knew that their sentiments would hardly be shared with white pollsters.

In 1963, the only matter pertaining to the media that actually concerned Malcolm was if he was getting too much recognition. Malcolm said that around 1961 he began to realize that envy and jealousy had arisen within the Nation of Islam, and that it was being said within the movement that he was trying to take over. In his autobiography he recounts how desperately he tried to make sure that the public remembered he was only the representative, and that Muhammad was the source. By 1963, he had become extreme in these efforts, even to the point of making gratuitous references to "The Honorable Elijah Muhammad" throughout his interviews and speeches—as if by repetition he could extinguish the flames of jealousy within the movement. The worse the criticism and jealousy became, the more Malcolm consoled himself with the assurance that "at least Mr. Muhammad knew that my life was totally dedicated to representing him." Malcolm later characterized his implicit trust in Muhammad's wisdom, love, and concern as being foolish, but while he was in the Nation of Islam he was a believer. Indeed, Malcolm so believed in the Messenger that he imputed to the rest of the movement the same faith he had invested in Muhammad: "All Muslims felt as one that without his light, we would all be in darkness."[4]

As for Martin Luther King, Jr., of course, if Malcolm had feelings of resentment, they pertained to King's philosophy of nonviolence and his politicized gospel of love for the oppressor. Not only did Malcolm believe King's philosophy put blacks at the mercy of white brutality and injustice, but he saw it as a means by which white liberals manipulated and controlled the black struggle in order to keep it pacified. After King's campaign in Birmingham, Alabama, Malcolm X criticized him for allowing children to participate in the march and consequently be arrested and jailed. "Real men don't put their children on the firing line," Malcolm said in a Washington, D.C., interview. Malcolm also said that the masses of blacks in Birmingham did not subscribe to King's nonviolent philosophy, and consequently white liberals had to send celebrity-leaders like Jackie Robinson and Floyd Patterson down to Birmingham to "head the next columns away from trouble."

In another Washington, D.C., interview, Malcolm expressed disapproval regarding the Birmingham campaign, and said that the Black Muslims "don't force ourselves upon people where we are not wanted," and that King's approach had been "one of an Uncle Tom." When the interviewer suggested that "talks" resulted from the campaign, Malcolm said: "You can't call it [']results['] when some [dog] has bitten your babies and your women and your children and you are to sit down and compromise with them and negotiate with them and then have to pay your way out of prison." Malcolm insisted that nothing had come out of the demonstration for blacks in the Birmingham area. A desegregated lunch counter was no advancement, he concluded.

As far as the Reverend King and demonstrations go, the activist pastor was probably disappointed when he was jeered outside of the Salem Methodist Church in Harlem in the summer of 1963. King had come to the Salem church to speak in an evening service and was greeted by booing and egg throwing critics in the crowd; and these were not just a few hecklers. Apparently the outburst approached the point of being threatening, and the car in which King was riding was damaged by the crowd. Malcolm X was immediately blamed because the day before he had purportedly told his followers to "go up there tomorrow and let Uncle Tom know that we are against him and do not believe in what he preaches." Malcolm X denied any culpability in the unfortunate incident, but to no surprise the police were quick to blame him for the crowd's raucous behavior, just as, in 1964, they would blame Malcolm for other problems in Harlem when he was thousands of miles away in Africa. Indeed, Jackie Robinson, who was no fan of the Black Muslims, made an interesting observation about the incident when he pointed out that "had there been adequate police protection, the egg-throwing might have been prevented." Not long afterward, Malcolm spoke in a Nation of Islam unity rally in Brooklyn, and though he remained critical of King's approach, he offered a backhanded compliment: "The Rev[erend] Martin Luther King is an intelligent man. When he sees his methods won't work, he'll try something else." Malcolm was obviously going out of his way to be kind. Not only was unity the theme of the Brooklyn rally, but he had recently made a public promise to promote unity among black leaders during a Nation of Islam rally in Harlem.

Malcolm's expressed commitment was prompted by a call for unity issued in the same rally by Muhammad's son Akbar, whose devotion to Sunni Islam proved to be a thorn in the flesh of the Messenger—the latter being caught between upholding his divine claim to "Islam" and obeying the correctives offered by his devout Muslim son.[5]

While criticism from a Black Muslim leader would not have surprised the Reverend King, he may have been fazed when word of evangelist Billy Graham's admonishment broke in the black press. According to the *Pittsburgh Courier*, Graham responded to King's Birmingham campaign by saying that he ought to "put on the brakes a little bit." Graham, quoted during a trip to New York City, referred to King as his "good, personal friend" but expressed concern that things in Birmingham required "a period of quietness in which moderation prevails." Not surprisingly, Graham used his visit to New York City as another opportunity to play the role of Dixie apologist. Pointing out that blacks in the North were "accepted as a race, but not as individuals," Graham seems to have been knocking Northern hypocrisy in order to compensate for the drama of segregation being played out in daily news reports from the South. In retrospect, Billy Graham's lukewarm approach to justice for African Americans is not surprising, though there were days when it appeared the dynamic young evangelist might prove to become quite a rebel in the camp of white religion.

In 1957, when the civil rights movement was gaining attention in the press, one of Graham's black staff members submitted an article about Graham to *Ebony* magazine. In "No Color Line in Heaven," the popular evangelist declared that the United States needed a revival to "wipe away racial discrimination." Calling God "color blind," Graham said that "racial prejudice looms as one of the most burning issues in the destiny of the United States." He also admitted that his own views about segregation had begun to change after the Supreme Court ruling on desegregation in 1953. Acting upon these new convictions, Graham desegregated his own crusades, even at the cost of intense criticism from white racists, including hate mail. Graham, who was becoming known as "an enlightened white fundamentalist" among blacks, may even have evoked secret hopes among African Americans that another John Wesley had been born, coming in the fullness of time to cry out against the injustices of white supremacy in the mid-twentieth century.

There is little doubt that Graham was willing to take some heat for his convictions. During an extended crusade at New York's Madison Square Garden in 1957, Graham had King open the July 18 service with prayer, and also invited him to address his crusade team on the topic of racism. The two churchmen seemed more than mere allies, Graham looking to King as inspiration for desegregating the church, and King looking to Graham's crusade methodology as a model for his own political campaigns. King even imagined doing a tag-team crusade with the popular evangelist, though if he had studied Graham closer he might have realized that his imagination had exceeded the limits of possibility. Still, Graham took risks in associating with King and was soundly criticized by white racists for his affiliation.[6]

As Graham's fundamentalist awakening continued, the *Pittsburgh Courier* recorded his sermon in a Charlotte, North Carolina, crusade in which the evangelist declared to whites: "We can think we are better than any other race, that we are God's pets. Well, there is no such thing as 'pet' in God's sight." Graham eased the statement by expanding it to a context of nationalism, but the racial intent was clear—the fiery evangelist was prodding his Southern Christian audience to abandon their commitment to white racial superiority. Along with saving souls, Graham successfully pushed his desegregated crusade throughout the South, being hindered only in Georgia, Alabama, and Mississippi. Meanwhile, Graham continued to build a solid relationship with King and even enlisted King's clergy associates, Gardner Taylor and Thomas Kilgore, on his crusade committee. Through this alliance, Graham met with King in three private meetings to discuss strategy, mass organization, and communication.

As racial issues heated up in the news and views of the media in 1959 and 1960, Graham seems to have wished to rise to the occasion. Invited to preach in apartheid South Africa, Graham disturbed the Dutch Reformed Church by refusing to preach before a segregated audience. Because of his stance on segregation, plus the fact that his crusades would only be conducted in English, the Dutch Reformed Church responded by withdrawing its support of Graham's proposed trip there early in 1960. In the summer of 1960, Graham brought his "God has no pets" theme to Brooklyn, where he preached to an audience of three thousand at the Cornerstone Baptist Church. Assuring his audience that racists would not make it to heaven, Graham declared: "I was born in the South. It was when I was converted that I looked at my brothers through the eyes of God and I saw all men as my brothers." He also expressed support for civil rights legislation.[7]

Graham spoke up again in 1960, this time in *Reader's Digest*, in an article prompted by his preaching expedition in Africa that same year. In the article, Graham discussed segregation in the U.S. church and advocated that "Christians should banish Jim Crow from their midst." Since segregation was a fundamental denial of the Christian gospel, Graham said, Christians should "dare to obey the commandments of love, and leave the consequences in God's hands." However, at this point Graham made it clear that he was not advocating large-scale changes in society. For his part, King undoubtedly saw the limitations of Graham's commitment to justice, which is probably why he encouraged him to "stay in the stadiums." According to Graham, King told him he could have a greater impact on "the white establishment" doing crusades than marching with him in the streets. According to Graham, the civil rights leader hoped the evangelist's white constituency would listen to him knowing they would not listen to black leadership. It is possible, however, that King was only telling him what he knew Graham wanted to hear—what he knew Graham would do anyway. To no surprise, as another source points out, Graham and King "tacitly agreed to confine their cooperation to privacy." Though Graham had begun with good intentions, his willingness to suffer for the sake of righteousness was short-lived as long as it involved challenging the status quo. As a critical biographer observed, Graham preferred "decorum to bold example, and he would never be comfortable with violent protest or even with nonviolent socially disruptive measures aimed at changing the standing order." As far as racial justice is concerned, Graham wanted to see the end of *de jure* segregation, just as he was in favor of ecclesiastical desegregation; but as to the *abolition* of white supremacy and its consequent social categories, it seems the evangelist was much like Abraham Lincoln in

Frederick Douglass's assessment: "In his interests, in his associations, in his habits of thought, and in his prejudices, he was a white man."

As Malcolm would also observe several years later on the pilgrimage to Mecca, Graham similarly pointed out in the *Reader's Digest* article that people naturally organize and function "along ethnic and nationalistic" lines. However, Graham wrote, when these organizations become prohibitively exclusive, they commit sin. Even blacks, Graham said, "feel more at home with their own forms of worship. . . . But they resent, and rightly, being forbidden." Graham stated that desegregating the church is a complex problem because the church is also a social club, "making racial intermingling more delicate than in transportation, stores, or even schools." As to blame, Graham was willing to place the onus of racial division equally on blacks, since "Negroes, too, practice prejudice." Christian love would obviously cover a multitude of sins, except for interracial relationships, Graham said, which would require discretion—by which he meant that such "unwise" unions should be avoided. Furthermore, Graham said, belligerence would have to be avoided, and integrationists would have to restrain themselves from "going too far too fast," because desegregation could not be forced. Graham closed out his article by talking about his own "pilgrimage to understanding the religious significance of the racial problem," and how even after being converted he thought of blacks in "the usual patronizing and paternalistic way." Only in 1950 when a white president of a black college took him aside and counseled him on the subject of race, Graham concluded, did he begin "thinking, praying—and searching the Bible." Ultimately, despite his commitment to desegregating the church, by the time of King's endeavor at Birmingham, Graham not only called for the wheels of black progress to stop rolling, but admitted that he even hesitated to call himself a "thorough-going integrationist."[8]

Malcolm X apparently kept an eye on Billy Graham, and had probably done so from the time of his incarceration. Graham had burst upon the national scene at the end of 1949, when an evangelistic campaign he was leading in Los Angeles won the attention of the newspaper magnate William Randolph Hearst, who used his publications to make Graham famous virtually overnight. After an extended crusade in Los Angeles, which lasted seven weeks, Graham's next stop was Boston, where Malcolm was incarcerated. Graham's crusade in Boston in early 1950 was equally spectacular, and it is hard to imagine that the incarcerated Malcolm did not become aware of the daily newspaper reports concerning the rising star of evangelical Christianity. If nothing else, thereafter Malcolm studied Billy Graham's evangelistic techniques, and when he finally embarked on his own crusade on behalf of Muhammad, he emulated the evangelist in one significant respect. According to Wilfred Little, Malcolm's eldest brother, when Malcolm began to move around the country and visited Nation of Islam temples that were already established, he employed the Billy Graham crusade method of acting as a supporting agent to the established church: "[H]e did it in a way where he included [the ministers] in it. He wasn't taking anything from them, he was adding something to them because the increase in attendance would help them also. Then he would leave and go on about doing the same thing somewhere else."[9]

Indeed, it is possible that Malcolm X inwardly perceived himself as a counterpart to Billy Graham. And while historians have naturally set Malcolm alongside Martin Luther King, Jr., comparing and contrasting the two in their roles as black leaders, it may very well be that *from Malcolm's perspective* such a comparison would seem far less significant or, at least, less challenging. In terms of black organizations in the civil rights era, of course, Malcolm was *not* Martin's counterpart, not until he became independent of the Nation of Islam. By then, of course, Malcolm was working toward collaboration with civil rights leaders, whereas he could only have seen himself from a more sharpened perspective as Graham's counterpart. Regardless, Elijah Muhammad was the head of the Nation of Islam, and as long as Malcolm represented Muhammad, he viewed King as one of the Pharaoh's magicians in competition with Muhammad, the black Moses. Indeed, in religious terms, King and Muhammad were the fountainheads of their respective movements—one leading the dark myriads of the Christian South, the other rallying Allah's black masses in the urban North. One opened the Bible and proclaimed a gentle, loving Jesus whose suffering beckoned black men, women, and children to the Calvary of civil rights; the other opened the Bible and called the lost-found Nation to separate themselves from their twentieth-century slavemasters. Whites did not—could not—have seen this religious reality. But Malcolm did, because he had helped to make it so.

In contrast, Malcolm X studied Billy Graham quite closely, as would become even more obvious after his departure from the Nation of Islam in 1964. Yet, even within the movement—perhaps *especially* in the movement—Malcolm may have reckoned himself as Allah's answer to the Billy Graham phenomenon. Malcolm clearly saw everything in terms of the advancement of Islam, and because he believed Allah was working in history to this end, it was no mere religious sentimentality that inspired his belief that Christianity must be defeated in every arena of life. This is certainly apparent in Malcolm's relationship with Cassius Clay, when the young fighter—shortly to become Muhammad Ali—faced Sonny Liston for the heavyweight boxing championship in 1964. Malcolm X was not only in his corner almost literally, but he sought to be Clay's advisor, lecturing the young fighter beforehand regarding the spiritual dimensions of the fight. "'This fight is the *truth*,' I told Cassius. 'It's the Cross and the Crescent fighting in a prize ring—for the first time. It's a modern Crusades. . . . Do you think Allah has brought about all this intending for you to leave the ring as anything but the champion?'" Certainly, when he was interviewed at Clay's camp in Miami, the contest between Christianity and Islam was the real fight unfolding in Malcolm's mind: "Fear magnifies what you're afraid of," he told George Plimpton. "One thing about our religion is that it removes fear. Christianity is based on fear."[10] There was one other time that Malcolm X the Black Muslim looked to Billy Graham as a kind of counterpart.

After the Los Angeles incident in 1962, in which police violently assaulted a Nation of Islam mosque, killing one member and seriously wounding several others, Malcolm was looking for the hand of Allah to descend upon the white man—especially since Muhammad refused to take any retaliatory action. Several days after the incident, Malcolm flew back to New York City to appear in a panel discussion with James Farmer, the director of the Congress on Racial Equality (CORE) and journalist William Worthy at the Palm Gardens in Manhattan. Prior to the program, Malcolm was interviewed outside the hall by Richard Elman of WBAI Radio. Malcolm explained the disturbing details of the attack, and when Elman asked him what course of action the Nation of Islam would take, Malcolm's answer not only reflected his disappointment in Muhammad's passivity, but also his actual belief that Allah would avenge the heinous injustice.

> We believe in God. We believe in justice. We believe in freedom. We believe in equality. And we do believe that God, our God, the Supreme Being, whose proper name is Allah, will execute judgment and justice in whatever way He sees fit, against the people who are guilty of this crime against our people in this country.[11]

What made this injustice all the more bitter for Malcolm was that a coroner's jury in Los Angeles had ruled the death of Ronald X (Stokes) a justifiable homicide because the officer who shot him claimed the Black Muslim had raised his hands as if to choke him. Malcolm sat through the hearing, his expression stoic, his eyes targeting the officer as he testified about shooting Ronald X. (Other men in the mosque had been shot in the groin or in the back; one, William X Rogers, age 26, was paralyzed for life.) "I listened to a man who admitted he killed a man in cold blood," Malcolm told a reporter afterward. "[A]s a religious leader I can only say that I am thankful there is a God in heaven to give real justice when necessary." Not long after this statement, real justice came, or so it seemed to Malcolm X. An airplane carrying one hundred and thirty people crashed in France, one hundred and twenty of those who perished being white Southerners from the state of Georgia—the land where Earl Little and Elijah Muhammad were born, the land whence they had fled.

Malcolm could hardly have restrained himself. He really had expected Allah's intervention, and the Nation of Islam had always been taught that Allah valued the life of one of his own over a hundred, maybe a thousand of the devils. Muhammad had failed to come through with an assertive response to white injustice, but Allah had not forgotten his bleeding children, nor had Malcolm's tears been wasted. Almost a year later, Malcolm told an interviewer: "I mentioned at the time as a religious man I really believed that God would bring disaster down upon the people who were responsible for allowing such an injustice to take place in a country that is supposed to be based upon freedom." Malcolm had openly and flagrantly delighted in this heaping portion of good, Old Testament justice and was defending himself for the entire year for having done so. "I mentioned at that time that I felt it was an act of God," Malcolm told his interviewer. "That was the same thing that Billy Graham mentioned in Chicago. He even mentioned that it was an act of God. But when Billy Graham mentioned it they didn't find anything wrong with it."[12]

In January 1963, Malcolm made an appearance in Charlotte, North Carolina, speaking at the Hi-Fi Country Club to an all-black audience. In that dramatic speech, he discussed Attorney General Robert Kennedy and the civil rights movement, and the hypocrisy of the Kennedy administration in dealing with the race problem. He also discussed a recent conference on racism in Chicago, in which representatives of the Protestant, Roman Catholic, and Jewish communities participated. In that conference, Malcolm pointed out, one white participant had called for input by a representative of the Nation of Islam. Malcolm commended this statement, pointing out that inviting "run-of-the-mill Negro leaders, who are nothing but Uncle Toms" to such a conference would yield no answers. Malcolm also made a less than flattering reference to Alex Haley, with whom he was engaged in the writing of his autobiography, though without mentioning his name. With regard to membership numbers of the Nation of Islam, Malcolm said that a recent article in the *Saturday Evening Post* had estimated there were six thousand Black Muslims, but "the same writer" had written in *Reader's Digest* in 1960 that there were between one hundred and two hundred thousand Black Muslims. "This shows you that they all write for the white man," Malcolm said, adding that this was an attempt on the part of whites to minimize the Nation of Islam and "sweep them under the rug." (Malcolm also seems to have had in mind the author of *Black Muslims in America*, C. Eric Lincoln, who estimated the movement had membership in the hundreds of thousands, but also came under harsh criticism by Malcolm for coining the term "Black Muslims.")

Haley's introduction to the Nation of Islam had indeed come with that piece in *Reader's Digest*, which Malcolm had initially greeted with contempt and suspicion. According to Haley's recollection in the epilogue of *The Autobiography*, both Muhammad and Malcolm were perhaps pleasantly surprised that his work for *Reader's Digest* was objective, and told him so. However, that Muhammad and Malcolm thought Haley's piece objective is a commentary on the general tendency in the media at that time to portray the Nation of Islam as a loathsome, dangerous, and violently hateful black organization. Haley's *Reader's Digest* piece was basically evenhanded, but not without its share of sensationalism. Yet compared with an article which ran later that year in the black magazine, *Sepia*, for instance, the Haley piece was quite objective. "The Trouble-Making Muslims" was an appalling presentation designed to evoke great disgust toward the Nation of Islam within the black community. *Sepia*'s writer not only sensationalized aspects of the movement's early years, but drew up a list of similarities between the Nation of Islam and Hitler's Nazis. Even captions placed under photos of Nation of Islam audience members were laced with cynical remarks (under the photo of an elderly Black Muslim woman: "The wisdom of her years lines this face, but is it wisdom or disillusionment that leads her life?"; under the photo of a man: "How could this young man ever qualify to lead his people after being indoctrinated with blind hate?"). Interestingly, though, Malcolm's reference in the Hi-Fi speech to Haley's initial estimation was incorrect; in the 1960 *Reader's Digest* piece, Haley actually suggested the Nation of Islam had an estimated membership of seventy thousand, not one to two hundred thousand members. In "Black Merchants of Hate," which Haley co-authored with Alfred Balk for the *Saturday Evening Post* in 1963, he suggested the Nation of Islam had only a "hard core of 5,500 to 6,000" members.[13] Despite Malcolm's complaint that Haley was minimizing the Nation of Islam, the truth is that this low estimate was far more realistic than the exaggerated figures of one to two hundred thousand that characterized writing on the Nation of Islam in the early 1960s. Of course, if anything good came of Haley's two pieces on the Nation of Islam, it was his subsequent interview with Malcolm X for *Playboy*, published in May 1963, which ultimately led them into collaborative work on *The Autobiography*. Besides his admitted distrust of people in general, given the manner in which journalists were writing about the Nation of Islam, it is no wonder that Malcolm greeted Haley's work with such skepticism. Even after they began to work together on *The Autobiography*, Malcolm told Haley he trusted him only "about twenty-five percent." In time, Malcolm's trust in Haley would increase, but his initial hostility toward him and other black writers must be understood in the context of the media's biased portrayal of the Nation of Islam in the early 1960s.

In the Hi-Fi speech, Malcolm also recalled the TV documentary "The Hate That Hate Produced," which had made the Black Muslims a nightmare sensation in the white community in 1959. This propaganda, Malcolm said, was designed to deny the religious nature of the Nation of Islam and portray Muhammad and his followers as a hate group.

> Hate, hate, hate, hate. They figured that Negroes would never go near him if they said he taught hate, because the average Negro don't want nothing to do with hate. He loves Jesus and he has been taught that Jesus didn't hate nobody, so he wants to be like Jesus and so he'll end up getting knocked in the head, brutalized, and he won't fight back because he says Jesus didn't fight back.

Malcolm also understood that African American Christianity was heavily infused with a biblical humanitarianism predicated upon the notion that Christ was passive and meek, and he believed that embracing such an image put blacks at a disadvantage. Consequently, Malcolm's response to the passive image of Jesus was to challenge it as a biblically incomplete representation: "You didn't read enough of that Bible. Maybe in Matthew, Mark, Luke, and John he didn't fight back, but when you find Jesus in Revelation, he's sitting on a horse with a sword dripping blood and he's fighting back."[14]

It has been said that Malcolm "never stopped reading Scripture, but he was drawn more and more in his last years to the wild apocalyptic visions of the Book of Revelation, in which the righteous make war against the wicked and even Jesus takes up the sword."[15] There is a point to this observation, though it is misleading. To the secular writer, perhaps the apocalyptic visions of the Book of Revelation seem wild, but they are—as Malcolm realized—the necessary out-working of the Christian gospel. The Christian conception of Jesus, particularly with regard to violence, was often based on an incomplete reading of Christ's life and words. Malcolm X could not tolerate the Jesus of the gospels, so he groped for a different Jesus, a Jesus with a sword, a Jesus who would fight—and he found him in the closing pages of the New Testament, returning to wreak havoc upon nonbelievers.

As to his first advent, Jesus came, if you will, as a tactical pacifist, his intention according to the gospel writers being to establish a spiritually oriented movement premised on his own willing sacrifice. The gospels do not portray Jesus as a prophet using love as a weapon to overcome evil—as if one so wise could be so foolish as to think that evil men could be overcome by love. This much Malcolm X understood, though Gandhi, another famous non-Christian, apparently did not. Malcolm's response to the prevailing "Christian" philosophy that undergirded the civil rights campaign was, in this sense, quite sound. He instinctively understood that Christ's famous words about loving one's enemies and turning the other cheek had been taken out of context and then politicized in order to placate the fears of white liberals. Malcolm X knew white people, and he knew that the only "Negro revolution" they would tolerate was one where black "revolutionaries" marched down the road unarmed, except with prayers and spirituals.

Jesus never intended his inwardly focused instruction to be appropriated as a tactic for a civil rights struggle. His so-called "Sermon on the Mount" was actually a private teaching to his apostles—the ones he had called to die in order to establish the alternative society he called his *ekklesia*, his church. Gandhi may not have understood this as well as the Reverend King, but the latter nevertheless incorporated the intensely spiritual and inwardly focused requirements of Christian discipleship into the campaign for civil rights. Unfortunately, Jesus had promised that the gates of hell would not prevail against his *ekklesia*; he said nothing about political campaigns. The folly of using the Jesus ethic of so-called nonviolence was obvious enough, at least to Malcolm X. Quite to the contrary, the gates of hell *did* prevail in the Southern rights struggle—men, women, and children being senselessly exposed to vicious dogs, brutalized and beaten by racists in and out of uniform; black and white activists murdered by the Klan; and little girls blown to sweet Jesus within the very sanctuary of the church—all sacrificed in the name of the nonviolent cross, but really being peace offerings to the Baal of racial supremacy reigning in the fearful heart of white America. What Malcolm X understood about the Gandhi-ized, politicized message of Jesus in the civil rights movement was that it had nothing to do with Jesus at all, and that the leaders of the civil rights movement, both white and black, had opted to march innocent people off like lambs to the slaughter because they deemed it far better to sacrifice black life and dignity than to do the unthinkable—to do what white people would readily have done for themselves: allow blacks to use just force against injustice. Malcolm recognized the political and religious hypocrisy of the civil rights philosophy and, right or wrong, imputed the worst aspects of it to Martin Luther King. Malcolm believed King was "primarily concerned with making the black man in this country see that the white man can change, that the white man is not as guilty as the Honorable Elijah Muhammad says."

> Martin Luther King's primary concern is in defending the white man—and if he can elevate the black man's condition while he's defending the white man at the same time, then the black man will be elevated. But if it takes a condemnation of the white man in order to bring about the elevation of the black man, you'll find that Martin Luther King will get out of the struggle.[16]

This, Malcolm seems to have been saying all along, was the problem with Christianity on a whole. "Christianity is a white man's religion. It is always emphasizing the role of the white man. Islam does not recognize color; it only recognizes the human personality."[17] In a 1963 interview with Kenneth Clark in which he reflected on his conversion in prison, Malcolm said:

Well, I had completely eliminated Christianity. After getting into prison and having time to think, I could see the hypocrisy of Christianity. . . . I firmly believe that it was the Christian society, as you call it, the Judaic-Christian society that created all the factors that send so many so-called Negroes to prison."[18]

In his famous *Playboy* interview, Malcolm observed that African Americans had been led to believe that Jesus was a white man. This was done "to maneuver him into worshiping the white man." Malcolm said that in his prison readings he came to realize that "the history-whitening process either had left out great things that black men had done, or some of the great black men had gotten whitened." As to racism in the United States, Malcolm told Haley that it was as much a factor in religion as in education, economics, and politics: "Even the religious philosophy is, in essence, white supremacy. A white Jesus. A white Virgin. White angels. White everything. But a black Devil, of course." When Haley asked him how he could verify that Jesus was actually a black man, Malcolm responded: "Sir, Billy Graham has made the same statement in public. Why not ask *him* what Scripture he found it in?"[19] Another aspect of the influence of white supremacy upon black religion, Malcolm said, was the financial support provided to the black church by the white community. Speaking before an audience of four hundred activists that had organized an economic boycott on white businesses in Jamaica, Queens, Malcolm stated that the church was favored because of its neutralizing role in the black community:

> Any preacher can build—any bank can get finance to build a church because the church probably does more to keep your mind in the sky. . . . that Negro preacher has a philosophy that is designed to absolutely make you helpless when it comes to doing something for yourself in this life, on this earth. . . . So the preacher is conditioning your mind to make you more susceptible to the tricky maneuvering that's going to be done upon you by the white businessmen in your community.[20]

Of course, if Malcolm's assessment of the African American church and Christianity were entirely correct, white racists would not have been bombing black churches in the South. To be sure, the black church was hardly above criticism, nor were its leaders pristine exemplars of the Christian faith, not even Martin Luther King, Jr. But in 1963 Malcolm X was still viewing the church through a Black Muslim lens, and while he was straining to see clearly, his scope was as narrow as it was exact. Malcolm X would never accept the nonviolent philosophy, just as he would never accept integration; but when he was able to see for himself and think for himself, he would undoubtedly see a worthy side to the black struggle in the Southern Christian arena, just as he would have to come to terms with the inadequacies of Muhammad's movement. One discerning writer in the *Washington Post* noted that with a few bombs thrown down in Birmingham, "a corresponding reaction of violence from the other side" was quite likely. The writer expressed concern over the growing influence of the Nation of Islam, especially since the South was becoming increasingly volatile. The Nation of Islam was as motivated by religious conviction as were many Christians involved in the South, he wrote. To be sure, the Christian influence in the civil rights movement was a tradition of faith rooted deeply in the black experience, "being part of the long, painful climb up from slavery." Yet the writer questioned if such a tradition would persevere, especially in light of the rising tide of black "Islam," which viewed Christianity as a white colonialist religion.

President Kennedy had his concerns, too, but not for the well-being of black Christianity. When the president was visited by a group of white newspaper editors from Alabama, Kennedy had virtually waved the Black Muslims in their faces in making a point about the dangers of rising "extremism" among blacks. News of the meeting, which was carried by the Associated Press and picked up by the *Washington Post* and the *New York Times*, drew a sharp response from Malcolm. His retort, which was carried in the *Times*, was that the president had shown the wrong "motivation," and instead of attacking racist organizations like the Klan, "Kennedy attacked Islam, a religion." The president, being a Roman Catholic, should have been more sympathetic, Malcolm continued, since Catholics had been discriminated against in the United States for many years.[21] Kennedy may have been goaded by the remark, but he had bigger fish to fry down South. Malcolm, too, had more important things to worry about. To be sure, there were still many devils to fight, but now there were also demons to cast out. As Allah would have it, however, before the finish of the year, President Kennedy would be dead and Malcolm would make that fateful declaration about chickens coming home to roost. Then the end would come and, finally, the beginning.

12

"Haunted by the Souls of Black Millions"

Christianity, Islam, and Malcolm X

Imitation is not discipleship. The Mohammedan Negro is a much better Mohammedan than the Christian Negro is a Christian because the Muslim Negro, as a learner, is a disciple, not an imitator.

—Edward Wilmot Blyden, *Christianity, Islam, and the Negro Race* (1887)

The whites want slaves, and want us for their slaves, but some of them will curse the day they ever saw us. As true as the sun ever shone in its meridian splendor, my colour will root some of them out of the very face of the earth.

—David Walker's *Appeal* (1830)

I had been a part of the tapping of something in the black secret soul.

—Malcolm X, *The Autobiography of Malcolm X*

"The Negroes of the United States are creating a new American foreign problem," wrote Pierre Crabités from Cairo sometime in 1932. Crabités, a white "Christian" from the United States, had been in Egypt since 1912 when President Taft had sent him there to fill a government post. For all of his expertise in the so-called Middle East, however, Crabités was also a racist who seems to have been prompted to write because of what he perceived as a disturbing trend. "Six months ago an American Negro came to Cairo without a saxophone and with no intention of playing in a jazz band," Crabités wrote. "He was as black as the Ace of Spades, his teeth a wall of ivory and his speech the drawl of the Southern plantation." As it turned out, the black man had announced to him and the Egyptians that "he was a Moslem and that he had come to this country in order to work his way to Mecca." Crabités was even more surprised to have learned from him that "Mohammedan congregations" were springing up all over the United States, in cities like Detroit, Chicago, Buffalo, and in Gary, Indiana.

These unlikely black "Mohammedan" communities were the source of a small but steady stream of converts determined to make their way to the Holy World of Islam. Crabités was primarily concerned because, heretofore, the Egyptians had associated "the name of America primarily with Caucasian civilization, Christian propaganda, and Protestant dogma." Not only were Egyptians suddenly getting the impression that the United States was a "black man's country dominated by Mohammedans," but these black pilgrims themselves did not realize that "in the Levant conversion, like naturalization, requires official red tape."

As Crabités saw it, these black converts were having the best of both worlds, converting to Islam and keeping their U.S. passports. Given his racist perspective, then, Crabités was fearful that soon "there will be a batch of black or near black babies added to the Cairo American community." Not surprisingly, he was not only disturbed by the darkening of the American image in Egypt, but worried that African American Muslims would become a problematic presence for "American consular and diplomatic officers." Crabités continued that the "Moslem propagandist who seeks to sell Islam to the colored people of America" could offer three "seductive propositions," one of which was polygamy. Given his skewed perspective on race, Crabités readily emphasized that because Islam also permitted concubinage, black converts with uncontrolled sexual appetites might "specialize in concubines"—and since, as he also admitted, color presented no social barrier in the Muslim world, it seems Crabités was burdened with the possibilities of black American men doing in Cairo what they would never be allowed to do back in the United States. Beyond these racist concerns, however, were the two other seductions of Islam: that Islam, theologically speaking, "is simplicity itself," and that it "symbolizes social equality." Even Crabités saw these as admirable strengths, though he seems to have preferred they remain within the context of Egyptian society. Crabités not only recognized that Islam had far exceeded Christianity in making converts in the dark world, but wondered aloud what might happen if it became "a black spot upon the American horizon."

If Islam remained a fascination with black expatriates, Crabités concluded, they would ultimately prove to be "petty annoyances and then disconcerting trouble" for U.S. diplomats. But if these converts brought Islam back to the United States, he wrote, "the ardent spirit of the neophyte and the sermons which they will preach make me shudder at the consequences which I see in store for America and particularly for the Southern States." As for those black American "Moslems" in Cairo, Crabités concluded that a "Negro convert to Islam, loose in the Near East, with an American passport in his pocket, is like a monkey with two tails. He is bound to attract attention." Such attention, he wrote, would evoke within him "that sense of vanity which has ruined many a good man," inevitably leading him to perdition.

Of course, this is the perspective of a "Christian" from the United States, whose published anxieties typify the dilemma of whites who venture outside the context of the United States and discover that the world does not necessarily conform to the social and cultural rules they had come to believe were laws of nature. In the nineteenth century, Frederick Douglass saw this, even in Europe, when he realized how differently whites responded to him as a man of color in comparison to whites in the United States. Indeed, as he traveled abroad, he repeatedly saw white men from the United States very similar to Pierre Crabités in Cairo, whose color prejudice exemplified what Douglass called a "species of aristocracy." "I have never found it abroad in any but Americans," he wrote. "It sticks to them wherever they go. They find it almost as hard to get rid of as to get rid of their skins." To be sure, skin—or to be more precise, the color of skin—has always been the most compelling factor in the United States. The great Filipino patriot José Rizal wrote that "men are like turtles; they are classified and valued according to their shells"—and if this was true under the "Christian" hegemony of Spain, it is most certainly the god awful gospel of U.S. "Christianity."[1] In late-twentieth-century U.S. society, of course, the debate over whether capitalism is the product or the source of racism seems less a question of the chicken-or-the-egg than it is about the chickens coming home to roost. This is especially the case regarding African Americans and Islam.

In 1887, the brilliant West Indian scholar and clergyman Edward Wilmot Blyden (1832–1912) published an insightful collection of essays called *Christianity, Islam and the Negro Race*. As a young man Blyden traveled in North and South America, and came to believe that blacks should build new, partially Westernized states in Africa. Emigrating to Liberia, West Africa, Blyden was schooled in education and religion, proving himself a brilliant linguist, classicist, theologian, and historian. An ordained Presbyterian minister, Blyden was also a prolific writer and academic administrator, among other things, but his views on race and religion are especially interesting. His thoughts on religion, as in other areas, were shaped by his pan-Africanist beliefs and, more so than even Marcus Garvey after him, Blyden was positively disposed toward Islam as a religion for blacks.

Blyden not only studied religion and theology, but he studied how Christianity had been mediated and consequently shaped by white Western culture. He likewise observed the widespread contempt of Western Christians toward Muslims, and having studied the impact of both religions upon black people, came to the controversial conclusion that Christianity was a significant hindrance to black advancement. Blyden himself never converted to Islam, though like Frederick Douglass in later life, he seems to have moved away from traditional Christianity. Still, Blyden differentiated between the essence of the religion of Jesus and that which it had become in the hands of whites.

To Blyden, European Christianity had skewed the "Semitic ideas promulgated in the Bible" by infusing them with Roman, Celtic, and

Teutonic thought and practice. Christianity was not the religion of Jesus, therefore, but a religion "modified to suit the European mind or idiosyncracies." As deeply rooted in the African-Asian context as Christianity was in its origins, Blyden said, it had "followed chiefly the migrations and settlements of members of the Aryan race," and even though it had spread more widely than any other religion, it did so only as it followed the course of European expansion. European Christianity turned the faith of Jesus into a "great objective mass of rites and dogmas, more stress being laid upon the material and visible than upon the unseen and spiritual," and manifested itself in constitutions and caste systems—a far cry from the Semitic orientation of the Bible, which perceived every man as "standing in direct relation to God." In terms of faith and life, Blyden believed that a black man in a Christian land could not be truly self-educated, because in order to be trained as a Christian he must be trained "not to be himself, but somebody else." Blyden wrote that even unconsciously, blacks are trained in the very basic, daily lessons of life to be the imitator, not the equal, of the white man. In contrast, the black Muslim is superior, Blyden contended, because he is a true disciple whose development and capacity for growth were not imitations, but inward realizations.[2]

The importance of Blyden's critique cannot be understated, not only because it may serve as a guide for another Reformation in the Christian world but also because it expresses a core spiritual perception in the black experience regarding Christianity, a perception that remains largely out of reach to white Christians. At the same time, in its own way, Blyden's analysis serves as a corrective to men like Elijah Muhammad, who treated the essence of Christianity contemptuously and, worse, without sincerity.

Blyden believed that no matter how sincere the faith of black Christians, they embraced the religion of Jesus primarily as "the only source of consolation in their deep disasters." Consequently, the kind of Christianity that resulted, however sweet and tender, "was necessarily partial and one-sided, cramped and abnormal," particularly because "tendencies to independent individuality were repressed and destroyed." Worse, those black Christians who could rise above this dilemma became "targets to their unappreciative brethren." That

Christianity lacked "cosmopolitan adaptation and power" was a fault that rested not on Jesus and his apostles, Blyden concluded, but upon the Christian nations that claimed the cross as their own.[3]

While blacks have long delighted in the psalmist's prophecy concerning Ethiopia stretching her hands out to God, it seems the real paradigm for black Christianity has been the biblical narrative of Simon of Cyrene—an African stretching his back to carry the cross of Jesus to Golgotha. The burden of the white man's cross fell heavily on black shoulders from the time of his introduction to the New World. While this cross was borne with amazing longsuffering and patience over two centuries of enslavement, blacks were able to revile it without surrendering their embrace of Christ. Of course, many were pacified in the process, while some fought back. As to the latter, most notable was David Walker (1785–1830), a North American abolitionist whose inspired, wrathful little epistle, *Appeal to the Coloured Citizens of the World*, made such an impact upon the Slave South that in some states its circulation was specifically outlawed. Walker clearly differentiated between the "pure and undefiled" religion of Jesus and the religion of the European, which seemed to him an oppressive plan fabricated by whites in league with devils. "But hark! My Master has taught me . . . that his gospel as it was preached by himself and his apostles remains the same, not withstanding Europe has tried to mingle blood and oppression with it." Walker held the "pretended" Christian pro-slavery preachers responsible as demonic examples for other whites who wished to abuse blacks. "Can any thing be a greater mockery of religion than the way in which it is conducted by the Americans?"[4]

In the *Appeal*, Walker not only cried out against the injustice of "Christian" slavery, but gave to the world an Africentric voice of great strength, mocking the hypocrisy of Thomas Jefferson and answering the folly of Henry Clay. However, to the chagrin of white abolitionists, Walker believed that pride and avarice had rendered whites generally the inferiors of blacks. He also advocated the use of force in overthrowing white oppression, and used language that anticipates the fiery appeal of Malcolm X: "[F]or we must remember that *humanity, kindness* and the *fear of the Lord*, does not consist in protecting *devils."*⁵ David Walker is remembered as an ideological and spiritual progenitor in the annals of black nationalism and liberation, yet the *Appeal* goes unrecognized in religious history, though it is one of the great prophetic masterpieces in modern Christian literature.

As Christianity goes, David Walker's *Appeal* is as much an inspired jeremiad as it is a superlatively provocative human rights document—and Walker, who died under mysterious circumstances in 1830, is as much a Christian martyr as any missionary fallen on "heathen" soil. Unfortunately, the depth and breadth of its biblical foundation notwithstanding, the *Appeal* will never be appreciated within the context of white Christianity. Jacques Ellul said it best when he wrote that "there is an immeasurable distance between all that we read in the Bible and the practice of the church and of Christians."⁶ He could also have written "of the church and of white Christians especially," but his failure to do so attests to the limitations even of his radical critique of "subversive" Christian religion. Ellul's Eurocentric biases seem to have blinded him to the virtual depravity that curses white Christianity because of its inherent race orientation, and the fact that he did not reckon white supremacy as a subversive factor is itself a commentary on white religion. The fact is, no critique of modern Christianity is adequate without the witness of Mother Africa and her children, and no discussion concerning twentieth-century white religion in the United States is relevant without the witness of Malcolm X. Of course, white Christianity, which cannot even swallow the dulcifying Martin Luther King, Jr., without a spoonful of processed sugar, is hardly prepared to accept a bitter cup from the American Cyrus.

Finally, Malcolm wrote that even while he was in the Nation of Islam he sensed his work was part of something deeper—that he was somehow connected with a great reservoir of black vitality that associated him with something buried within the depths of his people. "I had been part of the tapping of something in the black secret soul," Malcolm wrote in *The Autobiography*. His work, this "tapping" of which he wrote, was not his representative evangelism on behalf of Elijah Muhammad. The day came when Malcolm loathed the spiritual monuments he had erected on behalf of the Messenger. Deep within himself, however, Malcolm X had also tapped into a spiritual river of black resistance, and it was this that ultimately separated him from the Messenger. After all, men like Elijah Muhammad are, as the biblical writer says, clouds without water. But men like Malcolm X are like trees planted by a river. And so, *it is written.*

Contrary to the skewed expectations of Pierre Crabités, when Malcolm X was finally "loose in the Near East, with an American passport in his pocket," he was anything but a monkey with two tails, though he did draw a great deal of attention. In fact, having made his pilgrimage to Mecca in the *Hajj* season of 1964, Malcolm seemed more like a tiger with two tails. One of those tails was obviously political, and its wagging drew the special attention of the U.S. Department of State and the Central Intelligence Agency abroad, with the diabolical J. Edgar Hoover watching from a distance. Indeed, State Department officers in Africa sent frequent reports of Malcolm's appearances, speeches, and interviews to Washington, D.C. One interview, appearing in the Nigerian *Daily Express*, referred to Malcolm as a man "haunted by the souls of black millions," those who had died in the slave trade, on the plantations, and under racist oppression. This "Angry Man," the *Express* also reported, wanted to "establish a black Peace Corps which would carry black civilization to all African countries." When Malcolm appeared in Cairo in July 1964 to attend a summit of the Organization of African Unity with observer status, the State Department assured Washington that he lacked diplomatic success—but then admitted that his words to concerned African heads of state had likely done harm to the image of the United States.

Malcolm's other tail, of course, was religious, and it also wagged quite forcefully. The State Department took equal interest in Malcolm's religious work in the Muslim world. One detailed report in September 1964 recounted his interaction with the royal family and authorities of Saudi Arabia, his "little pilgrimage" to Mecca that same month, and his comments about personal spiritual development. In an interview at the U.S. Embassy, Malcolm apparently stressed his religious role and his determination to introduce traditional Islam to African Americans. According to his interviewer, Malcolm also stated that "the Black Muslims were basically ignorant of Islam and totally unwilling to admit their ignorance." Though the interviewer tended to misread Malcolm's good-natured manner and to underestimate his political awareness, it was nevertheless evident that Malcolm was now sharply critical of Elijah Muhammad, and that he preferred to identify himself as a "humanist" with respect to race relations.[7]

Neither did Malcolm hide his critical light under a foreign bushel. Early in October 1964, the *New York Times* published excerpts of a letter written from Saudi Arabia in which the former Black Muslim emphatically declared he no longer wore "Elijah Muhammad's 'strait jacket,'" and totally rejected the doctrines of the Nation of Islam as "racist philosophy" which had been "labeled 'Islam' only to fool and misuse gullible people." Malcolm acknowledged that he had not only been Muhammad's greatest helper in spreading this unfortunate religion by means of his own "evangelistic zeal," but had himself been "fooled and misused" by Muhammad. The article also revealed that Malcolm had been studying Islam in Mecca, and now he openly declared himself a true Muslim aligned with the religion of the holy world of Islam.

Not only did Malcolm declare himself a traditional Muslim, but he made it clear that he believed all men were brothers and equals before God, and that each man had a right to "believe whatever his intelligence leads him to believe is intellectually sound." Indeed, Malcolm acknowledged that "some of my dearest friends are Christians, Jews, Buddhists, Hindus, agnostics, and even atheists—some are capitalists, Socialists, and Communists—some are moderates, conservatives, extremists—some are even Uncle Toms." Denouncing Elijah Muhammad as a "faker," Malcolm presented himself as an openminded man but concluded that men such as Muhammad were able to exploit "unsuspecting people" because the West had gone to great extremes to "block out the knowledge of True Islam." In subsequent letters, reports of which were also published in the *Times*, it was revealed that Malcolm had been designated an official representative of the Islamic faith in the United States by the Muslim World League, and that he intended to open a Muslim Center in New York City. The Nation of Islam was scandalized, for obvious reasons.[8] The man who had masterminded the virtual deification of Muhammad as "the little lamb without spot or blemish" might just as easily demonize him, especially since Malcolm had made a public promise that he would "never rest until I have undone the harm I did to so many, well-meaning, innocent Negroes" who had embraced Muhammad because of him, and now even adored him "more fanatically and more blindly than I did."

Initially, of course, Malcolm X had not intended to use his independent political and religious stance as a platform to oppose the Messenger. In the first weeks of his independence, Malcolm wished to demonstrate his fidelity to Muhammad—his only dissent being a determination to take part in political action programs and even work with civil rights groups on behalf of black liberation. Interestingly, when he sought for a paradigm upon which to model his new action program, Malcolm did not look to Martin Luther King, Jr., but rather to King's "good friend," Billy Graham. "I have watched how Billy Graham comes into a city," Malcolm told an audience in April 1964, "spreading what he calls the gospel of Christ."

> But since it's the natural tendency for leaders to be jealous and look upon a powerful figure like Graham with suspicion and envy, how is it possible for him to come into a city and get all the cooperation of the church leaders? Don't think because they're church leaders that they don't have weaknesses that make them envious and jealous—no, everybody's got it.

Graham's method, Malcolm continued, was to spread the gospel and stir everyone up, but never start a church of his own.

> If he came in trying to start a church, all the churches would be against him. So, he just comes in talking about Christ and tells everybody who gets Christ to go to any church where Christ is; and in this way the church cooperates with him. So we're going to take a page from his book.

The page that Malcolm intended to borrow from Graham was purely tactical. Malcolm's intention was for his organization to act in a political manner comparable to the para-church Billy Graham Evangelistic Association. As the head of a kind of para-civil rights organization, Malcolm wanted to herald the "gospel of black nationalism" from city to city without posing a threat to established political or religious organizations in the black community. Like Graham, Malcolm X wanted to advance a core philosophy that would help the entire community despite variations in organization and opinion.

However, Malcolm offered a brief but insightful analysis of the evangelist as well. Graham's message, Malcolm said, was "white nationalism" and Graham himself was a "white nationalist." Malcolm had studied Graham closely, and he perceived that what the evangelist was preaching, though generally touted by Christians as "the simple message of the gospel," was actually a message that conformed to the requirements of white supremacy. What made Graham's message "white nationalism" to Malcolm X was that the evangelist consistently focused on issues of individual faith and private morality à la white interest—selectively omitting white racism and white supremacy as sins from which God was calling men to repent. To be sure, Graham had preached against race prejudice, a sin that anyone could commit. But he did not see racism in the larger context of white supremacy, nor was he willing to challenge systemic white racism in any significant manner. As an evangelist, Graham would never tell an adulterer to turn gradually from his sin, but when it came to white racism, the evangelist not only urged justice seekers like King to "put on the brakes" and show moderation, but he seems to have opted out of the struggle before it even began. His media hype and ecclesiastical heroism in a million Christian homes notwithstanding, Billy Graham disappointed his black Christian brethren and betrayed the entire black community with his silence at a time when he was most needed. If one white Christian minister in the twentieth century had an opportunity to disprove Blyden and put Malcolm X to silence, it was Billy Graham. Instead, he quickly confirmed that Malcolm was correct.

Charles Kenyatta, who followed Malcolm in and out of the Nation of Islam, recalls that when Malcolm was abroad calling for the United States to be brought before the United Nations for human rights violations, Billy Graham was interviewed on a New York television broadcast urging that Malcolm X "be watched very, very closely."[9] This is not surprising, given Graham's apparent disdain toward aggressive civil rights activity. Ultimately, the evangelist proved more loyal to the perfidious Richard Nixon than to Martin Luther King, Jr. Far too fascinated with the royal court, Billy Graham forfeited the prophet's hairy mantle for a shining robe of Teflon. Prophets die hard, but such dying would be left for his "good friend" the Reverend King, while Graham's calling, as it turned out, was to serve God *and* country—but mostly his country.

Graham's press release after King's death in 1968 was quite telling in this regard: "Many people who have not agreed with Dr. King can admire him for his non-violent policies and in the eyes of the world he has become one of the greatest Americans." Were these really the words of one of the few white men who enjoyed the privilege of calling King by his birth name, the evangelist who at one time had shared common goals with the civil rights leader and even hosted a banquet in King's honor at a convention of the Baptist World Alliance? In the end, according to Graham, what might redeem King in the eyes of white people was not his prophetic stand against racism and injustice but his commitment to nonviolence—the guarantee of white security and the protection of white sensitivities.

In 1965, when black Los Angeles could take no more of Mayor Yorty and Police Chief Parker, and their police had filled the cup of brutality to its brim, the City of Angels vomited up demons of fire and rage. Graham subsequently toured Los Angeles with the black clergyman E. V. Hill and recalled being "sickened by the violence and the wide-spread destruction we saw on every hand." Of course, in retrospect, Graham seems to have forgotten that it was not merely the destruction that disturbed him, but his political conception of the forces working behind it. According to another source, after Graham had surveyed the city from a helicopter, he declared the ruin "a dress rehearsal for revolution" instigated by "sinister forces trying to set race against race and class against class with the ruthless objective of overthrowing the government." Of course, this only confirmed what Malcolm had said the previous year about Graham being a white nationalist. Malcolm was dead by this time, but had he been alive he might have issued one of his famous smiles in approval of the rebuttal to Graham that appeared in the *Christian Century*:

What sinister forces, Mr. Graham? Are you implying with the John Birch Society that the Negro's rebellion is communist-inspired, communist-directed? Or do you mean by "sinister forces" the centuries-old rapaciousness of the white man, the white Christian's cold indifference to the plight of his Negro brother, the inactivity of genteel churches. . . . If you believe that the nation is being ruined by sinister forces, name them.

Billy Graham clearly opted for status quo acceptance and white nationalist sentiments instead of the prophetic role of truth-telling and racial justice. In the aftermath of the King assassination, when over one hundred cities in the United States had erupted in explosive riots, Graham had yet another opportunity to redeem himself and revolutionize white Christianity. Recognizing that the time was ripe, Graham's black associates approached him with the proposal that he "step into the gap and provide responsible leadership" in the racial crisis. But Graham took no assertive action, even refusing the wise suggestion that his evangelistic association should produce a film that would address racism. Instead, Graham leaned heavily on integrated crusades and increased the use of black musicians and celebrities in his ministry. "But he moved no closer to using, or even fully approving, King's tactics of prophetic confrontation and challenge of the establishment."[10]

In his last year, Malcolm X's *public* discourse on Christianity remained virtually the same as it had been while he was in the Nation of Islam. Not too many days before his assassination, when he was asked in a British interview why he had become a Muslim, Malcolm replied:

> Christian religion has been used to brainwash the [b]lack man. It has taught him to look for his heaven in the hereafter while the white man enjoys his heaven on earth. I chose to be a Black Muslim and a realist. The American whites talk but do not practice brotherhood; therefore it is my duty to fight this evil.[11]

When asked about his conversion to Islam, Malcolm invariably cited his first conversion to the Nation of Islam, though he seems to have intended his listeners to understand that his devotion to Islam had a certain continuity throughout his life, even when he was entangled in the Black Muslim movement.[12] Contrary to the wishful thinking of some black (and white) Christians, there is no sign that Malcolm was gravitating toward the cross prior to his death. The romantic notion that Malcolm would have embraced Christianity had he only lived longer is purely wishful thinking. That many black Christians prefer to imagine Malcolm stripped of the Islamic religion and coated in a sugary syrup of "love" says a great deal in confirmation of Blyden's analysis of black Christians and the white cross. White Christianity in the United States—which presupposes the equity of the ecclesiastical status quo and the good intentions of white religious leaders in matters of race—is merciless toward blacks who dare to suggest otherwise. Black Christians, though secretly sharing the indignant analysis of Malcolm X, are all too aware that white Christians see him as the quintessential "hate teacher," and therefore they can only accept him in some sterile, processed sense. Others, who feel it a betrayal to acknowledge truth when it comes from the mouth of a Muslim, are likewise inclined to impute to Malcolm an almost-conversion to Christianity, or simply dismiss him in deference to white Christian sensitivities. (Meanwhile, of course, many of these same black Christians willingly tolerate the insensitive social and political remarks of white televangelists and other right-wing Christian leaders in the name of Jesus, believing it their duty to bear up the cross of white religion in the name of Christian love.)

Of course, the public Malcolm X could not afford to tip his hat to Christianity, not only because he believed that Christianity as it was manifested in the world was oppressive, but because he was engaged in the advancement of Islam. Unlike William Blyden, who remained a Christian while praising Islam for its superiority vis-à-vis the black man, Malcolm embraced the religion of Muhammad the Prophet and it was in his best interest to emphasize the negative history of the Christian world. In *The Autobiography*, Malcolm echoed Blyden by saying that the Christian church "became infected with racism when it entered white Europe." Though the Western church had its roots in North Africa, Malcolm said, "[t]he Christian church returned to Africa under the banner of the Cross—conquering, killing, exploiting, pillaging, raping, bullying, beating—and teaching white supremacy."[13] It is possible that these closing remarks in *The Autobiography* were left over from earlier Black Muslim chapters, and that Haley edited them to fit "1965," the final chapter of the book. Nevertheless, even if this is the case, Malcolm's remarks are consistent with his general assessment of Christianity as a negative religious manifestation.

These two factors, Malcolm's political criticism of Christianity and his determination to advance Islam, shaped his public remarks about the Christian religion, and his lack of balance in discussing certain religious aspects was perhaps inevitable. For instance, in a speech he made before his Organization of Afro-American Unity on January 24, 1965, Malcolm broached the topic of the slave trade, the infamous slave ship *Jesus*, and the meaning and usage of spirituals by black slaves. His remarks were too simplistic and too convenient to reflect his private awareness about the roots of black Christian spirituality:

> The slaves had an old spiritual which they sang: "Steal away to Jesus, steal away home." You think that they were talking about some man that got hung on the cross two thousand years ago, whereas they were talking about a ship. They wanted to steal away and get on board that ship that was named Jesus, so that they could go back home on the mother continent, the African continent. . . . But you've got poor Negroes today, who have been brainwashed, still sitting in church talking about stealing away to Jesus.

Malcolm concluded that rather than singing "about that man that died supposedly on the cross, they were talking about a boat."

> This is what the spiritual came from. But they've got it in the church today, and that old dumb preacher has your and my —yes, dumb preacher—has your and my mind so messed up we think that Jesus is somebody that died on a cross, and we sit there foaming at the mouth talking about ["]you can have all this world, but give me Jesus.["] And the man took all this world, and gave you Jesus, and that's all you've got is Jesus.[14]

Malcolm's words must be weighed carefully, for while his point about the political use of Christian spirituals is undeniable, his contention that spirituals *originated* as political tools is problematic, even from Blyden's standpoint. To accept Malcolm's revisionist interpretation of the Christian spiritual in its entirety is to negate the essence of black Christianity which, even in its flaws and imperfections, represents a sincere appropriation of biblical faith and spirituality. Of course, the essence of black Christian faith was belief in the redemptive message of the Gospel story. Malcolm minimized this faith in his negative remarks about Christ's death on the cross, and in doing so he faithfully reflects the Qur'an's forceful denial of the crucifixion. Consequently, given his dual nature as a religious revolutionist, Malcolm's political reading of the black spiritual must be recognized as a religious reading as well.

Given these aspects of Malcolm's approach to Christianity, however, one must recall what he had expressed in his letter from Saudi Arabia, when he acknowledged having friends of differing faiths, whose beliefs he respected and perceived as being part of the larger human family. To the extent that Malcolm respected another person's faith, he also recognized that sincere faith transcended the political realm. After a speech he made in New York City on February 15, 1965, Malcolm was asked to comment on the difference between the teachings of the Nation of Islam and traditional Islam. His response was that "what Elijah Muhammad is teaching is an insult to the entire Muslim world." Malcolm concluded that the religion of Islam had nothing to do with color—and, almost in passing, he added: "There is *no* religion that has anything to do with color."[15]

Epilogue
Interview with a Christian Minister

After Malcolm's assassination in February 1965, the *Chicago Defender*, Elijah Muhammad's hometown paper, featured a brief interview with the Reverend Richard Gleason, a Baptist minister from the Windy City.[1] Gleason, who was twenty-eight years old the year of Malcolm's death, had met Malcolm X in Harlem following the latter's return from the pilgrimage to Mecca and a tour of Africa (May 21, 1964).

Gleason told the Defender: "Malcolm was completely committed to his people." The minister revealed that he had talked at length with Malcolm over lunch at Harlem's Theresa Hotel, where Malcolm had his organizational headquarters. Malcolm discussed the pilgrimage with Gleason, and how the experience had led him to change some of his views. Malcolm also told the Reverend Gleason that during a religious ceremony he and other pilgrims were dressed in a two-piece ceremonial garb, and they gathered in the formation of a circle, each kneeling on his own prayer rug.

It was then, Malcolm told Gleason, that he happened to glance up and realized he was in the presence of blue-eyed Muslims. When a ceremonial vessel was passed around the pilgrim circle, each handled it. Malcolm told Gleason it was a lot like the Christian rite of Communion and that before the experience of the pilgrimage, he was very anti-white, "but he seemed to have gained a broader view from the experience. He said he was able to see the overall view of the [Muslim] religion when he was in Mecca."

In retrospect, Gleason compared Malcolm X's struggles to those of

Christ because, he said: "As Christ reflected what the masses felt, reflected their needs, so did Malcolm. Politicians and other religious leaders killed him because he represented a threat. It was the same with Malcolm, who did not at all represent a few middle class Negroes who are successful." Gleason said that most black leaders talk "from outside the ghetto," whereas Malcolm was not concerned about City Hall.

Like Jesus, the minister concluded, Malcolm X was not interested in the elite of his age, he was concerned for the masses. "Malcolm had a quality about him that drew people to him. He was deep thinking," Gleason said, "and not at all arrogant or pretentious. He was a remarkable man."

Author's Postscript

During the Labor Day weekend of 1971 I went with my family to a religious convention in Washington, D.C., and found myself drafted into evangelistic service by one of the attending pastors leading a foray into the city. Barely fourteen years of age, I went along dutifully in the Lord's service, terrified by the prospect of passing out gospel tracts to strangers and fearful of the urban setting itself. A small-town pastor's son from western Pennsylvania, I was overwhelmed when I stepped off the bus onto a busy Georgetown street scented by marijuana and charged with revolutionary fervor. Wide-eyed, I wandered with a handful of tracts along a sidewalk cluttered with hippies and other societal rebels while acid rock blared from nearby speakers. Feeling lost, I nevertheless offered a tract to a young white man sprawled on the sidewalk smoking a reefer. He made a caustic remark about Christianity and waved me off. Walking farther down the street I came upon a man with a sidewalk table display of aromatic candles in various shapes and colors. A black man of dark complexion, the candle vendor was striking in his dashiki and sunglasses and he seemed approachable. My youth perhaps worked in my favor, for when I extended a tract he smiled guardedly, almost sympathetically—undoubtedly realizing I was feeling like a lost lamb. "I'll read yours if you read one of mine," he said firmly, and I immediately shook my head in agreement. It seemed a fair deal, after all, so we exchanged religious tracts—my Christian challenge for his Muslim counterchallenge.

The afternoon sun was pleasantly warm, and I was feeling more like a tourist—indeed an explorer—than a missionary, so I remained for a few moments to look over his candle display. Suddenly, down the street came strolling a lovely cinnamon-colored sister, sensuously clad in a summer dress. In that moment, both the Muslim candle vendor and the reluctant adolescent missionary were dumbfounded—though the candle man recovered immediately and proceeded to pour forth in eloquent exultation of her black beauty. She smiled and walked on and my apostate teenage eyes followed in wonder, until I realized that the candle man had stepped from behind his table and continued the ebullient praise, his adoring flirtations drawing her to stop, turn around, and smile at him. In an instant the candle man stooped low and twisted his head—as if to stare up the woman's dress—to the extent that his comical posture made him seem almost upside down. She smiled and continued walking, but I stood, shocked and embarrassed at the Muslim's unseemly behavior. Wandering back to the bus to wait for the rest of the adults, I kept thinking about the candle man and suddenly realized I had not yet looked at his tract. I pulled it out of my pocket and read its cover message, blazoned in bright red letters: *Christians Beware!* As it turned out, the tract was an anti-trinitarian polemic, warning Christians to cease and desist from proclaiming the divinity of Jesus lest we be guilty of sinning against the Spirit of God.

Interestingly, though, I was not fazed by this warning; it was the candle man's behavior that had made a bigger impression on my young mind. As a youth I assumed that the message of Islam (of course, like most people, I could not distinguish the Nation of Islam from traditional Islam at the time) was inferior to my religion, based simply on the candle man's behavior. In my immaturity, I dismissed Islam based on the behavior of one self-defined Muslim, just as the Western world tends to dismiss Islam with simplistic judgments based on the violent or immoral acts of certain Muslims portrayed by the media. In fact, until I read about Malcolm X, over a decade later, my conception of black Muslims was largely shaped by this experience, even though this man's behavior was certainly contrary to the teachings of the Qur'an—and most certainly would have been frowned upon by Malcolm X. Of course, it is easy to condemn any religion by observing the sins and hypocrisy of its followers. And though behaviors should reflect religious truth, and disciples should be held accountable for their behavior by their respective religious communities, I believe the ultimate integrity of any religion is based on its teachings. To me, the message of the Bible is far more believable than the message of the Qur'an, and so I am a Christian.

Later, after reading *The Autobiography of Malcolm X*, I learned that the Nation of Islam had likewise dismissed Christianity based on white Christian sin—an expansive array of historic and contemporary injustices ranging from slavery and colonialism to segregation in the church. I was immediately drawn to the prophetic message of *The Autobiography*, yet I was appalled by what I perceived as the reckless, irresponsible appropriation of the Bible by the Nation of Islam. It seemed to me then (and it still does) that throughout the story of the Nation of Islam, and especially that of Malcolm X, there is an ironic weaving of gold strands and straw—the confusion of a message of transcendent clarity and prophetic force with religious duplicity and distortion. Thus, in the case of Malcolm X, I have endeavored to excise one from the other, at least according to my Christian presuppositions. I have done so because I believe the force of Malcolm's life and message are well worth the effort.

Nevertheless, I suspect this book will bother Black Muslims and white Christians equally. Neither side will appreciate my critical treatment of their icons of leadership, and one or the other will suggest I have been unfair or prejudicial in my assessment of the duplicity of black "Islam" and white "Christianity." Those sympathetic to the Nation of Islam may contend that the founders of the movement were not really opposed to the essence of Christianity, only the tragic "white Christian" phenomenon. I believe this claim to be nothing but revisionist apology: if men like W. D. Fard and Elijah Muhammad had a sincere respect for the essence of Christianity, they would have made the logical distinctions between the religion of the white man and the religion of the Bible. Indeed, they would have made painstaking efforts to use the Bible constructively within the Christian context (as did Martin Luther King, Jr.) to demonstrate the real requirements of Christianity as it pertains to race and justice. Instead, these men ran roughshod over the religious essence of Christianity, damning and distorting it along with the European Roman Catholic and Protestant religious systems.

Others will suggest that I have imposed my religious and theological agenda upon the black community by raising the issue of hermeneutics—biblical interpretation—as a priority. After all, or so these critics might say, some of the biggest racists in white Christendom have been orthodox exegetes. Such critics may feel that I am nit-picking because I presume that black Christians ought to react to biblical abuse with the same force with which they would greet racial abuse. Of course, in many cases they have and continue to do so—though often it has been black religious leaders and scholars who seem to minimize doctrinal integrity as integral to a sound prophetic role. Some would even suggest that doctrinal integrity is a European fascination that is of no essential importance to the real life of the black believer. This is clearly the case with many black ministers who applaud Louis Farrakhan for his social analysis and wink at his religious distortions, apparently not perceiving that they are undermining their own spiritual roles in the community.

Today I am the pastor of a small urban congregation with a remarkably diverse composition, immigrants from what Malcolm liked to call the "dark world." The Asians and continental Africans in my community live as neighbors to Irish and Italian Americans, along with Latinos and blacks from the United States and the Caribbean. On the street in front of my church it is common to see Egyptian Muslim women walking in traditional veiled attire, and in the local C-Town Supermarket on a Sunday afternoon one may go from aisle to aisle and find people literally from all over the world, all shopping for their evening meal. Malcolm X would like my neighborhood. He would probably also smile if he saw my congregation.

The church I pastor was once a Norwegian congregation, their descendants eventually leaving the city and handing over the keys of the kingdom to "outsiders." In many ways, the building and its appearance are a reminder that Christianity, too, is undergoing changes. A century-old structure with a U.S. flag and a "Christian flag" at the front of the sanctuary, the church represents a religion that invariably required European immigrants to adapt to the necessities of white-mindedness and all it entailed. Like my congregation, however, Christianity in the United States is being refreshed and strengthened by black, brown, red, and yellow Christians, especially in our nation's urban centers. Churches in the city that have no sensitivity to people of color are very likely to close their doors, while the most successful churches have welcomed the new diversity and the breaking down of color barriers. Suburban-based denominations are now turning their attention to the cities (as are cults like the Mormons, who recently received new revelation as to the acceptability of blacks) and are groping for ways to in-reach to the city. This is no panacea, of course. Many of the attitudes and behaviors in the new Christian "racial reconciliation" movement (characterized most popularly by the Promise Keepers) are no better than the political missionary attitudes of white liberals during the civil rights era. Many white pastors who have come to reclaim the cities are paternalistic at best, and some are outright ecclesiastical "Massas" who have discovered that the Big House can be built in the city as easily as in the country.

If I could ask the reader to bear one thing in mind during the experience of reading this book it is that—for better or for worse—my motivations are pastoral. I did not originally conceive of the book in such a way, but during the real fleshing out of this work I went from being a "freelance religious educator" to an interim pastor, and finally to a full pastor of a church. The people who have contributed to my work are not just scholars and writers I have consulted, but Christians, Muslims, and Jews who have befriended me and taken the time to share their thoughts. However, I have written this book not only to extend my thesis of Malcolm X as a religious revolutionist, but also in the hope that it will affirm my religious community in its glorious diversity and perhaps even make a small contribution toward the coming of a new "world Christianity" purged of white supremacy and race-mindedness. I would like to think that in some measure such an endeavor is an apt tribute to Malcolm X, who ultimately hoped to make a noble endowment to the entire human race. Certainly, studying Malcolm X intensively over a number of years has helped to make me a better Christian, and his comfortable posture as a world citizen has equally been an inspiration to me in my little urban study.

To borrow from the words of Jesus, it is a time for new wine to be poured, but neither the Nation of Islam nor Christianity in the United States appear to be suitable vessels for the healthful advancement of wholistic spiritual development, particularly regarding race relations. New wine requires new wineskins, and it is the task of well-meaning Christians to craft wineskins untainted by racism. *"So let us not be weary in well-doing; for in due season we shall reap, if we faint not."*

LOUIS A. DeCARO, JR.
The parsonage, Vroom Street Evangelical Free Church
October 16, 1997
The 138th Anniversary of John Brown's Raid on Harper's Ferry

Appendix A

An Open Letter to Elijah Muhammad from Malcolm X, June 23, 1964

After Malcolm returned from his famous pilgrimage in the spring of 1964, he found himself caught up in an escalating conflict with the Nation of Islam sparked by the latter's determination to evict Malcolm and his family from their home. Malcolm responded by revealing to the press that Elijah Muhammad had sired a number of children in adulterous relationships with women in the Nation of Islam. Reprisals by the Nation of Islam included flagrant attempts on Malcolm's life and attacks on some of his followers. Malcolm wrote this open letter in the summer of 1964, shortly before he left again for his second, longer trip abroad that lasted from July to the end of November of that year. Malcolm's words to Muhammad not only reflect his post-Hajj perspective of the Nation of Islam, but also reveal his ability to use the Bible in an effective manner, his disappointment with Muhammad's non-action, and his sober sense of history. As to the latter, Malcolm's words concerning Muhammad's legacy have proven to be all but prophetic.[1]

I warned you three months ago that your followers in the Fruit of Islam were secretly arming themselves, and were being incited by your ministers to commit wholesale assault and even murder against those Afro-Americans who refuse to accept the so-called "divine" explanation you have given for your having fathered at least eight illegitimate children by six of your teenage secretaries. Despite the increasing acts of violence against fellow Afro-Americans . . . you have tried to give the public the impression that you are "aloof" (above and beyond) to what is going on, but as the leader of the Fruit of Islam your calculated silence will not enable [you] to escape the full blame for the explosive situation that is developing.

Since you didn't open your mouth and give the word to fight back when your faithful Muslim followers were brutally shot and beaten by white racists in Los Angeles, California . . . how can you justify now giving the word for your followers to declare war on each other, simply because some refuse to follow you any longer?

No matter how much you stay in the background and stir others up to do your murderous dirty work, any bloodshed committed by Muslim against Muslim will compel the writers of history to declare you guilty not only of adultery and deceit, but also of MURDER.

According to the Bible which you quote so often . . . [*King*] David became morally weak and committed adultery with the wife of his chief lieutenant, Uriah. In an effort to deceive his followers and keep them from deserting him because of his adulterous acts, David had his best friend, Uriah, killed by his own soldiers.

Although the innocent soldiers did the actual killing, it was David himself whom history records as the real murderer. I pray you will learn a lesson from David's history and call off this unnecessary bloodshed that you are driving your followers into before it is too late.

Instead of wasting all of this energy fighting each other, we should be working in unity and harmony with other leaders and organizations in an effort to solve the very serious problems facing all Afro-Americans. Historians would then credit us with intelligence and sincerity.

Malcolm X

Appendix B

*A Partial Transcript of a Sermon
by Malcolm X at Elder Solomon Lightfoot
Michaux's New York Church of God,
June 16, 1961*[1]

Michaux: Giving honor to God, we're proud to have Brother Malcolm X with us. I wanted you to know so you would understand us. And now we're going to try to understand you, and see whether our eyes are on the same God [*applause*].

Malcolm: To Elder Michaux, your charming wife, your brother over here, Dr. [*Lewis*] Michaux, and all of our beloved brothers and sisters, I am thankful to Allah for putting into Elder Michaux's heart to invite those of us who are Muslims here this evening to explain what the Honorable Elijah Muhammad is teaching that has the white man, as he said, so afraid. [*Audience voice: "That's right! Preach, brother!"*] You have to excuse me for being blunt, I only know that way, but I think that you have a wonderful elder, because anytime . . . [*applause*]. Today, whenever you see an open door, and he has opened his door here this evening to us, it's always a sign of an open heart, and an open heart is the sign of an open mind. And it is open-mindedness today that will save our lives, or narrow-mindedness that will cost us our lives. Our beloved leader and teacher, the Honorable Elijah Muhammad—and I think you should turn that name "Elijah" over in your mind—"Elijah" is a very important name according to the Bible, as Elder Michaux has so beautifully pictured to us already here this evening.

The Honorable Elijah Muhammad teaches us that we can learn a lesson from the bee. The bee is only an insect, but it goes from flower to flower. It doesn't land just anywhere, and it doesn't land just everywhere. Whenever a bee lands, he lands on a flower. He doesn't stay there all day, he stays there long enough to get the best of what that flower has to offer and then he goes on to another flower, and another and another and another, and finally when that bee does land, or make his home, he has honey. But when you sit in one place all of your life, you be like the fly. A fly lands there and says, "This is it," and a fly never has been known to make any honey. [*Laughter*] The fly's mind is closed but the bee's mind is open. And I think that all of us here this evening, the followers of Elder Michaux and the followers of the Honorable Elijah Muhammad, show by our ability to come together that those who are leading us and teaching us have created within us an open heart as well as an open mind.

Not long ago President Kennedy went half around the world and talked with Kruschev. Kennedy didn't think he was going to convert Kruschev, and Kruschev didn't think he was going to convert Kennedy. But Kennedy was wise enough to realize that Kruschev could destroy him. Kruschev was wise enough to realize that Kennedy could destroy him, and they thought that it would be better to sit down and talk with each other, get firsthand information about each other, so that they could better understand each other. And when you understand someone, though you have opposing views, you know how to live together on the same planet. This is very important today. It is important that all of us get a better understanding of each other. I'm thankful to Allah that Elder Michaux took the time that he did so that all of the Muslims who have come here tonight could get a better understanding of his doctrine—what he teaches, his conception of God, his conception of the prophets, his conception of the white man, and his conception of the black man. And in the couple of minutes that we have left, it is our desire and intention and hope to let you also understand our conception of God, our conception of the devil [*woman shouts from the audience: "Yeah!"*], our conception of the white man, and our conception of the black man. Then when you know how we believe as well as we know how you believe, we can better understand one another.

As many of you know, and as Elder Michaux has already pointed out, the Honorable Elijah Muhammad is probably the most controversial black man in America today. He's the most talked-about black man in America today, he's the most written-about black man in America today. And if the truth be known, in the mind of the white man he's the most feared black man in America today [*applause*]. He's not feared by the white man because he's bad. He's not feared by the white man because he has an army. He's not feared by the white man because he has weapons, but he's feared by the white man because the white man knows he's got a God behind him. [*A man shouts: "Right!" and applause*] The Muslims who follow the Honorable Elijah Muhammad are not political-minded, we don't believe in politics. We believe that every president that has ever sat in the White House has promised us and has never kept that promise. We believe that the politicians have used politics to trick us and to promise us falsely, and therefore today we reject politics, we reject the politicians, and we reject the political solutions set forth by the politicians to solve the serious problems that confront our people here in America today. And in rejecting that, we turn toward our own God, we turn toward the religion of our forefathers, we turn toward the God of our forefathers, we do the same thing that Moses taught his people to do in the house of bondage four thousand years ago. In fact, we who follow the Honorable Elijah Muhammad study the history of the Bible so that we'll better understand the condition and the things that face us here in America today. When we read the Bible and find out that there was slaves in there and that they too were held in bondage by a wicked slavemaster, we look around at ourselves and see that we too, 20 million black people, have been held here in bondage under the hands of the white man for the past four hundred years. And we feel that just as God, four thousand years ago, showed those people how to get out from under the bondage of their wicked slavemaster by raising them up someone from their midst to teach them and guide them—not into the religion of the slavemaster or the God of the slavemaster—but that prophet's job was to turn them back toward the God of Abraham, the God of Isaac, the God of Jacob, and the God of their own forefathers. [*Applause*]

I just have a couple of moments, I hope you'll be patient. When I met Elder Michaux this week in his brother's store, he was a very charming man. I was very surprised when I met him because usually the ordinary preacher and the Muslim doesn't hit it off. But I found that Elder Michaux was a different type of preacher than is commonly known here among the so-called Negroes here of America. We were able to . . . . [*Brief applause*] We were able—he's just like his brother, Dr. Michaux, who has the bookstore, and anytime you find a black man in America who will provide black people with books where they can read something about black people that elevates black people, when he has a brother like Elder Michaux, you know that both of them have got to be good men. So when he invited us out here to tell you what we believe in, we want to tell it to you just like that: We believe in one God whose proper name is Allah. We believe in the same God that Moses believed in, as he has already pointed out by reading from the Holy Qur'an [*Malcolm pronounces it "Ku-won" in imitation of Elijah Muhammad's pronunciation*]. We believe in the same God that Abraham believed in. We believe in the God that told Moses "an eye for an eye and a tooth for a tooth." [*Voices from the audience: "Yeah!" "That's right!" and applause*] We don't believe in any kind of God that tells slaves to turn the other cheek unless that same God is telling the slavemaster also to turn the other cheek. We don't believe in any kind of doctrine that teaches slaves to be passive and nonviolent. We believe in a God that will tell a man who is a slave how to get free, no matter what method is necessary to get him his freedom. And just as Moses called that God "Allah," and as Abraham called that God "Allah," and Noah called him "Allah" and Lot called him "Allah," and when Jesus was on the cross he likewise said "Allah Allah lama sabachthani"—those of you who have a knowledge of the language that Jesus spoke and know that Jesus called God by the name "Allah" I think you can better appreciate us today when you realize that we serve the same God that Jesus served, whose personal and proper name is "Allah." One God—not two Gods, three Gods, four Gods or five Gods, but one God. And as Elder Michaux will tell you, when you serve one God then you have unity. But when you serve more than one God, you have disunity. And the Honorable Elijah Muhammad teaches us that the disunity that has existed among the so-called Negroes of America has been your and my running around here after *ignorant* preachers, serving more Gods than one, and it has caused us to be divided. He has taught us that the religion of that God, in the language that Jesus spoke, would be called Islam. Jesus didn't speak English. Jesus didn't call the Supreme Being "God" because "God" is an English word and two thousand years ago when Jesus was walking the earth, the English-speaking people weren't speaking English. They were up in the caves and hills of Europe on their all-fours and they didn't know how to talk! [*Applause*] Please—because I only have a couple of moments—you might say, "Well, what difference does this make?" It makes a lot of difference. If you don't know where you were two thousand years ago, and you don't know where your slavemaster was two thousand years ago, you will be misled into thinking that you have always been a slave, or that you have always been a savage, and that he has always been up over you. So the Honorable Elijah Muhammad says you have got to take the black man today back into his past in order for him to get the correct understanding of what's going on right now. And he teaches us that in the language that Jesus spoke he called his religion "Islam." He called his God "Allah." And when Jesus met his disciples, as the Bible said, Jesus said, "Peace be unto you," that's how you say it in English. But actually when Jesus met his followers in those days he said, "Salaam Alaikum," and they replied "Walaikum Salaam,"— which means, "Peace be unto you" and in return, "And unto you be peace." And the Honorable Elijah Muhammad teaches us that anyone who believes in the religion that Jesus taught and in the God whom Jesus served, in the language of Jesus, that person would be called a "Muslim"—or as it is pronounced here in the West, a "Moslem." "Muslim" in the language that Jesus spoke only means "one who has submitted himself to the will of God, one who believes in obeying God, and one who will lay down his life for God and also lay down his life for his brother. This religion of Islam is religion of submission to the will of the Divine Supreme Being. But when a Muslim believes in a submissive religion, at the same time he's never taught to turn the other cheek. We are taught as Muslims, as followers of the Honorable Elijah Muhammad, as believers in the same religion that Jesus taught, to always seek peace—never look for trouble—but at the same time if we are attacked, our religion gives us the right to fight in defense of ourselves. [*Applause*] The reason that the white man is afraid of the Muslims and of the religion of Islam is because there are 725 million people in the non-white world, primarily in Africa and Asia, whose religion is Islam. There are 725 million of your and my brothers and sisters back in that area of this earth where the white man kidnapped us from, and brought us from in chains four hundred years ago. Our people back there turn toward the East, five times a day, and say in their language [*phonetically transcribed*]: "Ashado Allah illaha ashado an la hillahah il Allah, wa ashado ana Muhammadan rasool illah"—which in the language of our forefathers and in the langugage of Jesus, and the language of Abraham, and the language of Moses, and the language of all of the prophets means, "I bear witness that there is no God but Allah, and I bear witness that Muhammad is the messenger of Allah." When the white man hears you say that he shakes because he knows you're calling on a God then who will come to your rescue. And as many as—[*applause*] please! I only have a couple moments—as many of you probably read in the paper, when Dr. Billy Graham, a white Christian, a white theologian, returned from Africa last year, he said that the black man in Africa is turning away from the religion of Christianity back to toward the religion of Islam at a ratio of eleven to one. And Bishop Pike, an Episcopalian from San Francisco, in *Look* magazine, December, also pointed out that the black man in Africa is turning away from the religion of Christianity back toward the religion of Islam at a ratio of five to one. Why are the black people of Africa turning away from Christianity and back toward the religion of Islam? It's because the black man in Africa today is waking up. He's throwing off his chains; he's throwing off the yoke of his master; he's throwing the Europeans—who exploited him and colonized him in the past—out. And as that black man in Africa, who is your and my brother, and your and my sister, throws off the shackles of European colonialism and exploitation and oppression, he also gave that same European back the religion that he brought down there and used to make a slave out of him. And just as the masses of black people in Africa are turning away from the religion of Christianity back toward the religion of their forefathers, the religion of Islam, that same religion has leaked nine thousand miles across the Atlantic Ocean, and today is sweeping through the masses of black people right here in America under the spiritual guidance of the Honorable Elijah Muhammad. [*Applause*] Please!

The Honorable Elijah Muhammad is teaching the black man in America the language that he once had. He's teaching the black man in America the history that he once had. He's teaching the black man in America the complete culture that we once had in order to turn our hearts back in a direction and look at something that's great for our people, so that we can hold our heads high, instead of running around here with the inferiority complex that the slavemaster has brainwashed into us during our four hundred years of bondage here. [*Interference in recording*]

Elder Michaux, you have to excuse my Bible if it's a little worn out—it's worn out because I *use* it. If it was new you'd know I've been sitting on it a long time. [*Laughter*] But it's worn out because I use it, Elder. As Elder Michaux pointed out about Elijah in that Bible [*pounding his fist on the podium*], you first have to go back to the first prophecy to find out who was Elijah going to turn the hearts back to. Who were these people that Elijah was going to work on? In the 15th chapter of Genesis, in the 13th verse, God told Abraham: "Know for a surety, Abraham, thy seed will be strangers in a land that is not theirs"— think of that—thy descendants, thy offspring, will be strangers in a land that is not theirs, will be afflicted and enslaved for four hundred years. And the Negro preacher has been teaching you and me that that's the Jew. But the Honorable Elijah Muhammad says that it's the so-called Negro right here in America. Understand, it says "know for a surety that thy seed will be strangers in a land that is not theirs," and nobody has been more so treated like a stranger in a land that is not his than has the black man right here in America for the past four hundred years. But having been made blind, deaf, and dumb, we read the book and think it's about somebody else. Stranger—if I come to your house and you tell me where to sit, I'm a stranger there. If I'm not free to come and go anywhere in that house that I desire, I'm a stranger there. And here in America, Uncle Sam has a house in which there are fifty rooms, and the black people of America cannot come where they want or go where they want despite the fact that we were born here, despite the fact that we were enslaved here, despite the fact that we have fought and died in every war the white man has ever had, still we're treated like strangers in a land that is not ours. And no one can deny that. [*Applause*] Please.

So the Bible is a good book. It's the Word of God. But you have to understand it. The book says when it's about to close: "Blessed are those that read and understand." It don't say reading it will make you blessed. You've got to understand it to be blessed. If reading the Bible [*pounding his fist on the podium*] would make you blessed, there wouldn't be a Negro in America suffering. But nobody reads Bibles more than the Negro and no one catches more hell than the so-called Negro here in America. [*Break in tape recording*] . . . black people who are strangers in this land right now. Strangers so much so you're called a second-class citizen. Strangers so much so that you are *not* granted civil rights. Strangers so much so you have to ride on the back of the bus up North as well as down South. Is that right or wrong? [*Audience: "Right!"*] But the Bible says, and God says in this book, "but also that nation whom they shall serve will I judge. And afterward they shall come out with great substance." And the Honorable Elijah Muhammad says that that's America, and that nation that is doomed to be judged by God is America. It's Uncle Sam who today is guilty for the crime that he has committed against these twenty million black people. If God condemned Pharaoh for enslaving those people, and God condemned Nebuchadnezzar for enslaving those people in Babylon, and a man here today more vicious than Nebuchadnezzar ever was, more vicious than Pharaoh ever was, has enslaved our people and brutalized our people in this house of bondage for longer than four hundred years. And if you think that God judged Pharaoh for what he did, and that God judged Nebuchadnezzar for what he did, and God is going to forgive the [*pounds fist on the podium*] American white man who has brutalized you worse than anybody ever has, I say you got the wrong understanding. [*Applause*]

As Elder Michaux said, we're living at the end of the world. But what world? Solomon said "generations come and generations go, but the earth abides forever" [Ecclesiastes 1:4]. God is not going to destroy the earth. God is going to destroy people. There's more than one world on this earth. There's an eastern world and a western world. There's a dark world and a white world. There's an old world and a new world. There's a righteous world and a wicked world. Now which world is God going to destroy? He says in this book, "Behold . . ." [*pounding his fist lightly, Malcolm pauses from his fiery diatribe and begins to speak in a very gentle fashion*]. Excuse me for going a little fast. But you know it's like the Honorable Elijah Muhammad has explained it to us and [when] you see our people misunderstanding, it gets you excited sometimes. And when you see a house getting ready to blow up that your beloved brother is in, and he's sitting there dumb and doesn't know that that house is about to go up, you feel sorry for him, and it makes you get a little excited. But look what He said: God would judge that nation whom they shall have served. And beloved brothers and sisters, that's none other than America—you're in Babylon, you're in a modern Babylon, you're in a modern Sodom, you're in a modern house of bondage that you thought was Egypt four thousand years ago.

And many of you will say, "If God is going to judge this nation with fire, how are his people going to escape?" He told Moses, in Deuteronomy [18:18], "I will raise them up a prophet like unto thee. I will put my words into his mouth, and he shall teach them all that I shall command him." And the white man has always known that right here in America a prophet, a man of God, would be raised up from the midst of these slaves, and it would be his job to do the same thing for his people today that Moses did for his people four thousand years ago. Moses never went to the slavemaster and said, "Let us integrate," Moses told the Pharaoh, "Let my people go." Please! At no time did Moses say integration—"Let my people go" means separation! Let us get away from you, let us have some land of our own, where we can set up a house to worship our own God, where we can set up a house in which will be the religion of our own God.

So the Honorable Elijah Muhammad teaches us that God told Moses, "I will raise up a prophet just like thee, and he shall speak unto them all that I shall command him." And all of that, if you understand it, pertains to the day and time that you and I are living in right now. And you have to look for a prophet like Moses, and Elder Michaux actually put his finger on it there in Malachi, when he read the part where Malachi said, or rather God said it through the words of Malachi, "Behold before the coming of that great and dreadful day, I will send you Elijah"

[Malachi 4:5]. Elijah is a man like Moses, Elijah is a man like Moses who will be raised up from the midst of the so-called Negroes in the last days. Moses was an ex-slave. Moses was a stranger in a house that wasn't his. Moses's people were strangers in a land that didn't belong to them, and yet God appeared [*pounding his fist on the podium*] among those slaves who were strangers in that house and picked up one of their own kind and told him exactly what to tell that slavemaster. His job wasn't to make friends between the slave and the master. His job wasn't to lessen the gap between the slave and the slavemaster. Moses's job was to separate those slaves from that slavemaster. And that modern Moses must do the same work that the ancient Moses did, but the prophet says the modern Moses would be a man named Elijah. And we who follow the Honorable Elijah Muhammad here in America today look upon him as that man named Elijah. We look upon him as that one who lined up the Baal prophets and told them to call on their god. And the Baal prophets to us means everyone of the so-called Negro preachers here in America who have been teaching our people to believe in mystery gods and strange gods. Today the Honorable Elijah Muhammad tells every Negro preacher in America combined to call on their god, and they're calling on the same god that the slavemaster does. Go to their church—they're going into the same church that the slavemaster does. But when all of them combined finish calling on their god and trying to work those miracles, the God that the Honorable Elijah Muhammad is serving, the God that the Honorable Elijah Muhammad is representing to the black people of America—not the white man. We're not here to teach the white man anything. We don't let him in our meetings. But we are warning him and teaching black people. Moses's job was to warn the slavemaster and teach the slaves. Elijah's job is to warn the slavemaster and teach the slaves. The Honorable Elijah Muhammad is warning the slavemaster today and teaching the black people. He's teaching you the truth about yourself, the truth about your own kind, the truth about your history, and the truth about the righteous life you should be living instead of that wicked life that you have learned from following after the white man.

The followers of the Honorable Elijah Muhammad—if you'll notice, all of them are young, yet they don't drink, yet they don't smoke, not even cigarettes. They don't take narcotics or reefers or anything else. To live in New York and not get drunk you're going some. But the followers of the Honorable Elijah Muhammad, as young as they are, [*sounds like Malcolm is accenting these remarks by slapping the back of his hand into the palm of his other hand*] they don't smoke, they don't drink, they don't take narcotics, they don't gamble, they don't lie, they don't cheat, they don't steal, they don't use profanity, and they try their best to be as polite as it is possible to be. At the same time they don't commit fornication or adultery. This has been completely eliminated from the followers of the Honorable Elijah Muhammad, and he has done it simply by teaching us that we are the righteous people who originally came from God. But as long as you are taught that you were a savage in the jungle when the white man caught you, why you'll be running around here trying to imitate the white man because you think that he's better than you. But the Honorable Elijah Muhammad teaches us the truth about ourselves. We are God's people. We come out of God's house and the white man is the son of Satan, just like the black man is the son of God. [*Applause*] [*Unintelligible phrase. A woman shouts: "Preach brother, preach!"*]

Just—please—as the Honorable Elijah Muhammad has successfully reformed all of his followers to that point, also he has completely eliminated fornication and adultery. He makes the black man who follows him respect the black woman, protect the black woman, elevate the black woman—this is our religion. You may say, "What about the white woman?" The white man takes care of the white woman. The white man will lynch a black man about a white woman. Now who is around here protecting the black woman? She has no protection. She has no one to elevate her. She has no one to respect her. So we who follow the Honorable Elijah Muhammad cannot be a Muslim unless we learn how to respect our own woman. The black man, he tips his hat to white women. He grins his teeth at white women. He shakes and scratches his head when he gets around them. None of you can deny that. But at the same time the black woman, especially here in America, has never had anyone to respect her or to protect her, nor to elevate her. This is all a part of our religion, and because this is one of the primary ingredients of our religion, this religion is sweeping among black America like a forest fire. And it has the white man worried. Women, our women who haven't had any protection in the past, are getting out of that church where these Negro men have not protected them, where the Negro men been patting them and pawing them all the while they've been in there—I'm not speaking [*about this church*], I'm speaking about those crooked churches that you yourself have been to now! [*Laughter and applause*]

Notes

NOTES TO THE PREFACE

1. *The Autobiography of Malcolm X*, with Alex Haley (New York: Ballantine Books, 1972), 38.

2. Nathan I. Huggins, "Martin Luther King, Jr.: Charisma and Leadership," *Journal of American History*, September 1987, 479.

3. Interestingly, one fine scholar simultaneously patted me on the back and slapped me on the hand in response to my first book on Malcolm X. "Not being a social scientist," he said, I had "skewed" the nature of the Nation of Islam by calling it a cult. My lack of credentials as a social scientist notwithstanding, my critic knows that I have only affirmed the analysis of the sociologist of religion, Milton Yinger, who recognized the problematic religious nature of the Nation of Islam as early as 1957. Yinger's analysis was unfortunately put aside by C. Eric Lincoln's thesis in his popular *The Black Muslims in America* (1960). However, since the Nation of Islam has consistently failed to emerge as a plausible sect of Islam it seems that Yinger the social scientist was correct after all: the Black Muslims were, and continue to be, a "Muslim" cult. See review by L. H. Mamiya, *Choice*, March 1996.

4. The use of "Black Muslim(s)" is properly enclosed in quotation marks because the Nation of Islam has never used this term as a self-designation and, actually, resents the term because it forces a distinction between them and the rest of the Muslim world. In his days as a spokesman for Elijah Muhammad's Nation of Islam, Malcolm X fought with the media over their use of "Black Muslims." However, my choice to use the term without enclosing it in quotations is solely for the purpose of writing convenience and should not be understood in any derogatory manner. I refrain as much as possible from referring to the Nation of Islam members as Muslims (though when I do I use "Muslims") because I make a firm distinction between Elijah Muhammad's followers and believers in traditional Islam. Similarly, when I refer to the Black Muslim religion as "Islam," I use quotation marks.

5. Amiri Baraka, *The Autobiography of LeRoi Jones/Amiri Baraka* (New York: Freundlich Books, 1984), 319.

NOTES TO THE INTRODUCTION

1. The use of the popular term "race" is problematic and its prevalence as a conceptual category in the minds of whites and blacks in the United States is itself indicative of the extent of racism's impact upon our society. Neither the Christian nor the Muslim can find justification for the skewed concept of "race" as a biological unit in our respective canons; we must ultimately reject "race" as a real human category if we are ever going to achieve any kind of equitable human solution in the ongoing conflict between blacks, whites, and other peoples of color in this society. On the other hand, the terms "race" and "racial" are so much a part of our language that enclosing them in quotations in every usage is tedious and overbearing for the writer, the editor, and the reader. Despite my intellectual and spiritual objection to the rubric of "race" I have opted for ease in writing and reading, and have therefore left them unmarked by quotations.

2. For example, one of Elijah Muhammad's followers, Abass Rassoull, formed the "United Nation of Islam," a faction at odds with Farrakhan's Nation of Islam. See Peter Noel, "Raising Elijah," *Village Voice*, October 28, 1997, 46–48.

3. Malcolm X once told a Nation of Islam audience: "Do you know, people have come to Muhammad's Mosque and no matter whether they believed in what Mr. Muhammad was saying or not they never could go back and sit in church." In Benjamin Karim, ed., *The End of White World Supremacy: Four Speeches by Malcolm X* (New York: Seaver Books, 1971), 39.

4. See Thomas Hauser, *Muhammad Ali: His Life and Times* (New York: Simon and Schuster, 1991), 111–12; *Malcolm X: The Last Speeches*, ed. Bruce Perry (New York: Pathfinder Press, 1989), 147.

5. Sonya Ross, "Brother Ben: Former NAACP Head Joins Nation of Islam," *Vibe*, August 1997, 44.

6. Guy Trebay, "Sins of Omission," *Village Voice*, October 22, 1996, 18.

7. Rev. Wyatt Tee Walker, "An Open Letter to Louis Farrakhan & Others," [September?] 1995.

8. Conversation with the Rev. Charles Kenyatta, October 1995.

9. With tear-filled eyes, Farrakhan recalled Malcolm's assassination and told *Emerge* magazine: "My loyalty was with the Honorable Elijah Muhammad. But the pain that it created. . . . And a vicious enemy, sitting back watch-

ing this, with agents on both sides feeding the fire with fuel, culminating in Malcolm's assassination." "Farrakhan: Some Straight Talk and a Few Tears for Malcolm from the Minister," interviewed by George E. Curry, *Emerge*, August 1990, 32; Farrakhan quote from "Brother Minister: The Assassination of Malcolm X," produced by Lewis Kesten, directed by Jack Baxter and Jefri Aalmuhammed (X-ceptional Productions, 1994).

10. I found it interesting that in a conversation with Charles Kenyatta, who followed Malcolm throughout the Nation of Islam years and thereafter, he spoke of Malcolm's posture immediately after the assassination as being a figure of the crucifix. The tragic photograph of Malcolm taken moments after the shooting featured with a story by Gordon Parks for *Life* magazine, however, shows only one of Malcolm's arms outstretched. The fact that Kenyatta remembers Malcolm as dying with both arms outstretched says a great deal about the messianic implications of his work in the minds of those who followed him—implications that the FBI apparently also perceived in Malcolm as well. The photo is found in "The Violent End of the Man Called Malcolm X," *Life*, March 5, 1965, 26.

11. I Corinthians 2:11. All biblical quotations are from the New American Standard translation unless otherwise stated.

NOTES TO CHAPTER 1

1. It is not necessary to give a detailed account of the founding and history of the first Nation of Islam. I have provided a brief account in chapter 2 of *On the Side of My People*, 22–29. An account is found in Claude Andrew Clegg III, *An Original Man: The Life and Times of Elijah Muhammad* (New York: St. Martin's Press, 1997), 20–36, though Clegg's well-written biography suffers from serious deficiencies. Throughout my analysis of the first Nation of Islam, however, I am heavily indebted to Sahib's important work, "The Nation of Islam," which interestingly represents the second Nation of Islam just before Malcolm X's release from prison in 1952. Sahib presents a great deal of information based on extended interviews with Elijah Muhammad, providing excellent insight into the founding of the original Nation of Islam and Muhammad's involvement with W. D. Fard. See Hatim Sahib, "The Nation of Islam," Master's thesis, University of Chicago, 1951.

2. While the influence of the Moorish Science Temple movement is apparent in the early years of the first Nation of Islam, it is more interesting to consider the possibility that Fard may actually have been involved in the black nationalist movement of Marcus Garvey, the Universal Negro Im-

provement Association (UNIA). Documentary scholar Paul Lee first observed the uncanny resemblance of one Garveyite organizer in San Francisco named George Farr. In description and sentiment, Farr—who appears in Naval Intelligence reports made in the early 1920s—seems like Fard. Since Fard claimed to have worked on behalf of black liberation on the West Coast prior to coming east to Detroit, and since he is documented as having a criminal record on the West Coast as well, the possibility that Farr is Fard is all the more enticing. If Fard was a Garveyite, this would not only account for the paramilitary style of the organization but might also suggest that Fard had dissented from the strong Christian orientation of the Garvey movement. Farr clearly acknowledged using the Bible's "prophesies" to "awaken" black people. It is possible that Farr decided he could do a better job of awakening them with his own home-made version of Islam. Mr. Lee revealed his scholarly observation of George Farr in personal conversation with me in the spring of 1992. See Robert A. Hill, ed., *The Marcus Garvey and Universal Negro Improvement Association Papers*, vol. 4 (Berkeley: University of California Press, 1985), 233–37, 311–12, 339, 678.

3. Deen Muhammad Wallace/[Warith Mohammed] , *As the Light Shineth from the East* (Chicago: WDM Publishing, 1980), 27; Sahib, "The Nation of Islam," 69; Clegg, *An Original Man*, 20; C. Eric Lincoln, *The Black Muslims in America* (Boston: Beacon, 1961, 1973), 14.

4. Clegg, *An Original Man*, 20–21; Clifton E. Marsh, *From Black Muslims to Muslims: The Transition from Separation to Islam, 1930–1980* (Metuchen, N.J.: Scarecrow Press, 1984), 51; Sahib, "The Nation of Islam," 69.

5. Note that Warith Mohammed (nee Wallace Muhammad), the son of Elijah Muhammad, says that Fard "studied Drew Ali's approach" and imitated the "package" the latter had used to convey his ideas. Muhammad, *As the Light Shineth from the East*, 107.

6. "Their knowledge of Christianity and the Bible is not much better than their knowledge of Islam and the Koran [*sic*]. In fact, they are ignorant in both. My observation reveals that the best of these followers might know two or three verses of the Bible, but even these few verses he does not understand." Sahib, "The Nation of Islam," 103.

7. Erdmann Doane Beynon, "The Vodoo Cult among Negro Migrants in Detroit," *American Journal of Sociology*, May 1938, 896.

8. One example of Fard's "mathematical" type questions contained in a catechism of thirty-four problems is as follows: "The uncle of Mr. W. D. Fard lives in the wilderness of North America surrounded and robbed completely by the cave man. Therefore, he has no knowledge of his own, nor any one else,

but his mind travels twenty[-]four billion miles per second which is considered the average speed of thought per second. How many round trips will he make in ten seconds to the far planet Platoon?" And another: "The total atoms equal 10,000,000,000,000,000,000,000,000,000,000,000, 000,000, 000,000,000,000,000,000,000,000,000,000,000, 000. How many atoms are there in North America?" See Sahib, "The Nation of Islam," 148; and Arna Bontemps and Jack Conroy, *Anyplace but Here* (New York: Hill and Wang, 1966), 220.

9. Sahib, "The Nation of Islam," 70.

10. It is interesting that in preparing his thesis, Hatim Sahib, a traditional Muslim, took a moment to express his personal disgust for Fard's treatment of the Nativity story. In a searing footnote, Sahib declared: "[The Qur'an] considers such accusing individuals as being atheists and non-Moslems [*sic*] and states that they will be punished in the after life by being put in Jehanna [*hades*]." Sahib, "The Nation of Islam," n. 2, 70.

11. Beynon, "The Voodoo Cult," 900.

12. Ibid.

13. G. W. Grogan, "Dispensationalism," *The New International Dictionary of the Christian Church* (Grand Rapids, Mich.: Zondervan, 1981).

14. The terms "premillennialism" and "postmillennialism" are characteristic of the Christian category of theology referred to as eschatology, the doctrine of last things. Premillennialism simply implies belief that the return of Christ will precede his millennial reign on the earth; postmillennialism consequently implies that Christ's return will occur after some sort of extended period of spiritual enlightenment and renewal on earth. The former anticipates a worsening of the human condition, culminating in a divine interruption and an enforcement of God's Kingdom, while the latter anticipates a heightening of the influence of the Christian church, the success of evangelism, and the preponderance of Christian faith culminating in the return of Christ. A third view, perhaps the most reasonable and historically grounded in the context of the original New Testament reader, is amillennialism (or nonmillennialism), which sees the thousand years of Revelation chapter 20 as a biblical metaphor for the apostolic age and the blossoming of the Christian church. In the case of premillennialism, however, a classical form has existed from the days of the early church and is based only on a reading of the controversial Revelation 20 passage. In contrast, Dispensational premillennialism makes skewed, grotesque, and hackneyed work of other apocalyptic texts in the Hebrew and Christian scriptures, and is generally fixated on the modern State of Israel with a bizarre, theo-political focus.

The Dispensational school thus tends toward titillation and its popular adherents inflate everyday political and social events to the level of prophetic fulfillment, often basing their bold pronouncements on the mere occurrence of events in Israel or the so-called Middle East. Not surprisingly, during the recent Gulf War, many Dispensationalist Christians were heralding Armageddon and the arrival of the antichrist in the person of Saddam Hussein.

15. William A. Maesen, "Watchtower Influences on [']Black Muslim['] Eschatology: An Exploratory Story," *Journal for the Scientific Study of Religion,* Winter 1970, 324.

16. Williston Walker, *A History of the Christian Church* (New York: Charles Scribner's Sons, 1970), 515–16; Robert C. Newman, "Ellen Gould White," *The New International Dictionary of the Christian Church,* 1043.

17. Maesen, "Watchtower Influences," 322; Beynon, "The Voodoo Cult," 900; Sahib, "The Nation of Islam," 71.

18. Beynon, "The Voodoo Cult," 904. A generation after Beynon, one popular black magazine resurrected the speculations surrounding Fard's connection with the Japanese underground in order to cast a negative light on Elijah Muhammad's Nation of Islam. See "The Trouble-Making Muslims," *Sepia* (December 1960), 19. As noted above in note 2, if the Garveyite George Farr was actually W. D. Fard, the connection between the Japanese underground on the West Coast and the founder of the first Nation of Islam may have substance and also explain the attempt on the part of the Japanese to exploit Fard's movement in Detroit. See Hill, *The Marcus Garvey and Universal Negro Improvement Association Papers,* 311 and 339.

19. Sahib, "The Nation of Islam," 84–85.

20. In contrast to what Elijah Muhammad apparently reported to Sahib, in another publication of his Nation of Islam, Muhammad says that Fard was deported from Detroit on May 26, 1933. Elijah Muhammad, *The Supreme Wisdom: Solution to the So-Called Negroes' Problem* (1957; rpt. Newport News, Va.: National Newport News and Commentator, n.d.), 15.

21. E. U. Essien-Udom, *Black Nationalism: The Search for an Identity in America* (Chicago: University of Chicago Press, 1963), 44. Elijah Muhammad told Essien-Udom specifically that he saw Fard off at the airport. Sahib, "The Nation of Islam," 71 and 94; Lincoln, *The Black Muslims in America,* 199.

NOTES TO CHAPTER 2

1. Henri M. Yaker, "The Black Muslims in the Correctional Institution," *Welfare Reporter,* October 1962, 165.

2. Abraham J. Heschel, *The Prophets*, vol. 1 (New York: Harper Colophon Books, 1962), x.

3. Paul W. Valentine and Joel D. Weisman, "Elijah Muhammad, Muslim Chief, Dies," *Washington Post*, February 26, 1975, A8.

4. Sahib, "The Nation of Islam," 87–89; Bob Lucas, "First Magazine Interview with Elijah Muhammad, Black Muslim Leader," *Cavalier*, January 1964, 91.

5. Austin Scott, "Elijah Muhammad, Muslim Leader," *Washington Post*, February 26, 1975, C5; *The Crisis* [NAACP], January 1916, 145.

6. Sahib, "The Nation of Islam," 89.

7. Ibid., 88–89; *The Autobiography of Malcolm X*, 207–8.

8. Lucas, "First Magazine Interview with Elijah Muhammad," 91; *The Autobiography of Malcolm X*, 207; Sahib, "The Nation of Islam," 93.

9. *The Autobiography of Malcolm X*, 207–8; Elijah Muhammad, *Message to the Blackman in America* (Newport News, Va.: United Brothers Communications Systems, n.d.), 178; Marsh, *From Black Muslims to Muslims*, 53; Sahib, "The Nation of Islam," 90.

10. Benjamin Quarles, *The Negro in the Making of America* (New York: Collier Books, 1964, 1978), 97; August Meier and Elliott Rudwick, *From Plantation to Ghetto* (New York: Hill and Wang, 1976), 216; E. Franklin Frazier, *Black Bourgeoisie* (New York: Collier Books, 1962), 81; Sahib, "The Nation of Islam," 91.

11. Lucas, "First Magazine Interview with Elijah Muhammad," 91; Sahib, "The Nation of Islam," 90–93, 123; Hans J. Massaquoi, "Elijah Muhammad: Prophet and Architect of the Separate Nation of Islam," *Ebony*, August 1970, 88; Scott, "Elijah Muhammad, Muslim Leader." Elijah's physical description is based on the words of Osier Muhammad, his grandson, in Steven Barboza, *American Jihad: Islam after Malcolm X* (New York: Doubleday, 1993), 107. The Savior's Day convention is a tradition that has been continued by Louis Farrakhan's contemporary version of the Nation of Islam.

NOTES TO CHAPTER 3

1. Sahib, "The Nation of Islam," 92–93.

2. Clegg, *An Original Man*, 23; Sahib, "The Nation of Islam," 96, 94.

3. Clegg, *An Original Man*, 24–25; Beynon, "The Voodoo Cult," 901.

4. Sahib, "The Nation of Islam," 78–79, 94; Clegg, *An Original Man*, 26.

5. Sahib, "The Nation of Islam," 80, 86–87; Clegg, *An Original Man*, 26; Beynon, "The Voodoo Cult," 906; Essien-Udom, *Black Nationalism*, 64–66.

6. Essien-Udom, *Black Nationalism*, 67; Clegg, *An Original Man*, 80, 97; Sahib, "The Nation of Islam," 75.

7. Clegg, *An Original Man*, 95–96.

8. Sahib, "The Nation of Islam," 97–98.

9. "[H]e had been on a quest for spiritual fulfillment for most of his life prior to meeting Fard." Clegg, *An Original Man*, 24. See my discussion regarding Malcolm X's primal experience in DeCaro, *On the Side of My People: A Religious Life of Malcolm X* (New York: New York University Press, 1996), 35–37, 88–89, 103. I have drawn this term from Ivring Hexham and Karla Poewe, *Understanding Cults and New Religions* (Grand Rapids, Mich.: Eerdmans, 1986), 60–62.

10 Sahib, "The Nation of Islam," 98. Another source says Fard had given Muhammad a list of 104 titles to read. Clegg, *An Original Man*, 80.

11. Clegg, *An Original Man*, 80; Sahib, "The Nation of Islam," 76–77.

12. Sahib, "The Nation of Islam," 233.

13. Clegg, *An Original Man*, 87; Sahib, "The Nation of Islam," 241; Edward Jones, interviewed by the author, June 17, 1992, New York City; Osier Muhammad, quoted in Barboza, *American Jihad*, 107. Emphasis in the text.

14. Sahib, "The Nation of Islam," 81–84, 245; Clegg, *An Original Man*, 98; Marsh, *From Black Muslims to Muslims*, 117; Muhammad, *As the Light Shineth from the East*, 17, 19–20.

NOTES TO CHAPTER 4

1. Mark L. Chapman, *Christianity on Trial: African-American Religious Thought before and after Black Power* (Maryknoll, N.Y.: Orbis Books, 1996), 64–65.

2. See Nat Hentoff, "I Still Mourn the Future of Malcolm X: Is That Spaceship for Farrakhan?" *Village Voice*, June 10, 1997, p. 22. For a substantial discussion about the mythology of the Nation of Islam, including the tales of Yakub and the mother ship (or mother plane), see Clegg, *An Original Man*, 41–67.

3. Clegg, *An Original Man*, 38; *On the Side of My People*, 108.

4. Louis E. Lomax, *When the Word Is Given* (New York: World Publishing, 1963), 118.

5. Elijah Muhammad, *The Supreme Wisdom*, vol. 2 [reprinted without original publication date] (Newport News, Va.: United Brothers Communications Systems, n.d.), 31.

6. Elijah Muhammad, "Mr. Muhammad Speaks: The Truth Has Come,"

in *The Truth*, vol. 2, May 2, 1959. Compiled and edited by Sam Shabazz Muhammad (Compton, Calif.: Genealogy Society, n.d.), 48.

This two-volume set is actually a collection of photocopied clippings of the syndicated "Mr. Muhammad Speaks" column, which preceded the newspaper of the same name. Unfortunately, while this collection is an extremely valuable representation of Muhammad's published articles, the editor's tendency was to present the clippings without full or consistent citation of the original publication. Hereafter, *The Truth*.

7. Elijah Muhammad, "Mr. Muhammad Speaks: The Bible and the Holy Qur-an," *The Truth*, vol. 2, 10.

8. Elijah Muhammad, "Mr. Muhammad Speaks," *Pittsburgh Courier*, May 11, 1957, sec. 2, 2.

9. Chapman, *Christianity on Trial*, 61.

10. Elijah Muhammad, "Mr. Muhammad Speaks: The Truth," *The Truth*, vol. 1, 24.

11. Elijah Muhammad, "Mr. Muhammad Speaks: Battle in the Sky," *The Truth*, vol. 1, 21; id., "Mr. Muhammad Speaks: America Will Destroy Itself," *The Truth*, vol. 1, 61.

12. Sahib, "The Nation of Islam," 186, 241.

13. Elijah Muhammad, "Mr. Muhammad Speaks: Who Is That Mystery God?" *The Truth*, vol. 2, 7.

14. Elijah Muhammad, "Mr. Muhammad Speaks: What Shall We Expect to See? A Spirit or a Man?" *The Truth*, vol. 2, 8.

15. Lomax, *When the Word Is Given*, 123, 127; Muhammad, "Mr. Muhammad Speaks: Who Is That Mystery God?"

16. While it is hardly consistent with the older biblical account of the conception of Jesus as a divine incarnation, the Qur'an clearly teaches that Jesus was miraculously born of the Virgin Mary: "She said: My Lord! How can I have a child when no mortal hath touched me? He said: So it (will be). Allah createth what He will. If He decreeth a thing, He saith unto it only: Be! and it is." Sûrah III:47 quoted from *The Meaning of the Glorious Koran: An Explanatory Translation* by Mohammed Marmaduke Pickthall (New York: Mentor Books, n.d.), 66.

17. The Greek term appears in Luke's gospel (1:35) as "overshadow," *episkasei*, a verb in the future tense whose root meaning is directly related to the Hebrew *shekinah*—the cloud that appears, for instance, in the story of Moses as a sign of God's presence.

18. Lomax, *When the Word Is Given*, 123–24. In between Malcolm's two trips abroad in 1964, he became entangled in an escalating war with the Na-

tion of Islam prompted by the latter's relentless efforts to oust him and his family from their home in Queens, New York City. In retaliation, Malcolm revealed the details of Muhammad's sexual violations to the press. One FBI "Elsur" (Electronic Surveillance) made from Malcolm's home telephone recorded a conversation between him and a woman (perhaps) from the Nation of Islam, in which he expressed certainty that the Messenger would use violence in response to these revelations to the press. "You mean the Messenger is that ruthless?" the unidentified woman asked. "Any man who will go to bed with his brother's daughter and then turn and make five other women pregnant is a ruthless man," Malcolm responded. See Clayborne Carson, ed., *Malcolm X: The FBI File* (New York: Carroll and Graf, 1991), 470.

19. Clegg, *An Original Man*, 186–87.

20. Conversation with Charles Kenyatta. In our ongoing discussions regarding Malcolm X and the Nation of Islam beginning in the fall of 1994, Kenyatta (formerly Charles 37X) recounted his experience of following Malcolm X out of the Nation of Islam, and the conflict that took place between Malcolm and the Black Muslims over Muhammad's "secretaries." This reference is based on Kenyatta's account of the testimony given by one of the young victims to Malcolm X, which the latter had also tape recorded. Kenyatta repeated this account on numerous occasions. See also Bruce Perry, *Malcolm: The Life of a Man Who Changed Black America* (Barrytown, N.Y.: Station Hill Press, 1991), 230–31.

For all of his claims to be the fulfillment of certain biblical prophecies, there is a certain irony— at the very least poetic—in the way that some biblical descriptions of the "false teacher" resonate far more authentically as descriptions of Elijah Muhammad. In particular, see 2 Timothy 3:4–7 and 2 Peter 2:14–15.

21. Malcolm X, *Malcolm X: The Last Speeches*, 124–25. See also DeCaro, *On the Side of My People*, 267–68.

22. DeCaro, *On the Side of My People*, 153.

23. Clegg, *An Original Man*, 141–42.

24. Ibid., 142. A copy of the first page of a letter of Malcolm X to Alex Haley "from Mecca," dated "Friday 9 AM—April 25, 1964," is found in the original hard-cover edition of *The Autobiography of Malcolm X* (New York: Grove Press, 1965), photo section, [p. 12]. Emphasis in the text.

25. See DeCaro, *On the Side of My People*, 254–57.

26. Elijah Muhammad, "Mr. Muhammad Speaks: History of Jesus," *Pittsburgh Courier*, August 3, 1957, 10.

NOTES TO CHAPTER 5

1. I have made no effort here to provide a historical description or out-line of the Garvey movement. I have provided a thumbnail sketch of Garvey and religion in *On the Side of My People*, 11–20. The authoritative text on Garvey and the UNIA is Tony Martin, *Race First: The Ideological and Organizational Struggles of Marcus Garvey and the Universal Negro Improvement Association* (Dover, Mass.: The Majority Press, 1976), in which Dr. Martin provides a substantial and fascinating discussion on the UNIA and religion in chapter 4.

2. *The Autobiography of Malcolm X*, with Alex Haley (New York: Ballantine Books, 1965; Rpt., 1987), 1–4, 385–94. Henceforth the 1987 edition is used.

3. Ibid., 14; Jan Carew, *Ghosts in Our Blood: With Malcolm X in Africa, England, and the Caribbean* (Chicago: Lawrence Hill Books, 1994), x. Also see Ted Vincent, "The Garveyite Parents of Malcolm X," *The Black Scholar*, April 1989, 10–13; and my discussion about Malcolm's parents in *On the Side of My People*, 38–43; Marcus Garvey, *Message to the People: The Course of African Philosophy, No. 7*, edited by Tony Martin (Dover, Mass.: The Majority Press, 1986), 50–59; Martin, *Race First*, 74.

4. Garvey quoted in Gayraud S. Wilmore, *Black Religion and Black Radicalism: An Interpretation of the Religious History of Afro-American People* (Maryknoll, N.Y.: Orbis Books, 1994), 149.

5. Randall K. Burkett, *Black Redemption: Churchmen Speak for the Garvey Movement* (Philadelphia: Temple University Press, 1978), 5–6, 157–65; Martin, *Race First*, 73–74; W. B. McDougall, reporter, "News and Views of U.N.I.A. Divisions: Milwaukee, Wisconsin," *Negro World*, February 5, 1927, 8.

6. *The Autobiography of Malcolm X*, 6–7; "Mr. Muhammad and His Fanatic Muslims?" *Sepia*, November 1959, 26. Essien-Udom, *Black Nationalism*, 63; James A. Wechsler, "The Cult of Malcolm X," *The Progressive*, June 1964, 24.

7. *The End of White World Supremacy: Four Speeches by Malcolm X*, ed. Benjamin Karim (New York: Seaver Books, 1971), 25.

8. Malcolm X, *Malcolm X: The Last Speeches*, 31.

9. Frank M. Snowden, *Blacks in Antiquity* (Cambridge, Mass.: The Belknap Press of Harvard University, 1970), 218; David Brion Davis, *Slavery and Human Progress* (New York: Oxford University Press, 1984), 37; Sahib, "The Nation of Islam," 183.

10. Note, for example, Garvey's remark concerning Christ: "It is evident that Christ had in his veins the blood of all mankind and belonged to no par-

ticular race"; or his thoughts on race propaganda: "All propaganda comes from the arranged desire of individuals and not from a race as a whole. It is the thinkers and leaders who originate propaganda. By insisting on its wide distribution they get other people to think as they like." Garvey, *Message to the People*, 51, 129.

11. *The Autobiography of Malcolm X*, 4, 6. I prefer to use "wholistic" rather than "holistic" because the former seems to express the view of humanity from a Hebrew-Christian view, while "holism" is often associated with "new age" or alternative views that equate wholeness with holiness. This is the distinction I make below with reference to Louise Little's "holistic belief system."

12. Interview with Wilfred Little Shabazz by author, August 15, 1992, Detroit.

13. *The Autobiography of Malcolm X*, 6, 12–15; Eugene V. Wolfenstein, *Victims of Democracy: Malcolm X and the Black Revolution* (London: Free Association Books, 1989), 96.

14. *The Autobiography of Malcolm X*, 7–8.

15. Carew, *Ghosts in Our Blood*, 113, 130–31. Readers, and particularly scholars, should approach Carew's work with great caution as it appears to be unreliable as a historical resource. While I am sympathetic with his approach and appreciative of his writing, Carew has conflated memory with imagination in order to "reconstruct" several conversations he had with Malcolm X shortly before his assassination. Carew says he had long been struck by the lack of reference to Malcolm's Caribbean heritage and was "impelled to write" in order to bring "new dimensions" of Malcolm's life to light (pp. x–xi). However, even a cursory reading leaves one asking why such a detailed, complete recollection of an encounter with Malcolm should suddenly emerge three decades later (certainly three decades late), and how it is that the eminent author published no preliminary remarks over the years even hinting at the importance of Malcolm's Caribbean heritage and his conversations with him. To be sure, Carew says he did not become convinced of the "missing Caribbean link" until 1980 (p. ix), yet this means Carew chose to write nothing for over a decade. Indeed, Carew's reconstructed conversations sound more like Carew's autobiographical reflections vis-à-vis Malcolm, the latter serving as a literary device instead of a re-created historical figure. Ironically, the Malcolm X characterized in David Graham DuBois's novel, *And Bid Him Sing . . .* , is far more believable, and his words authentically reflect that writer's 1964 encounter with Malcolm X in Egypt. In this light it is difficult to avoid concluding that Carew's reasons for writing have more to

do with the recent Malcolm X craze, despite the validity of his emphasis on Malcolm's "Caribbean link." Sadly, even the interview materials in the book are not entirely free of Carew's imaginative interpolation. For example, Carew has Wilfred Little Shabazz, Malcolm's eldest brother, saying that his mother had sequestered Marcus Garvey during a flight from the FBI (p. 118). This is flatly incorrect, for Garvey never fled the FBI and, as Wilfred assured me in a recent telephone conversation, Garvey never stayed in the Little home. Here, Carew needlessly fabricated details in order to dramatize Wilfred's recollection of his mother's involvement as a writer and reporter in service to Garvey's movement. The same applies to Wilfred's supposed reference to Malcolm's style of walking as "tiger-boy" (p. 112), which Wilfred told me he knew nothing about. Telephone conversation with Wilfred Little Shabazz, November 21, 1997.

16. See DeCaro, *On the Side of My People*, 50–51; interview with Wilfred Little Shabazz by author, with Paul Lee, August 14, 1992, Detroit.

17. Garvey, *Message to the People*, 56.

18. Ibid., 56–57.

19. Burkett, *Black Redemption*, 162–64; Martin, *Race First*, 72; Vincent, "The Garveyite Parents of Malcolm X," 10–13.

20. *The Autobiography of Malcolm X*, 172; Robert Millette and Mahin Gosine, *The Grenada Revolution: Why It Failed* (New York: Africana Research Publications, 1985), 20; David Lowenthal and Lambros Comitas, eds., *The Aftermath of Sovereignty: West Indian Perspectives* (Garden City, N.Y.: Anchor Books, 1973), 173.

21. Carew, *Ghosts in Our Blood*, 117.

22. Garvey, *Message to the People*, 31.

23. Interview with Wilfred Little Shabazz by author, with Paul Lee, August 14, 1992; *The Autobiography of Malcolm X*, 7. Emphasis in the text. In a subsequent interview with Wilfred, he pointed out that he clearly remembered the same incident portrayed by Malcolm in *The Autobiography*, but that the disagreement did not characterize an ongoing debate in the household. According to Wilfred, his father went along with his wife's dietary preferences, though he apparently had different convictions about eating meats. Telephone conversation with Wilfred Little Shabazz, November 21, 1997.

24. *The Autobiography of Malcolm X*, 16–17; interview with Wilfred Little Shabazz by author, with Paul Lee, August 14, 1992.

25. *The Autobiography of Malcolm X*, 19.

26. Note this well-intentioned observation: "In general, the influence of

the Negroes on the Pentecostal movement must not be underestimated." In fact, given the extent to which the Pentecostal movement represents the influence of black culture on U.S. religion (and by extension, many other parts of the world), this is a scholarly understatement. Walter J. Hollenweger, *The Pentecostals* (London: SCM Press, 1972), 23, 30.

27. Carew, *Ghosts in Our Blood*, 126. Note that when Paul Lee and I asked Wilfred Little about the roots of his mother's spiritual perspective, he replied: "Well, the way she would talk about it, most of it she got from the Caribe Indians—she's from the Caribbean area—and by spending time around them." Interview with Wilfred Little Shabazz by author, with Paul Lee, August 14, 1992.

28. Interview with Wilfred Little Shabazz by the author, with Paul Lee, August 14, 1992.

29. *The Autobiography of Malcolm X*, 156.

30. Ibid., 17.

31. Carew, *Ghosts in Our Blood*, 116; interview with Wilfred Little Shabazz by the author, August 15, 1992.

NOTES TO CHAPTER 6

1. Perry, *Malcolm: The Life of a Man Who Changed Black America*, 76, 108; *The Autobiography of Malcolm X*, 154.

2. See reference to Samuel Laviscount and young Malcolm in *On the Side of My People*, 57–58. Biographical material on Rev. Laviscount was obtained from a bio-sketch entitled "Reverend Samuel Leroy Laviscount," published on the Website of Laviscount's granddaughter, Marla Blakey, at http://www.io.org/~picsell/mbhome.htm.

3. Letter of Malcolm X Little to Rev. Samuel L. Laviscount, November 14, 1950. Same source as biographical material on Laviscount in note 2. Note that Malcolm used "saviour."

4. Lucas, "First Magazine Interview with Elijah Muhammad," 12. Emphasis in the text; Elijah Muhammad, "Mr. Muhammad Speaks: Brotherhood of Black Mankind," May 4, 1959, in *The Truth*, vol. 2, 93.

5. Elijah Muhammad, "Mr. Muhammad Speaks: The Truth Has Come," May 2, 1959, in *The Truth*, vol. 2, 48.

6. *The Autobiography of Malcolm X*, 223–24. Job speaks of the resurrection in Job 19:25, David in Psalm 16:10. Essien-Udom, *Black Nationalism*, 91. Emphasis in the text.

7. Perry, *Malcolm: The Life of a Man*, 114.

8. Elijah Muhammad, *The Supreme Wisdom* (The Nation of Islam, 1957; rpt. Newport News, Va.: The National Newport News and Commentator, n.d.), 7–8.

9. Letter of Malcolm X to Laviscount. Upper case in original; *The Autobiography of Malcolm X*, 182.

10. Letter of Malcolm X to Laviscount.

11. Letter of Malcolm X Little to Philbert X Little, July 28, 1950.

12. Letter of Malcolm X Little to Henrietta Shah, September 25, 1950; emphasis in the original.

13. *The Autobiography of Malcolm X*, 169–70; letter of Malcolm X Little to Philbert X Little, July 28, 1950.

14. Letter of Malcolm X Little to Philbert X Little, July 28, 1950.

15. Claude Frazier Sharieff, interviewed by author, New York City, June 17, 1992; Essien-Udom, *Black Nationalism*, 180, 221.

16. Letter of Malcolm X Little [to Philbert X Little], December 9, 1954; emphasis in the original.

17. Essien-Udom, *Black Nationalism*, 101.

18. Perry, *Malcolm: The Life of a Man*, 122.

19. Letter of Malcolm X to Philbert X Little, March 19, 1955. Emphasis in original; Malcolm X, "We Arose from the Dead!" *Moslem World & the U.S.A.*, August–September 1956, 24–27; emphasis in the text. Also see *On the Side of My People*, 137–40, on the relationship of A. B. Naeem with the Nation of Islam.

20. Wilfred Little Shabazz, interviewed by author, with Paul Lee, Detroit, August 14, 1992.

21. Excerpted from Paul Lee, "The James Booker Row: An Alternative Reading," December 1995, 2; courtesy of Best Efforts, Inc.; emphasis in the original.

22. *The Autobiography of Malcolm X*, 411; "The Story of Ramza," an unpublished, undated autobiographical sketch in the archives of Best Efforts, Inc. Also see "Ramza: Jeweler for New Malcolm X Movie," *Your Black Books* [Newport News, Va.], February 1992, 1.

23. Justice Jawn Sandifer (ret.), interviewed by the author, New York City, March 28, 1992.

24. Ibid.

25. Malcolm's description of the Johnson X incident is found in *The Autobiography of Malcolm X*, 233–35. For a detailed account of the incident and references, see *On the Side of My People*, 111–15.

26. Justice Jawn Sandifer interview.

27. Robert Haggins, interviewed by author, March 28, 1991, New York City. Unfortunately, the postcard is no longer extant.

Far less poignant, my other favorite postcard story pertains to the famous *Playboy* interview with Malcolm, conducted by Alex Haley (which eventuated in the writing of *The Autobiography*). According to Haley, Malcolm was highly skeptical about the sincerity of *Playboy* in publishing the interview. "You know that devil's not going to print that!" he told his future co-author. Shortly after the interview was completed, the editors at *Playboy* were shocked to receive a color postcard picturing a coiled rattlesnake poised to attack. On the flipside was written: "Greetings from the middle of the Desert," and it was signed, "X." Apparently, Malcolm had subsequently reported to Elijah Muhammad's winter home in Phoenix, Arizona, and had sent the card along to cap off the interview with a little shock. While the editors took the postcard as an expression of visceral contempt, they unfortunately missed out on the fact that Malcolm was simply having fun at their expense. Cf. *The Autobiography of Malcolm X*, 385; June Cochran, "Playbill," *Playboy*, May 1963, 3.

NOTES TO CHAPTER 7

1. William Worthy, "The Nation of Islam: Impact and Prospects," *Midstream*, Spring 1962, 36.

2. Elijah Muhammad, "Mr. Muhammad Speaks: Islam the True Religion," in *The Truth*, vol. 2, 13; idem, "Mr. Muhammad Speaks: Islam for the So-called Negro," in *The Truth*, vol. 2, 12; idem, "Mr. Muhammad Speaks: The Coming of God," in *The Truth*, vol. 2, 6; Abdul Basit Naeem, "Moslem Convention—1957," *Moslem World & the U.S.A.*, March–April 1957, 12–13; Elijah Muhammad, "Mr. Muhammad Speaks: Allah Offers You a Future," in *The Truth*, vol. 1, 19.

3. Elijah Muhammad, "Jesus Is Killed," *Pittsburgh Courier*, September 7, 1957, 10.

4. Elijah Muhammad, "Mr. Muhammad Speaks: Islam versus Christianity," *Pittsburgh Courier*, January 11, 1958, 10.

5. Elijah Muhammad, "Mr. Muhammad Speaks: Christianity versus Islam," *Pittsburgh Courier*, January 25, 1958, 12; idem, "Mr. Muhammad Speaks," in *The Truth*, vol. 1, 65.

6. Letter of the Rev. William Holmes, "Mr. Muhammad Draws Some Fire," *Pittsburgh Courier*, October 12, 1957, sec. 2, 7; letter of Venora M. B. Scott; "What Courier Readers Think," ibid., November 16, 1957, 8; letter of

Venora M. B. Scott, "Voice of the People; What Courier Readers Think," ibid., July 14, 1956, 10.

7. Letter of the Rev. Joseph P. King, "What Courier Readers Think," *Pittsburgh Courier*, October 19, 1957, 7; letter of Rev. Benjamin F. Reid, ibid., October 19, 1957, 7; letter of Rev. M. C. McKenney, ibid., November 22, 1958; letter of Rev. Arthur McGiffert, ibid., October 25, 1958, 9; letter of Hattie B. Perryman, ibid., July 14, 1956; letter of Progressive Pentecostal Young People's Meeting of Chicago, ibid., October 25, 1958, 9; letter of J. M. Gerval, ibid., October 12, 1957, sec. 2, 7.

8. Peter Goldman, *The Death and Life of Malcolm X* (Chicago: University of Illinois Press, 1979), 42.

9. Memo from SAC, New York, to FBI Director, "Malcolm K. Little; Internal Security-Nation of Islam," November 16, 1962, 13, Reel 1, Scholarly Resources, Inc., microfilm of the FBI headquarters file on Malcolm X, published as *Malcolm X: FBI Surveillance File* (Wilmington, Del., 1978); hereafter *SR*. New York Office Report, "Malcolm K. Little, Internal Security-NOI," May 19, 1959, 30, Reel 1, *SR*; New York Office Report, "ML; SM-NOI," April 30, 1958, 37, Reel 1, *SR*; New York Office Report, "MKL; SM-NOI," April 23, 1957, 57, Reel 1, *SR*.

10. See *The End of White World Supremacy*, ed. Karim, 55; *The Autobiography of Malcolm X*, 167.

11. "Religion Must Not Be Separate—Muslim Says," *Saint Louis Argus*, January 30, 1959. This article documents Malcolm's appearance on "The Editor Speaks" program, WLIB Radio, New York, along with George Schuyler of the *Pittsburgh Courier* and Chuck Stone of the *New York Age*.

12. New York Office Report, "MKL; IS-NOI," May 19, 1959, 8–9, 16, Reel 1, *SR*. Malcolm seems to have been alluding to the first verse of this popular evangelical Christian hymn: "On a hill far away stood an old rugged cross, the emblem of suffering and shame; and I love that old cross, where the dearest and best, for a world of lost sinners was slain." George Bennard, "The Old Rugged Cross" (Rodeheaver Co., 1941).

13. New York Office Report, "Malcolm K. Little; Internal Security-NOI," May 17, 1960, 34, 46, 50, Reel 1, *SR*; New York Office Report, "ML; SM-NOI," April 30, 1958, 24, Reel 1, *SR*; New York Office Report, "MKL; IS-NOI," May 19, 1959, 10, Reel 1, *SR*.

14. A transcript of Muhammad's speech and remarks by Malcolm X from the 1957 "Saviour's Day" convention are found, respectively, in "Islam: The Remedy for the So-Called Negroes' Ills," and "Moslem Convention—1957," *Moslem World & The U.S.A.*, March–April 1957, 19–22, 14–15.

15. Letter of Elizabeth Kinnear, *Moslem World & The U.S.A.*, May–June 1957, 2.

16. The editor, Abdul Basit Naeem, was a guest at "Saviour's Day" 1957, and praised Elijah Muhammad as "a great Moslem" who provided the greatest possibility of leading blacks into "the fold of Islam *en masse*." In the next issue, Naeem acknowledged that his goal was to maximize black converts "in the shortest possible time." See "Moslem Convention—1957," *Moslem World & The U.S.A.*, March–April 1957, 23–24; "American Moslems of African Descent," *Moslem World & The U.S.A.*, May–June 1957, 7.

17. H. D. Quigg, "Malcolm X, No. 2 Muslim, Says Black Man 'Original,'" *Daily Defender* [Chicago], June 19, 1963, 9; Brian Glanville, "Malcolm X," *New Statesman*, June 12, 1964, 901–2.

18. *The Autobiography of Malcolm X*, 85, 297; *The Negro Protest: James Baldwin, Malcolm X, Martin Luther King Talk with Kenneth B. Clark* (Boston: Beacon Press, 1963), 21. The scandalous photographs of the minister's affair appeared with the captions "Trapped!" and "Confusion!" in the *New York Amsterdam News*, August 2, 1958, 3.

19. *The Autobiography of Malcolm X*, 211.

20. Wilfred Little Shabazz interview, August 14, 1992.

21. Malcolm's discussion about the "little lamb" analogy and his reflective description of Black Muslim rallies with Muhammad are found in *The Autobiography of Malcolm X*, 211, 250–57; emphases in the text. Goldman, *The Death and Life of Malcolm X*, 48–49, 79.

22. *Malcolm X: Speeches at Harvard*, ed. Archie Epps (New York: Paragon House, 1991), 118–19; Lomax, *When the Word Is Given*, 169.

23. Hakim Jamal, *From the Dead Level: Malcolm X and Me* (New York: Random House, 1971), 187; SAC (97–145) to SE [redacted], "Nation of Islam; NOI-IS," June 6, 1957, 105-8999-464, 1–2.

NOTES TO CHAPTER 8

1. See reference to "The Hate That Hate Produced" in *The Autobiography of Malcolm X*, 238, and *On the Side of My People*, 134–35; Goldman, *The Death and Life of Malcolm X*, 61; "Says Many Misleading Followers: Malcolm X Hurls Challenge at Negro Preachers," *Pittsburgh Courier*, April 12,1958, 8; "Defends Muhammad's Teachings: Malcolm X Blasts Negro Ministers!" *Pittsburgh Courier*, August 9,1958, 7.

2. "Another Preacher Beaten in Alabama; Lashed until His Blood Ran!" *Pittsburgh Courier*, April 28, 1959, 8; Trezzvant W. Anderson, "Birmingham

Minister Prays during Beating; 'Lord, Forgive These Men,'" *Pittsburgh Courier*, April 28, 1959, 8.

3. Elijah Muhammad, "Mr. Muhammad Speaks: Brotherhood of Black Mankind," May 4, 1959, in *The Truth*, vol. 2, 93.

4. Ibid.

5. Rev. George C. Violenes, "Christian World," *New York Amsterdam News*, December 28, 1957, 30. "Christian World" also appeared in the *Amsterdam News* on December 7, 1957, 17, and on December 14, 1957, 7.

6. "Pastor, Baptist Church, Join Muslims," *New Crusader*, February 3, 1962; Dan Burley, "Truth about Muhammad: How Christians Fit into Black Muslim World," *New Crusader*, February 10, 1962, 9.

7. *The Reminiscences of Ed Edwin*, a self-interview (Columbia University, Oral History Research Office), May 6, 1963; *The Autobiography of Malcolm X*, 242; see Stephen Neill, *A History of Christian Missions* (New York: Penguin, 1980), 249–52; *The History of Christianity in West Africa*, ed. O. U. Kalu (London: Longman Group, 1981), 147.

8. Or so he alludes to "God's Angry Men" in *The Autobiography of Malcolm X*, 237; Malcolm X, "God's Angry Men," *New York Amsterdam News*, in FBI file 105-8999-450; idem, "God's Angry Men," *Los Angeles Herald-Dispatch*, November 14, 1957, FBI file 105-8999-584; October 31, 1957, FBI file 105-8999-585; November 28, 1957, FBI file 105-8999-602.

9. Malcolm X, "God's Angry Men," *Los Angeles Herald-Dispatch*, October 10, 1957, FBI file 105-8999-543; October 3, 1957, FBI file 105-8999-542; November 7, 1957, FBI file 105-8999-569; February 13, 1958, FBI file 105-8999-638; April 10, 1958, FBI file 105-8999-731; December 5, 1957, FBI file 105-8999-613.

10. Ibid., November 28, 1957, FBI file 105-8999-602; October 10, 1957, FBI file 105-8999-543.

11. Elijah Muhammad, "Mr. Muhammad Speaks: America Will Destroy Itself," in *The Truth*, vol. 1, 61; Elijah Muhammad, "Mr. Muhammad Speaks: Islam for American So-Called Negroes," *Pittsburgh Courier*, February 23, 1957, 21; Hakim, *From the Dead Level*, 177; Malcolm X, interviewed by Alex Haley, in *The Playboy Interview*, ed. G. Barry Golson (Los Angeles: Wideview Books, 1980), 43; Ralph Mathews, Jr., "Has Anything Really Changed since Malcolm X Talked to AFRO in 1963?" *The Afro-American* [Baltimore], May 23, 1981, 14.

12. Malcolm X, "God's Angry Men," *Los Angeles Herald-Dispatch*, December 19, 1957, FBI file 105-8999-616; December 26, 1957, FBI file 105-8999-618; *The Autobiography of Malcolm X*, 237. The editor of the *Amsterdam News* later

recalled that Malcolm X "finally admitted to me that Muhammad wanted to write it. He saw that Malcolm was becoming the biggest thing in New York blackwise." Goldman, *The Death and Life of Malcolm X*, 61; Malcolm X, "God's Angry Men," *Los Angeles Herald-Dispatch*, October 10, 1957, FBI file 105-8999-543; January 9, 1958, FBI file 105-8999-619; February 27, 1958, FBI file 105-8999-680; October 24, 1957, FBI file 105-8999-546; September 26, 1957, FBI file 105-8999-541.

NOTES TO CHAPTER 9

1. August Meier, "The Black Muslims," in *A White Scholar and the Black Community, 1945–1965: Essays and Reflections* (Amherst, Mass.: University of Massachusetts Press, 1992), 134–35. This essay originally appeared in *Liberation,* April 1963, 9–13. Meier actually debated Malcolm X at Morgan State University in March 1962, during which Malcolm apparently referred to the scholar as one of the "blue-eyed devils." Afterward, Meier went to say goodbye to Malcolm, who "turned, took my hand, and said 'Professor Meier, I hope you don't mean good-bye.'" Meier says he regrets that he never looked up Malcolm when visiting New York City (p. 32).

2. *Malcolm X Speaks*, ed. George Breitman (New York: Grove Press, 1982), 199.

3. Jamal, *From the Dead Level*, 178, 179, 192; memorandum from Detective Ernest B. Latty to Commanding Officer, Bureau of Special Services, "Muslim Rally, 125–126th Sts. at 7th Ave. Manhattan," May 30, 1960, in New York Police Department, Bureau of Special Services files, hereafter *BOSS*; "A Choice of Two Roads." Malcolm X debates Bayard Rustin, hosted by John Donald, WBAI-FM Radio, New York, November 7, 1960 (Los Angeles: Pacifica Tape Library, #BB 3014).

4. "A Choice of Two Roads."

5. "Meeting of Muhammad's Temple of Islam, Embassy Auditorium," Los Angeles, April 16, 1961, 10, 13, 14, *BOSS*.

6. Ibid., 27, 29.

7. Lucas, "First Magazine Interview with Elijah Muhammad," 90.

8. "Meeting of Muhammad's Temple of Islam, Embassy Auditorium," 1, 8; *The Autobiography of Malcolm X*, 237; S. Alexander, "Nationalism Is the Badge of Self Respect," in Alfred Q. Jarrett, ed., *Muslims' Black Metropolis* (Los Angeles: Great Western Books, 1962), 30; Jamal, *From the Dead Level*, 213. Jamal says that when Muhammad's column began to run in the *Herald-Dispatch,* the men of the Nation of Islam were required to sell the paper—an-

other aspect that enhanced the working relationship of Malcolm with Alexander; New York Office Report, "Malcolm K. Little," November 17, 1961, 9, *SR*, Reel 1; New York Office Report, "Malcolm K. Little; NOI," November 19, 1958, 7, *SR*, Reel 1.

9. Elijah Muhammad, "Mr. Muhammad Speaks: Justice for the American So-Called Negroes," *Pittsburgh Courier*, August 22, 1959, 12.

10. "An African American's Dream" flier (Washington, D.C.: Saints' Missionary Foundation, 1993?); Lillian Ashcraft Webb, *About My Father's Business: The Life of Elder Michaux* (Westport, Conn.: Greenwood Press, 1981), 80–81, 156; letter of Deacon Jasper W. Sturdivant, Gospel Spreading Church of God, Washington, D.C., to author, September 4, 1992.

11. Michaux vs. Muhammad event ad in *Happy News*, September 1961; description based on photos from same event in "Elder Michaux Defends Teachings of Christ," *Happy News*, October 1961, 8; Webb, *About My Father's Business*, 80–81; memo from Detective William K. De Fossett to Commanding Officer, Bureau of Special Services, September 1, 1961, "Subject: Activities of the Nation of Islam (Bus Motorcade to Washington, D.C., on September 10, 1961), *BOSS*.

12. Elijah Muhammad, "Mr. Muhammad Speaks: The Blindness of the Negro Preachers," in *The Truth*, vol. 1, 27; letter of Deacon Jasper W. Sturdivant to author, September 4, 1992; memo from SAC, Chicago to SAC, Indianapolis, "Nation of Islam; IS-NOI," August 25, 1961, 1–2, FBI file 105-8999-2443.

13. Memo from Detective William K. De Fossett to Commanding Officer, Bureau of Special Services, "Activities of the Nation of Islam," June 28, 1961, *BOSS*; date of Malcolm's sermon is confirmed in letter from Sturdivant to author, September 4, 1992, 1; "Footnotes on Black History" postcard featuring Robert L. Haggins's photograph of Malcolm X, Lewis H. Michaux, and Muhammad Ali, and notes by Paul Lee (Highland Park, Mich.: Best Efforts, Inc., 1983).

14. All quotations are based on the author's transcription of "Elder Michaux and Malcolm X in New York City, June 19, 1961." See Appendix B for a partial transcript; *The Autobiography of Malcolm X*, 4–5.

15. C. Eric Lincoln, *My Face Is Black* (Boston: Beacon Press, 1964), 98–99.

16. All quotations transcribed by author from Malcolm X on "Community Corner" with Bernice Bass, WADO Radio, New York, n.d., but internal evidence suggests July 1, or July 1–2, 1962 [possibly a late-night show]). Dating of this recorded interview was provided by Paul Lee of Best Efforts, Inc., Highland Park, Michigan.

NOTES TO CHAPTER 10

1. *The Autobiography of Malcolm X*, 365; Goldman, *The Death and Life of Malcolm X*, 92, 63.

2. Elijah Muhammad, "Mr. Muhammad Speaks: The Blindness of the Negro Preachers," in *The Truth*, vol. 1, 27.

3. "Say Moslem Leader Preaches Race Hatred; Mags Blast Muhammad," *Pittsburgh Courier*, August 15, 1959, 10; see also "Is New York Sitting on a 'Powder Keg'?" *U.S. News & World Report*, August 3, 1959, 50–51, and "Races: The Black Supremacists," *Time*, August 10, 1959, 24–25; "Dr. King, Keating Blast Muslims Group," *Pittsburgh Courier*, August 29, 1959, 6; Trezzvant W. Anderson, "Deny Him Use of Auditorium; [Georgia] Church Group Afraid of Dr. King," *Pittsburgh Courier*, May 31, 1958, 3; Derrick Bell, text of statement made over KDKA Radio, Pittsburgh, n.d., in "Says Conditions Make Muslims," *Pittsburgh Courier*, September 5, 1959, 2.

4. Note again that after Muhammad's official recognition in the Muslim world, the Nation of Islam stopped calling their sanctuaries "temples" and started calling them "mosques" in order to appear more consistent with the Muslim world.

5. For more details on the Los Angeles police assault, see Goldman, *The Death and Life of Malcolm X*, 97–99; *On the Side of My People*, 184–85; Jamal, *From the Dead Level*, 217–27.

6. L. I. Brockenbury, "Ministers Call Muslims Hate Group," *Pittsburgh Courier*, June 2, 1962, 1, 4.

7. Malcolm X on the "Barry Farber Show," WOR-AM Radio, New York. It is not clear whether this broadcast took place on June 28, 1963, or August 9, 1963.

8. "Billy Graham Raps New York Tensions," *Pittsburgh Courier*, January 17, 1959, 8. See chapter 10 for more discussion about Graham and civil rights; *Annual Report 1960 of the City of New York Commission on Intergroup Relations*, Stanley H. Lowell, Chairman, Frank S. Horne, Executive Director, April 1, 1961, 6–7; see *On the Side of My People*, 115–17.

9. "But around 1963, if anyone had noticed, I spoke less and less of religion. . . . And the reason for this is that my faith had been shaken." *The Autobiography of Malcolm X*, 294; "Mr. X Tells What Isla[m] Means," *New York Amsterdam News*, April 21, 1957, in FBI file 105-8999-421. Several days before his assassination, Malcolm said on a radio broadcast that the Nation of Islam had "right-meaning persons" in its ranks. See *Malcolm X Speaks*, ed. Breitman, 189; Jamal, *From the Dead Level*, 183; "Malcolm X Preaches from Pulpit

of Abyssinian Bapt[ist Church] in New York," *Pittsburgh Courier*, June 15, 1957, in FBI file 105-8999-465.

10. "Malcolm X Proclaims Muhammad as Man of the Hour," speech at Yale University, October 1960, in *Rhetoric of Racial Revolt*, ed. Roy L. Hill (Denver: Golden Bell Press, 1964), 304, 312.

11. *Malcolm X: Speeches at Harvard*, ed. Epps, 115–16.

12. I have addressed these aspects more fully in *On the Side of My People*, 135–58; *Malcolm X: Speeches at Harvard*, ed. Epps, 126.

13. See the creation story of the Nation of Islam as described in Clegg, *An Original Man*, 42.

14. See *On the Side of My People*, 94; New York Office Report, "Malcolm K. Little," November 17, 1959, 52, *SR*, Reel 1; "Islam Held Ahead in Africa Contest: Graham Says Christianity Needs More U.S. Negro and Native Missionaries," *New York Times*, May 13, 1960, 14.

15. *The Autobiography of Malcolm X*, 190, 265.

16. John Aigner, "The Handshakers," *New York Citizen-Call*, October 1, 1960, 17; New York Office Report, "Malcolm K. Little," November 17, 1959, 32–33, *SR*, Reel 1; Memo from Detective Ernest B. Latty to Commanding Officer, New York City Police Department Bureau of Special Services, "Muslim Rally on Saturday, September 7, 1963 on Lenox Ave. Between 114th & 110th Streets, Manhattan," September 9, 1963, 2, *BOSS*; Laurence Henry, "Malcolm X Lives," *Cavalier*, June 1966, 92.

17. Partial transcript of "Pro and Con," WMCA-AM Radio, New York, March 3, 1960, with Malcolm X and the Rev. William M. James, hosted by William Kunstler; memorandum, New York Office, March 18, 1960, "Re: Nation of Islam," 3–4, in New York Office Report, "Malcolm K. Little," November 17, 1959, *SR*, Reel 1. Also in *Malcolm X: The FBI File*, ed. Clayborne Carson (New York: Carroll and Graf, 1991), 180–90. The article to which Kunstler referred on the program was Michael Clark, "Rise in Racial Extremism Worries Harlem Leaders," *New York Times*, January 25, 1960, 1, 18.

18. Malcolm X on "Pro and Con," 5; "Malcolm X Proclaims Muhammad as Man of the Hour," 315; see *On the Side of My People*, 157–58.

19. David Gallen, *Malcolm X as They Knew Him* (New York: Carroll and Graf, 1992), 60; Gil S. Joel, "Thinking It Thru: Black Muslim Approach," *Patent Trader* [Mt. Kisco, N.Y.], April 25, 1963, 3; *The Autobiography of Malcolm X*, 293; Lucas, "First Magazine Interview with Elijah Muhammad, Black Muslim Leader," 11, 93. See Alex Haley's descriptive comparison of Malcolm and Muhammad in Mary Seibert McCauley, "Alex Haley, a Southern Griot:

A Literary Biography" (George Peabody College for Teachers of Vanderbilt University), Ph.D. diss., 1983, 99.

NOTES TO CHAPTER 11

1. "King's Kwips: King on Malcolm X," *Pittsburgh Courier* (Georgia Edition), May 25, 1963, 1.

2. Washington, D.C., Field Office Report, "Malcolm K. Little, Also Known as Malcolm X; Internal Security-Nation of Islam," May 23, 1963, 7, Reel 1, *SR*; Stephen B. Oates, *Let the Trumpet Sound: The Life of Martin Luther King, Jr.* (New York: New American Library, 1982), 251–52; New York Office Report, "Malcolm Little," April 30, 1958, 14, Reel 1, *SR*; Joseph T. Friscia, "Malcolm X and His Black Muslims," *Saga*, July 1962, 73. Malcolm told Friscia that King made Susskind promise "never to allow me to appear on his TV show," but it is more likely that King's only fear was that Malcolm would appear on Susskind's show when he was on it. Malcolm was thereafter a guest on the Susskind show more than once, but never with King present; Flier, "Harlem Freedom Rally at 7th Avenue at 125th Street, Saturday, May 28th, 1960," in *BOSS*; Memo from Detective Ernest B. Latty to Commanding Officer, Bureau of Special Services, "Muslim Rally, 125–126th Sts. at 7th Ave. Manhattan," May 30, 1960, *BOSS*.

3. King, along with other civil rights leaders, was invited to participate in a unity rally sponsored by the Nation of Islam in Harlem on August 10, 1963. King declined the invitation, and did not even send a representative. A recording of Malcolm's entire speech at this rally has been published as *The Wisdom of Malcolm X* (Rahway, N.J.: Audiofidelity Enterprises, n.d.); memo from John L. Kinsella, Commanding Officer, Bureau of Special Services, to Chief Inspector, "Street Rally on Lenox Ave. At 115th Street, Man., Sponsored by the Nation of Islam," August 13, 1963, 1–3, *BOSS*.

4. *The Autobiography of Malcolm X*, 289–91.

5. "Malcolm X, in DC, Raps Jackie, Floyd, Dr. King," *New York Amsterdam News*, May 25, 1963, 20; Washington, D.C., Field Office Report, "Malcolm K. Little, Also Known as Malcolm X; Internal Security-Nation of Islam," May 23, 1963, 14–15, Reel 1, *SR*; "Malcolm X Inspires Egg Throwing Attack," *Call & Post* (Cleveland), July 6, 1963, C7; Jackie Robinson, "Egg-Throwing and Dr. King," *New York Amsterdam News*, July 13, 1963, 11. In the spring of 1964, when the media began to broadcast news of a Harlem "hate gang" that did violence to whites, the police pointed toward Malcolm X. At the time he was in Africa, after having made the pilgrimage. Upon returning, he participated in a

forum and addressed this "scare." See *Malcolm X Speaks*, ed. Breitman, 64–71; Martin Arnold, "Brooklyn Rally Held By Muslims," *New York Times*, July 28, 1963, 44; memo from Patrolman Frederick Jenoure to Commanding Officer, Bureau of Special Services, "Muslim Rally," July 17, 1963, 2, BOSS.

    6. "Negroes Moving Too Fast? 'Put on the Brakes,' Urges Billy Graham," *Pittsburgh Courier*, April 27, 1963, 1; "No Color Line in Heaven," *Ebony*, September 1957, 99–100, 102, 104; Taylor Branch, *Parting the Waters: America in the King Years 1954–63* (New York: Simon and Schuster, 1988), 227–28; Billy Graham, *Just As I Am: The Autobiography of Billy Graham* (San Francisco: Harper and Zondervan, 1997), 314; William Martin, *A Prophet with Honor: The Billy Graham Story* (New York: Quill/William Morrow, 1991), 235. According to one hagiography of Graham, the evangelist published an earlier article in 1956 called "Plea for an End to Intolerance" in *Life* magazine. See Curtis Mitchell, *Billy Graham: The Making of a Crusader* (New York: Chilton Books, 1966), 24.

    7. "No Group God's Pets, Graham Says," *Pittsburgh Courier*, October 25, 1958, 3; "Billy Graham: Heaven Won't Let Racists In," *New York Amsterdam News*, July 20, 1957, 1; Branch, *Parting the Waters*, 227; "Billy Graham Says Church Must Eliminate Jim Crow," *Pittsburgh Courier*, July 30, 1960, 36.

    8. Billy Graham, "Why Don't Our Churches Practice the Brotherhood They Preach?" *Reader's Digest*, August 1960, 52–56; Graham, *Just As I Am*, 426; Branch, *Parting the Waters*, 228; Martin, *A Prophet with Honor*, 172; reference to Lincoln in Frederick Douglass's speech at Lincoln Park, Washington, D.C., April 14, 1876, in *The Life and Times of Frederick Douglass* (Secaucus, N.J.: Citadel Press, 1983), 492.

    9. "Brief Biography of Billy Graham" (Wheaton, Ill.: Billy Graham Center Archives at Wheaton College), http://www.wheaton.edu/bgc/archives/bio.html; interview with Wilfred Little Shabazz by the author, August 15, 1992.

    10. *The Autobiography of Malcolm X*, 306–7; George Plimpton, "Miami Notebook: Cassius Clay and Malcolm X," *Harper's*, June 1964, 58.

    11. Transcript of Malcolm X interview by Richard Elman, WBAI Radio, New York, May 1, 1962, in the Rare Book and Manuscript Collection of Columbia University, New York. This transcript has been published in *Malcolm X: As They Knew Him*, ed. Gallen, 101–7; however, the editor failed to date the interview, and errs in placing the forum at the Manhattan Center and in saying that Bayard Rustin participated in the program. The forum, moderated by Murray Kempton, did not include Rustin and was held at the Palm Gardens Hall, also in Manhattan. See also *The Crisis of Racism* (N. Hollywood, Calif.: Pacifica Radio Archive, n.d.), tapes #BB3049 a & b.

12. "Slain Musli[m], 29, buried; cop freed," *Afro-American* (Baltimore, Md.), May 26, 1962, 19; Chet Coleman, "'62 Muslim Riot Victims End Visit to Hometown," *Philadelphia Tribune*, March 12, 1963, 3; Gordon Parks, "What Their Cry Means to Me," *Life*, May 31, 1963, 78; Transcript of Malcolm X on "The Ben Hunter Show," Los Angeles, Channel 11 television, March 29–30, 1963 (a late-night show), in letterhead memorandum from Los Angeles office, [caption redacted], April 8, 1963, 4–5, Reel 1, *SR*.

13. Transcript of Malcolm X speaking at the Hi-Fi Country Club, Charlotte, North Carolina, January 30, 1963, in letterhead memorandum enclosure from FBI Field Office, Charlotte, "Re: Nation of Islam; Internal Security—Nation of Islam," March 13, 1963/NO1/HQ, 25-330971-8-20, 9; Alex Haley, "Mr. Muhammad Speaks," *Reader's Digest*, March 1960, 100–104; *The Autobiography of Malcolm X*, 383–85, 389; "The Trouble-Making Muslims," *Sepia*, December 1960, 18–21; Alex Haley and Alfred Balk, "Black Merchants of Hate," *Saturday Evening Post*, January 26, 1963, 74.

14. Malcolm X speaking at the Hi-Fi Country Club, 21; regarding "The Hate That Hate Produced," see *The Autobiography of Malcolm X*, 238, and *On the Side of My People*, 134–35.

15. Goldman, *The Death and Life of Malcolm X*, 79.

16. Malcolm X on *Program P.M.*, WINS Radio, New York, June 13, 1963. Author's transcription from audiotape.

17. M. S. Handler, "Malcolm X Starting Drive in Washington," *New York Times*, May 10, 1963, 14.

18. *The Negro Protest*, 21–22.

19. Malcolm X interviewed by Alex Haley, in *The Playboy Interview*, ed. Golson, 44–45; emphasis in the text.

20. Malcolm X addresses the Rochdale Movement, Queens, New York, November 28, 1963. Partial transcript by author of tape in New York University, Institute of Afro-American Studies; SAC, New York, from SAC, Phoenix, "Nation of Islam; IS-NOI," December 6, 1963, FBI file 105-8999-3950. See also "Malcolm X Endorses Boycott," *New York Amsterdam News*, December 7, 1963, 29.

21. Marquis Childs, "Bombs in Alabama Aid Black Muslims," *Washington Post*, March 15, 1963, A18; "Kennedy Reported Concerned about Negro Extremism," *Washington Post*, May 15, 1963, A6; "Kennedy Fears Negro Extremists Will Get Power if Moderates Fail," *New York Times*, May 15, 1963, 26; M. S. Handler, "Malcolm X Scores Kennedy on Racial Policy," *New York Times*, May 17, 1963, 14.

NOTES TO CHAPTER 12

1. Pierre Crabités, "American Negro Mohammedans," *Catholic World*, February 1933, 559–66; Douglass, *The Life and Times of Frederick Douglass*, 250; José Rizal, *Noli Me Tangere*, trans. Leon Ma. Guerrero (Manila: Guerrero Publishing, 1995), 2.

2. *Black Spokesman: Selected Published Writings of Edward Wilmot Blyden*, ed. Hollis R. Lynch (London: Frank Cass & Co., 1971), xi–xxviii, and Blyden, "A Vindication of the African Race," 178; Edward W. Blyden, *Christianity, Islam and the Negro Race* (London: W. B. Whittingham, 1887; rpt. Edinburgh: Edinburgh University Press, 1967), xiv, 37–38, 241.

3. Blyden, *Christianity, Islam and the Negro Race*, 12–13, 246.

4. David Walker, *Appeal to the Coloured Citizens of the World; But in Particular, and Very Expressly, to Those of the United States of America*, edited by James Turner (Baltimore: Black Classics Press, 1993), 55–63.

5. Ibid., 44–45.

6. Jacques Ellul, *The Subversion of Christianity* (Grand Rapids, Mich.: William B. Eerdmans, 1986), 7.

7. Airgram from American Embassy, Lagos, Nigeria, to U.S. Department of State, "Press Coverage of Malcolm X's Visit to Nigeria," May 14, 1964, 1–2; airgram from American Embassy, Cairo, Egypt, to U.S. Department of State, "U.A.R. Press Coverage on Malcolm X," August 28, 1964, 2; airgram from American Embassy, Jidda, Saudi Arabia, to U.S. Department of State, "Activities of Malcolm X," September 29, 1964, 2.

8. M. S. Handler, "Malcolm Rejects Racist Doctrine; Also Denounces Elijah as a Religious 'Faker,'" *New York Times*, October 4, 1964, 59; "Malcolm X Reports He Now Represents World Muslim Unit," *New York Times*, October 11, 1964, 13; "Malcolm's Plans Irk Muslims Here; He Is Denounced as His Return Is Awaited," *New York Times*, November 8, 1964, 48.

9. Telephone interview with Rev. Charles Kenyatta by the author, July 31, 1997. Kenyatta has alluded to Graham's comment in our frequent conversations over the past few years, but he gave a specific recollection of Graham's remark in this interview and recalled that Graham had appeared on Channel 7 television in New York City.

10. Martin, *A Prophet with Honor*, 351; Branch, *Parting the Waters*, 227, 314. Graham personally addressed King as "Mike"; Graham, *Just As I Am*, 427; Arna Bontemps and Jack Conroy, *Anyplace but Here* (New York: Hill and Wang, 1966), 274–75.

11. Malcolm X, *February 1965: The Final Speeches*, ed. Steve Clark (New York: Pathfinder Press, 1992), 43.

12. Please note my discussion on Malcolm's "Muslim continuity" in *On the Side of My People*, 211–13.

13. *The Autobiography of Malcolm X*, 368.

14. *Malcolm X on Afro-American History* (New York: Pathfinder Press, 1988), 32.

15. Malcolm X, *Malcolm X: The Last Speeches*, 147; emphasis is mine.

NOTE TO THE EPILOGUE

1. "Likens Malcolm X, Christ," *Chicago Defender*, February 27–March 5, 1965, 1–2.

NOTE TO APPENDIX A

1. "An Open Letter to Elijah Muhammad," June 23, 1964, enclosed in Philadelphia Airtel to FBI Director, "OAAU; IS-MISC; OO: NY; MMI; IS-MMI; OO: NY," July 15, 1964, FBI Headquarters file on the Organization of Afro-American Unity, #12.

NOTE TO APPENDIX B

1. Transcribed and edited by Louis A. DeCaro, Jr., from the tape recording, *Elder Michaux and Malcolm X in New York City, June 19, 1961*, Washington, D.C., Church of God. Courtesy of Deacon Jasper W. Sturdivant, the Church of God, Washington, D.C.

Index

About the Author

Louis A. DeCaro, Jr., holds graduate degrees from Westminster Theological Seminary and New York University and is the author of *On the Side of My People: A Religious Life of Malcolm X* (NYU Press, 1996). He is also a coeditor of and contributor to *Signs of Hope in the City: Ministries of Community Renewal* (Judson Press, 1997) with Robert D. Carle.

Lou was reared in the Italian American Pentecostal movement, schooled in the Reformed Protestant tradition, and educated and enlightened by his involvement in two black congregations for over a decade (the Elim International Fellowship in Bedford-Stuyvesant, Brooklyn, and Bethel Gospel Assembly in Harlem). After completing his Doctorate of Philosophy in Religious Education, he was ordained in the African American church and has since taken the pastorate of a New York City–area congregation.